ZAHA HADID

ZAHA HADID

Guggenheim MUSEUM

Published on the occasion of the exhibition
Zaha Hadid
Organized by Germano Celant and Mónica Ramírez-Montagut

Solomon R. Guggenheim Museum, New York
June 3–October 25, 2006

This exhibition is made possible by  Oldcastle Glass

Additional support is provided by   Deutsche Bank ▢

The Leadership Committee for *Zaha Hadid* is gratefully acknowledged.

ISBN: 978-0-89207-346-7

Guggenheim Museum Publications
1071 Fifth Avenue
New York, New York 10128

Available through
D.A.P./Distributed Art Publishers
155 Sixth Avenue, 2nd floor, New York, New York 10013
Tel.: (212) 627–1999; Fax: (212) 627–9484

Distributed outside the United States and Canada,
by Thames & Hudson, Ltd., 181A High Holborn Road
London WC1V7QX, United Kingdom

Design: 2x4, Inc., Natasha Jen, Susan Sellers
Production: Minjee Cho, Melissa Secondino
Editorial: David Grosz

Printed in Germany by Cantz

Cover: *Z-Wave*, 2006.
Proposed site-specific intervention for *Zaha Hadid*, Solomon R.
Guggenheim Museum, New York; digital rendering

Inside covers: front, *Tektonic* (detail), painting; back, *Tatlin Tower
and Tektonic "Worldwind"* (detail), painting. *The Great Utopia:
The Russian and Soviet Avant-Garde, 1915–1932*, Solomon R.
Guggenheim Museum, New York, 1992.

CONTENTS

SPONSOR'S STATEMENT

The impact that Zaha Hadid has made on the world of architecture is already very significant. Widely recognized as both a pioneer and leader in her field, Hadid was also the first woman to be named Laureate of the prestigious Pritzker Architecture Prize. Oldcastle Glass is proud to sponsor her well-deserved exhibition, *Zaha Hadid*, at the Guggenheim Museum.

For more than twenty years, Zaha Hadid has received countless awards and accolades for her groundbreaking approach to architecture. *Zaha Hadid* offers further proof of the enormous contributions Hadid continues to make to her profession, and Oldcastle Glass is delighted that this exhibition will expose hundreds of thousands of Guggenheim visitors to her creative brilliance. She inspires all who are involved in architecture, the arts, and real estate development. Zaha Hadid shows us what can be done when one is truly committed to testing the boundaries of architecture, urbanism, and design.

Hadid's impact has inspired Oldcastle Glass to continue matching the challenges she presents to all those associated with, and affected by, great architecture. As a proud sponsor of this extraordinary exhibition, we look forward to witnessing the delight and joy the public will come to know by experiencing her work at the Guggenheim.

Edwin B. Hathaway
Chief Executive

FOREWORD

Zaha Hadid is the most comprehensive exhibition to date devoted to one of the most visionary architects of our time. The first woman to be awarded the distinguished Pritzker Architecture Prize, in 2004, Hadid is internationally known both for her theoretical and academic work, as well as a portfolio of daring built projects that have challenged the traditional geometry of modern buildings. This well-deserved exhibition provides an in-depth look at thirty years of revolutionary experimentation and research in the interrelated fields of urbanism, architecture, and design.

Born in Baghdad in 1950, Zaha Hadid went to schools in Switzerland and England before undertaking the mathematics program of the American University in Beirut. She then pursued architectural studies at London's Architectural Association (AA) in 1972 and finished with a Diploma Prize in 1977. Shortly after, she joined the Office of Metropolitan Architecture (OMA) founded by Rem Koolhaas and Elia Zenghelis, her former professors. In 1979, she opened an independent practice in London and started teaching at the AA. Hadid garnered international recognition in 1982, when her project The Peak won the competition for a leisure club in Hong Kong, and since then several audacious buildings have been built, a result of her ongoing exploration of challenging ideas.

This retrospective consists of an interdisciplinary approach to architecture. The exhibition presents an overview of Hadid's work that makes evident the shifts in her body of work. It includes a wide range of mediums: paintings, sketches, drawings, urban plans, competitions, models, relief models, animations, furniture, and design objects. At the outset of her career, Hadid's architectural practice followed Suprematist and Constructivist ideals. Based on floating lines and planes frozen in time and space, her early representation of architecture presented broken, compound angles with acute interstices that expressed considerable tension. These early projects were most commonly represented in large-format paintings. Her reconsideration of the architectural drawing, through nontraditional floor plans with spatial configurations open to interpretation, had a major impact on her architecture. Since then, she has moved from abstraction and fragmentation to fluidity and seamless complexity. Her first fractured forms have given place to a more recent system of fluid and undulating shapes best represented in her latest work, the Phaeno Science Center in Wolfsburg, Germany.

The Solomon R. Guggenheim Foundation has a distinguished history of inviting major architects to create compelling exhibition design. In 1992, Hadid collaborated with the Guggenheim by designing *The Great Utopia*, the largest exhibition in the museum's history. Her brilliant conception unified the Frank Lloyd Wright spiraling white ramp with the Suprematist and Constructivist painting and sculpture at the heart of the show. Over the years, other great architects have designed exhibitions for the Guggenheim, such as Arata Isozaki (*China: 5,000 Years*, 1998), Frank Gehry (*The Art of the Motorcycle*, 1998), and Jean Nouvel (*Brazil: Body and Soul*, 2001). The Foundation has also presented important exhibitions on architecture, most recently *Frank Gehry: Architect* (2001).

Zaha Hadid comes at a moment when her projects—cultural, infrastructural, residential and commercial architecture, including master plans—are being realized in more than ten countries. With this exhibition, the Guggenheim is giving the public the opportunity to become better acquainted with Hadid's unique architecture, while also expressing a strong commitment to engage architecture that is shaping our lives and our times.

An exhibition of this magnitude could not have been accomplished without the full commitment of Zaha Hadid and her remarkable colleagues. Nor would it have taken the shape it did without the exceptional talent and dedication of our New York staff, led by Lisa Dennison, Director of the Solomon R. Guggenheim Museum. I am especially grateful to Germano Celant, Senior Curator of Contemporary Art, and Mónica Ramírez-Montagut, Assistant Curator of Architecture and Design. The many other people who made important contributions to this show are listed elsewhere in this catalogue.

Such an ambitious retrospective could not take place without the generous support of our sponsor. We would like to extend our sincerest thanks to Oldcastle Glass, whose commitment to innovation in architecture is expressed through their support of this landmark exhibition and accompanying symposium. In particular, I would like to thank Edwin B. Hathaway, Chief Executive Officer, for his vision and leadership. In addition, I would like to thank Deutsche Bank for its ongoing commitment and support of exhibitions at the Guggenheim. This exhibition also benefits from the support of the Leadership Committee chaired by Pentti Kouri , and including Lu Pat, Raja Sidawi, and other generous individuals.

Thomas Krens
Director, The Solomon R. Guggenheim Foundation

PREFACE/ ACKNOWLEDGMENTS

Zaha Hadid is an ambitious undertaking. This exhibition could not have been accomplished without the collaboration and unconditional support of above all Zaha Hadid. We wish to express our gratitude to Zaha Hadid Architects for their tireless efforts, generosity, and commitment to seeing the success of this exhibition through. The absolutely outstanding team of Zaha Hadid Architects is credited on the Project Team listing. We would also like to specially acknowledge Woody Yao and Ana Cajiao's contributions to the catalogue. The close collaboration and partnership of Zaha Hadid Architects with our museum staff team contributed to the realization of this historic exhibition.

We wish to express our sincerest gratitude to Jessica Ludwig, Exhibitions Project Manager, for her unique devotion to the project.

We would like to acknowledge in the Project Team credit page the hard working team that participated in the realization of this exhibition. We deeply thank you all.

We are indebted to the contributing authors Patrik Schumacher, Partner Zaha Hadid Architects; Joseph Giovannini, Architectural Critic; and Detlef Mertins, Professor of Architecture and Chair, Department of Architecture, University of Pennsylvania. We would also like to thank Nicholas Boyarsky for allowing us to publish interviews of Hadid by his father Alvin Boyarsky.

An exhibition of this magnitude would not have been possible without the generous collaboration of Zaha Hadid's clients. We are especially grateful to the lenders: Herbert Resch, Zumtobel, Dornbirn, Austria; Paolo Moroni and William Sawaya, Sawaya & Moroni, Milan; Glenn D. Lowry, Director, and Paola Antonelli, The Museum of Modern Art, New York; Nuria Lopez de Guereñu, Consejera de Transportes y Obras Publicas del País Vasco, Spain; Simon Parris and Kenny Schachter, Kenny Schachter ROVE, London; Joseph Giovannini, New York; Pablo de la Cal, Expoagua Zaragoza 2008 S.A., Spain; Alasdhair Willis, Established & Sons, UK; Manuela Pinna, Ernestomeda Spa, Pesaro, Italy; Mario de Biase (Mayor of Salerno) and Lorenzo Criscuolo (Project Manager), Comune di Salerno, Italy; Pablo Otaola, Comisión Gestora para el Desarrollo de Zorrozaurre, Bilbao; Linda Shearer, Contemporary Arts Center, Cincinnati; Michael Janssen, BMW Werk Leipzig, Germany; Alberto Alessi and Francesca Appiani, Museo Alessi, Omegna, Italy; Inge Wolf and Inka Plechaty, City of Weil am Rhein and Deutsches Architektur Museum, Frankfurt am Main; Francesca Alati and Carla Recchi, Treno Alta Velocita, Rome; and Massimo Fucci, DuPont Europe.

Due to the tireless efforts and generosity of all these individuals and organizations, the Guggenheim is pleased to present this retrospective exhibition, a unique contribution to the achievements of architecture in our contemporary world.

The unique architectural forms of the Guggenheim Museum's Frank Lloyd Wright building have played an important role in the conception of the *Zaha Hadid*. The exhibition is organized chronologically, presenting Zaha Hadid's early projects on the lower ramps and latest achievements on the upper spaces. Disrupting the linear chronology, thematic approaches are interwoven within the narrative. The thematic approaches, lines of research set forth by Hadid, link different projects of different times. Some of the themes, such as the concepts of fields, folds, ribbons, and clusters, are present on the ramps to be experienced by our audience. The exhibition will provide a first-hand experience of some of the concepts that have today become major points of departure when discussing the production of contemporary space. We hope this exhibition will contribute to a better understanding of Zaha Hadid's audacious architecture within the wonderful setting of Frank Lloyd Wright's Guggenheim.

Germano Celant
Senior Curator of Contemporary Art

Mónica Ramírez-Montagut
Assistant Curator of Architecture and Design

PROJECT TEAM

ZAHA HADID ARCHITECTS

Zaha Hadid
Patrik Schumacher, Partner
Woody Yao
Ana Cajiao
Melodie Leung
Thomas Vietzke
Helmut Kinzler
Tiago Correia
Roger Howie
Sarah Schuster
Ken Bostock
Muthahar Khan
Jevin Dornic
Miya Ushida
Andrea B. Caste
Josefina del Rio
Antonio de Campos (artist consultant)

GUGGENHEIM MUSEUM

Curatorial
Germano Celant, Senior Curator of Contemporary Art
Mónica Ramírez-Montagut, Assistant Curator of Architecture and Design

Curatorial Interns
Ting-Chi Wang
Bianca Cabrera
Jennifer Parsons

Art Services and Preparations
David Bufano, Chief Preparator
Derek DeLuco, Technical Specialist
Mary Ann Hoag, Lighting Designer
Barry Hylton, Senior Exhibition Technician
Elizabeth L. Jaff, Associate Preparator for Paper

Conservation
Julie Barten, Conservator, Exhibitions and Administration
Nathan Otterson, Conservator, Sculpture

Construction
Michael Sarff, Construction Manager

Development
Peggy Allen, Special Events Coordinator
Julia Brown, Manager of Membership
Lisa Brown, Corporate Development Associate
Stephen Diefenderfer, Special Events Manager
Renee Schacht, Manager of Institutional and Capital Development
Nick Simunovic, Director of Corporate Development, Americas
Helen Warwick, Director of Individual Development

Director's Office
Katerina Bernstram, Assistant to the Director
Sarah Cooper, Administrative Assistant
MaryLouise Napier, Deputy Chief of Staff

Education
Ryan Hill, Education Program Manager
Kim Kanatani, Gail Engelberg Director of Education
Elizabeth Lincoln, Education Coordinator, Public Programs
Sharon Vatsky, Senior Education Program Manager, School Programs
Christina Yang, Senior Education Manager

Exhibition Design
Ana Luisa Leite, Manager of Exhibition Design
Melanie Taylor, Exhibition Designer Coordinator

Exhibition Design Interns
Kelsey Harrington
Naomi Munro

ZAHA HADID: ADVENTURE IN ARCHITECTURE

Germano Celant

During the 1970s, while studying at the Architectural Association (AA) in London and working for the Office for Metropolitan Architecture (OMA), Zaha Hadid began to gain an awareness of the languages of the visual and constructive arts and to cultivate an identity in these disciplines. This period marked a radical turning point in these fields, carried out by a range of figures—from Archigram to Superstudio, Robert Smithson to Arata Isozaki, Hans Hollein to Frank Gehry, Raimund Abraham to Aldo Rossi, Robert Venturi to Peter Eisenman, Tokyo Ito to Richard Meier—who pushed the proliferation of creativity— eccentric and chromatic, structural and technological, material and formal—into the relationships that arise between the reality of a project and its image. The process was no longer integrative but explosive. Thus the resulting construction, even while responding to a functional and social need, could also have an imaginative, figurative, and therefore implicitly artistic side. This was an abandonment of univocality—according to which architecture is an echo chamber of use-demands and economic demands— in favor of an open multiplicity of purpose, where what matters is not mere usefulness, but the uselessness and immateriality linked to the communication of signs in which the construction is also posited as a conveyer of messages and images. The illusion of constructive thought as self-contained, logical, and central, with no residue, falls by the wayside, as the idea now becomes fragmentary, decentralized, and excessive.

Design production at this point becomes more poetic. It offers not only remedies—making the building practical, serviceable, and governable—but also reflects a subjective component: the architect's creative thought. The latter takes form in an image that illuminates the language of architecture with new meanings. The notion of pure, reductive production, impersonal and abstract, enters a state of crisis, and what emerges is a figuration that brings with it a strong iconic identity and therefore a quality that is highly original and diverse compared to the integrative forms of architecture that make up the modern urban landscape. The sensational, spectacular exceptionalism and obviousness of this iconic architecture bring visibility back to the fore alongside invisibility, and the emphasis is now on exteriority over interiority, surface over structure. Architecture thus approaches the notion of monument as a double of the planner and patron who leave their signatures on the product, in a gesture that has something publicly vainglorious and narcissistic about it. The communicative function alters the relations between architecture and society in the same way, pushing them to adapt the imagination to the imposed terms of consumerism and the mass media. It must show that it can resist the perpetual mutation of the strategies of communication, which in global contemporary industry undergo daily changes on the level of product as well as market. At the same time, the image/logo/signature must remain constant and display itself in the building as the continual affirmation of an eternally renewed spectacularity that thrives on the excesses of temporal occurrences. The edifice is transformed into a terminal where surprising, hyperbolic visions and news are generated and regenerated. The urgency for information modifies the architectural event, rendering it performative so that it may survive in the ever-changing labyrinth of functions and representations produced and solicited by society. In this way one is forced to rethink the fundamental values of architectural design— which have always been based on schematic, abstract, metahistorical rules—as places of transit for practices linked to the variants of history.

This, then, is architecture as kaleidoscope, and it accepts the acceleration of time, events, and unexpected incidents. Making no secret of its interest in giving priority to the image, it moves closer to other arts conceived through sudden apparitions and mediums to convey conceptual and emotional contents. This movement does not allow itself to fall into the trap of any one specific message, but rather thrives on instability and surprise, on confusion and the mingling of positive and negative, the particular and the universal. Architecture sets out in search of a narrative, the transcription of a vision, either subservient or critical, that arises in the interrelationship between the personal and the social, and yields an architectural result whose power is alternative to the univocal, Manichaean, and moralistic perspectives of twentieth-century international modernism. This position is a skeptical, disillusioned one that does not preclude the realism of a concrete response to human needs, but also contains anarchistic aspirations with respect to past and present values.

At this moment the architect becomes aware of her inability to resolve all problems, but at the same time she is no longer open to a purely tactical approach that denies her imagination and conceptual powers. To regenerate these, she puts her trust in the image, which theoretically implies a cultural project, conceivable and realizable, whose roots lie not only in economics and functionalism, but also in fantasy and the dream. And in order to take her first steps in this new adventure, she initially relies on defining images—on paper or in maquettes, on canvas or on the screen—that will represent her vision. With their sudden, modifiable appearance, she crystallizes the multiplicity of a design or a residue of a design that is not yet concrete but still imaginary; that is, it simulates meaning and reality.

When, in 1977, on the occasion of her graduation from the AA, she begins to elaborate an architectural territory with which to identify herself and offer a vision of her own, she does so by presenting a project for a bridge over the Thames—Malevich's Tektonik (London, 1976–77)—which is an abstraction on paper, a conceptual hypothesis inspired by the Suprematist artist. This point of departure is fundamental to an understanding of the architect's later methodological developments. First of all, Hadid looks to an architecture that draws inspiration from art's autonomy and becomes, in Malevich's terms, a *form of pure art*. Thus it corresponds to creative demands of construction, which are therefore independent of reality, to give the project a strongly imaginary bent, in accordance with the conceptual schema of an abstract and painterly tradition that runs from Suprematism to the work for OMA. Except that the metaphysical beauty of Malevich's *Alpha Architekton* (1920), a source of inspiration for Hadid's London bridge, is translated into a utilitarian hypothesis, a referential entity, in essence. In this sense Hadid articulates a reality that is without origin and not concrete. She creates a colored image—one that can be on paper or canvas—an image that precedes reality, a simulation in which the vestiges of the world do not exist: they are virtual. This hyperfuturistic, visionary conception short-circuits art history, transforming Malevich's original paintings and models (Fig. 01), which were imaginary, into a claim to reality. It is a process that translates Suprematist and Constructivist iconography, which is Utopian and experimental in character, into a potential instrument for use. An image of something that does not exist, like the pure and absolute space of a work of art, seeks to establish a concrete manifestation in a bridge with multiple levels of function.

The choice to take an image from the art world and turn it into architecture is an entirely novel proposition. It implies the recourse to a prophetic, messianic approach, that of an art uprooted from reality, and to architecture's necessary concreteness and realism. Moreover, the use of creative simulation—on paper, canvas, or screen—with its mutable virtuality, liberates thought and forms, allowing them to roam freely without having to mirror an imposed socioeconomic

demand. The image can overflow, radiating openly into a combination of models in a weightless, atmosphereless hyperspace. All of Hadid's future work will hinge on this dichotomy between the artistic and the imaginary, the virtual and hyperspace. As an artist-architect, she works first on signs and figures, which short-circuit energy, and then on the concrete future of the images.

We can thus understand the definition of her projects as *paintings*, just as we can grasp her adoption of an external, almost aerial view suggesting the disorienting perspective of maps and urbanistic charts, as in the drawings for the Irish Prime Minister's Residence (Dublin, 1979–80) and the Parc de la Villette (Paris, 1982–83). The view from an external, imaginary point reminiscent of the satellite's eye is fascinating and surprising, going so far as to give the project an ominous, astounding aspect not unlike that encountered in Suprematist works like Gustav Klucis's *Dynamic City* (1919) or El Lissitsky's *Prouns* (Fig. 02). It turns the architect into a vagabond and nomad in the space he is supposed to design, inserting him in a correct constellation of solutions and figures. At the same time, the aerial perspective is accompanied by a weightless, directionless condition that leaves one free to explore the subject according to the optics of reality as well as the dream. Hadid's Hong Kong project, The Peak (1982–83), attempts to span, in Suprematist fashion, the stratifications of a city that has grown up vertically, and proposes an almost seismic sweep of this space, one capable of upending the system of habitation. The topography of the planned building is interpreted in terms of a geology that includes the striations of social and subjective life. The resulting proposition succeeds in establishing a disturbing, surprising separation between the subterranean strata and the aerial voids of the construction, which when seen in perspective looks like a vehicle that has landed on a mountaintop during a voyage of discovery. It is the outer limit of

architecture, made up of abstract, personal forms. This sort of new world takes shape in the painting *The World (89 Degrees)* (1983), which depicts a portion of planisphere and an extraterrestrial topographical map that could be considered a chromatic, formal photograph of the interplanetary voyage Hadid has taken through the universe of imaginary and artistic architecture from the days at the A A to the definition of her own professional identity.

The phantasmagorical observation of a chaotic, disorienting, and magmatic city is a subject that has been transformed into imagery numerous times. The totality consists of fluids and grids, colors and bewildering volumes, and it has a constant presence in the architect's imagination. In works ranging from Halkin Place (London, 1985), to the installation *Metropolis* (Institute of Contemporary Art, London, 1988), the exasperating urban mass of London is depicted in all its articulated levels and multiple centers. These urban interpretations confront the expanded stage of the metropolis, but they do so according to the bold hypothesis of art, whereby the world is displaced by an image, as Marcel Duchamp was able to do. This displacement, which takes the observer's gaze outside the object and the city, involves, in Hadid's projects, a creative treatment, as in the painting *Berlin 2000* (1988), and Victoria City Aerial (Berlin, 1988), where the aerial navigation inside the volumes of the city of Berlin produces chromatic and volumetric corridors that divide the city into sections that are no longer political but functional, such as shopping centers, offices, and hotels. The orbital and artistic perspective highlights traffic patterns, which become abstract lines, and the clustering of buildings, to the point where the evolution of Barcelona, in A New Barcelona (1989, Fig. 03), takes a form whose dense weaves of lines and wedges lead to a redefinition of its urban context.

Since they are portions of territory, Hadid's paintings are "cutouts" of an astral, spherical vision and appear as partial framings of the city. Specular fragments of a whole image, they can also be subjected to free rearrangements and montage. They can appear over the electronic media n books or reviews, on monitors and movie screens, freely cut up or edited. What matters, in fact, is their value as information on the project. This communicative construction, typical of the 1990s, makes more and more room for the computer and computer simulations, a technological tool that allows one to simulate an internal and external journey that *seems* real. This reinforcement of the architect's imagination helps to construct an absolutely realistic image of a building that does not exist in reality. It helps to define the body of the edifice, as both skin and flesh, entering inside its nervous system and vital channels. The latter metamorphose into road beams and highways, while the stratifications of muscle become mobile stratifications following changeable trajectories. The significance of this transition from the painted concept to the complex, articulated superform is highlighted in the project's visibility and potential factuality.

The painting's calligraphy and its dialectical relationship with the elaboration of a concrete project creates, *ex novo*, an attitude in which need dominates the result but keeps the imagination of forms alive. The Office Building on Kurfürstendamm 70 (Berlin, 1986) continues to echo the Suprematist-Constructivist position, but it responds to the use-demand for a reduced, compressed urban space. In this case the building rises up off the ground, suspended like Vladimir Tatlin's *Corner Counter-Reliefs*, and is composed of heterogeneous materials presented for their specific visual qualities. It constitutes a living space osmotically placed within the fragmented, broken urban space of Berlin, but asserts itself as a dynamic, nonobjective image, which, although restricted to an economy of space, thrives on a multiplicity of perspective orientations and material transparencies and opacities—a kind of sailboat building that floats and travels freely through the monolithic ensemble of German city planning. Projecting out from it are protuberances and wedges of negative and positive space, triangular and elliptical articulations that insinuate themselves into the urban fabric, breaking through its linearity and becoming counter-

spaces—multiform technological magmas which in their disunity absorb all contrasts and transform themselves, as Tatlin (Fig. 04) puts it, into a "unity rich in initiative." These same counterspaces are proposed in Los Angeles (West Hollywood Civic Center, 1987), Abu Dhabi (Al Wahda Sport Centre, 1988), and Hamburg (Hafenstrasse Office and Residential Development, 1989); and these projects, in their fragmented appearance and heterogeneous forms, establish a whole that shatters the existing morphology and acts as a figural and functional reagent.

Concrete realization translates first into monument and then into architecture. Material and sculptural surprise informs *Folly 3* (1990), executed for Expo '90 in Osaka. An open hollow of surfaces in compressed cement, its different geometries and colors are arranged as paths, and the whole seems to combine a strong reference to the monumental and political architecture of Walter Gropius and his *Monument to the Fallen of March* (Weimar, 1920), as well as to the language of Richard Serra's sculpture, as in *Joplin* (1970), and *Shift* (1970–72). At Osaka, the dynamics of the inclinations and angles induce transit and rest, but more than anything else they define architectural culture as a tool of information based on variable planes and screens. The process is similar to scientific activity, where the elements are reproducible but in perpetual motion—a process that stands apart from traditional production. Here the definition of architecture mutates. It is not repetitive but conceptual; it does not imitate reality but formulates ideas that shed light on the activity of living. It aims at making discoveries and creating from novelty a presence that is an energetic interweaving of image and project, as in the Vitra Fire Station (Weil am Rein, Germany, 1990–94), a testimonial to a different mode of architectural production.

The space is broken up, creating a play of perspectives in an attack on the orthodoxy of form and visual control. Indeed the complexity of the architectural montage, which corresponds to an urban vision and functions as a crystallization of the road system of the industrial complex of

Vitra, aims to create a weave, a three-dimensional construction half-*Proun*, half-Persian rug, where the complexity of the threads and grids should be seen as open circularities and multiplicities.

The explosion of surfaces, however, is problematic, because it attempts to reconcile formal disaggregation with practical organization, an architectural operation that reflects a contemporary idea based on a causality that is no longer linear and singular, but complex. That is, it is perfectly circular; there is no before and after, no entrance or exit, high or low, left or right, but only an open swarm of all the components. The Vitra Fire Station is thus a work of architecture that emerges on the ground, in which every fragment contains information on the whole image, but does not sum it up. In fact its existence presents an almost natural order, that of a flowering; the material is inanimate, but it structures itself as if it were alive. Visually and sculpturally, it does not correspond to any static order where everything solidifies at a point of arrival; rather, it attempts to create an evolutionary movement based on the variants resulting from an active display—based on the stretching, cutting, bending, and slicing of the structures. This filmlike montage thrives on cuts—so much so that its edges are sharp and its graftings brutal—and on blendings and contrasts between all the transparencies, lights, and cement surfaces, so that the parts are interconnected and susceptible to specular variations in continuous transformation. In the end, the "architectural" object is broken down into parts in such a way as to allow one to understand the mechanisms anatomically, then put back together according to a complex, dramatic juxtaposition and collision between its primary components.

The circularity lives in a transitory state between fullness and emptiness and makes Hadid's architecture an unstoppable stream, a sequence of points and viaducts, of volumes and surfaces that flow into one another, juxtaposing mutability and stasis. Entering it, one has the impression of a variable space with no destination, something contingent on the vicissitudes of the lives of the inhabi-

01 Kazimir Malevich, *Gota*, 1923, reconstructed in 1989. Plaster, 33 ¹/₂ x 18 ⁷/₈ x 22 ⁷/₈ inches (85.2 x 48 x 58 cm). Musée national d'art moderne, Centre Georges Pompidou, Paris

02 El Lissitzky, *Proun (Entwurf zu Proun S.K.)*, 1922–23. Gouache, india ink, pencil, conté crayon, and varnish on buff paper, 11 ³/₄ x 8 ⁷/₁₆ inches (29.8 x 21.4 cm). Solomon R. Guggenheim Museum, New York, Gift, Estate of Katherine S. Dreier 53.1343

03 A New Barcelona, 1989. Painting

04 Studio view of Vladimir Tatlin's model *Monument to the Third International* (1919–20)

05 Philharmonic Hall, Luxembourg, 1997. Digital rendering

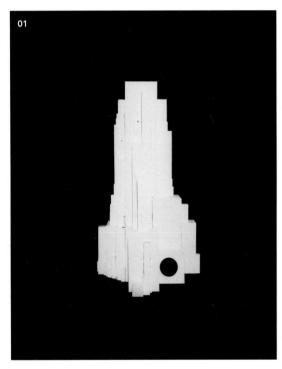

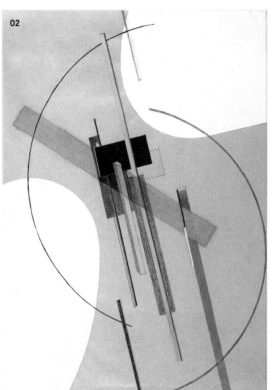

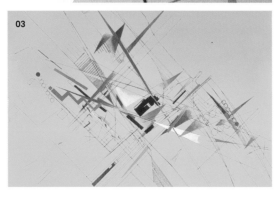

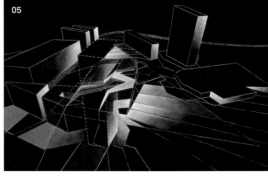

cants and visitors. No direction is given, as though it is left up to our impulses and desires, which can always change their objects and destinations, to determine which path to take. Vitra Fire Station is a network of interconnected canals full of liquid matter that is not static but mobile.

Transit is the fundamental subject of the projects LFOne/Landesgartenschau (Weil am Rheim, Germany, 1996–99), and Car Park and Terminus Hoenheim-Nord (Strasbourg, France, 1998–2001). Here the displacement and flux create linear and surface dislocations that become fields and routes in which one finds automobiles, taxis, and buses, as well as passersby and travellers. Looking at the architect's drawings for the Car Park and Terminus, one realizes that the project is essentially topological, that is, it is a sequence of passages both horizontal and vertical; whereas with LFOne, a hall for an international gardening show, the lines lead her to construct a space that is neither metaphysical nor rational, like that for the cars, but natural and organic. The former project is rationally empty and the latter fluidly full, laden with oscillations and hidden rules. LFOne is a complex of connections and junctures that form felicitous networks of conjunction and displacement, as in a natural labyrinth. Architecture and landscape here become a single reality, the one emerging inside the other and vice versa, creating a continuum based on a mutual absorption of differences.

In the period from 1992 to 2000, the concepts of fluidity and circularity, expressed through virtual instruments, inspire many urban projects in which the imaginary vector drives Hadid to paint designs that present themselves as exploratory maps of ideas and forms (Fig. 05). Based largely on a displacement and chromatic fluidity drawn again from the sphere of the Russian avant-garde and the architectural fantasies of Yakov Chernikov, the site-plan painting of landscape for the Carnuntum Museum (Bad Deutsch-Altenburg, Austria, 1993), and the exploded aerial view of the Cardiff Bay Opera House (Wales, 1994–96) are the designs of a diviner who aspires to find and compose urban entities structured according to an organicity that thrives in a halo of prickles and waves intended to produce a polycentric condition of life.

The quest for a multiplicity of places, materials, surfaces, and hollows defining Hadid's adventure in architecture is fully affirmed in the Lois and Richard Rosenthal Center for Contemporary Art (Cincinnati, 1997–2003). Here the tension is directed toward a space without rules, which favors dramatic effects and a monumental proliferation of hollows and materials. Conceived as a kind of Mies van der Rohe building gone mad, the Rosenthal Center is made up of architectural blocks highlighted by protuberances and the materials themselves, as underscored by the volumes and museum spaces that stagger the geometry of the building's sides. Hadid uses these elements to disturb the linearity and volumetrics of the city. She energetically alters the external whole, dislocating and disarticulating the parts and making them autonomous, in order to produce an entity that is neither closed nor hierarchicized. The idea is to reflect the mission of the institution, its dedication to contemporary art—that is, to a mobile, variable language, which has a center but develops in different directions, depending on different colors and materials. The Rosenthal Center becomes something suspended in space and time, unpredictable, as underscored by its entrance and lobby, which function as an "urban carpet," a magical, aerial vehicle—like art itself, whose travel is guided by imagination—that nevertheless remains anchored in the life of the polis. In the constructed body of the institution, what reigns is the loss of center and the fluctuation of itineraries, architectural motifs that mark the entire adventure of Hadid's interiors, whether designed for exposition or habitation. We have mentioned the vegetable and carnal flowering in her works, but in this case we might also add the image of a rocky fringe that cancels out the ground's rigid physiognomy and reveals its mobility; alternately, we could speak of a labyrinthine itinerary conforming to a formless, larval geography. The idea is to express an immersion in a uterine cavity in order to incubate a second birth, the birth of the gaze and aesthetic taste, the necessary entry into the universe of art.

In the MAXXI National Centre of Contemporary Art (Rome, 1997–ongoing), the internal fluidity of the Rosenthal Center is externalized and becomes a multiplicative extension of lines and volumes, an architectural field that is a controlled proliferation of itineraries and habitats, and a continuum without center, a weave of material signifying the circulation of ideas and images. Here too the monolithic, centralizing representation of architecture dissolves and becomes a grid laden with an explosion of signs over the constructed ground. Indeed the building is conceived as a garment or a second skin covering the body of one part of the city—a light, woven envelope reminiscent of ancient Roman inlay as well as the landscape of Latium. Echoing the sinuous lines of LFOne, the MAXXI Centre inhabits its context like a painting whose canvas stretches softly over the earth's strata, adheres and fills its hollow spaces, renouncing the rigid formula of autonomous, imposed architecture, which is monolithic and central. There is no closure to the design; rather, it is open to infinite projection, producing the lines of force that make up the museum and branch out over the surrounding space. Here the edifice is transformed from a self-contained entity into a moment in a formal and spatial dialectic with the dynamic elements of the city. It represents the interaction between two nuclei—the museum and Rome—or, alternately, the split of a central nucleus—the institution—which expands and becomes a root that nourishes and self-nourishes, a hollow of itineraries and lights, spiral, explosive, and charged with vital lymph.

Such openness also implies an absence of repetition and linguistic uniformity, an identity that is fundamental for this museum that always projects outward toward an unknown horizon. For this reason, the project for the Guggenheim Museum (Taichung, Taiwan, 2003) is conceived as a stone continuity of space and time, a perpetual conti-nuity of forms that inside seems crossed with paths leading in every direction. What matters is the continuity of the museum and of art: the organic uniformity of the life of visual culture, which does not end at some given point, but rather indicates possible horizons suggesting a movement toward something, like the baroque with its journey through a space that can be articulated ad infinitum. Continuity is thus conceived as a breaking of limits, foreshadowing a telescopic vision of the city—that is, reflecting the exploratory approach of science toward new universes, new perspectives, from the central to the elliptical, from Bramante to Borromini.

Having singled out decentralization as modus operandi, in order that construction present itself as an open weave with no reference to a privileged signifier to orient it or confer meaning on it, Hadid's architecture can be consid-ered a mingling of organic culture and baroque culture. Its aim is to move between energetic incandescence and solidifications of folds and joints, between nature and an artifice that terrifies because it supports surprises and deviations from the normal course of the architectural narrative. Her construction is mental, like her paintings, and it is organized in visions where chaos and order, form-lessness and figuration intersect—where the dynamism becomes the finished work because it leaps into the void of the edifice's membranes, a void mastered as the sign of energy expansion.

A void sprouting up from the earth and spreading into the air is allegorically evoked by Hadid's Bergisel Ski Jump (Innsbruck, Austria, 1999–2002), where the leaping and falling rhythms produce an aerial sculpture, a kind of periscope that turns about to watch the landscape and weaves a ski-jump ramp of streaking speed. This taut, fluid architecture recalls one of Claes Oldenburg's "colos-sal monuments" and expresses a telluric force yawning in the emptiness. The spiral and the whirling wheel amplify the heavenly detachment of the ski jumper, who breaks free into the void and flies. In the Napoli-Afragola High-Speed Train Station (Naples, 2003–ongoing), the motion becomes more serpentine and recalls a snake slithering with ease through nature.

The project highlights an elastic approach to building that shifts the center and contours in relation to the slid-ing motion typical of mobile machines such as a city sub-way. Although this is a station, its form contradicts the moments of stasis and pause, conveying instead a sense of mobility and velocity. It presents itself as a bridge between different moments in the life of the city.

Hadid's architectural works can be seen as soft draperies displaying wondrous cavities that slice the air and open up new horizons—autonomous, self-sufficient coverings that form an envelope that is at once substance and empti-ness, a body that is not an immobile shape but shifts and displaces itself with respect to the perspective, tirelessly moving about. The Phaeno Science Center (Wolfsburg, 2000–05) is an animal-like body that celebrates its tri-umphs in its outer skin and movement. Bathed in light, the tissue of scales and transparent openings making up its organically geometrical shell, the Phaeno Center pulsates in space and is packed with surprises and obstacles cor-responding to scientific discoveries. An intellectual and virtual fire circulates in this space, fed by concrete as well as intuitive power. This is why its form is multiple and elu-sive; it lives in a dialectic of opposites, which, as they encounter one another, create new solutions that are based on a structural method. It is a volume built on cones that are positioned inside and outside, to avoid superim-positions of construction and create instead a "crater landscape" supporting the whole. The metaphor of lavalike ebullition and explosion is consistent with the scientific functions of an institution where opposing forces produce results. The crater is thus the material nucleus serving as the support for the architecture and the center for thought and research. The spirit and nervous vitality of discovery hover above it, the same spirit that allows us to approach an architectural object that is no longer displayed before our eyes but dark and hidden, secret and indecipherable, if we limit ourselves to a single, rigid perspective. The archi-tecture comes to life because the gaze not only resorts to its intellectual tools but also brings experience into play; that is, it succeeds in tapping an architectural modeling that is perpetually variable. In the Phaeno Center, the appearance of continuity prevails over that of rupture. Right angles and solid surfaces are eliminated; curves and pores predominate, as though it were a body whose skin breathed and perspired illuminations. The whole thing is plied and flexed, because fluctuation prevents the estab-lishment of a rigid law and a definitive order. Inflection underlies shaping and modeling: it is a quest. At the same time, this work is enigmatic; it has a questioning tension about it, for it plays out on multiple registers of meaning and visibility, all equally valid and powerful, in order to con-struct an intermediary whole at once suspended and sus-pensive, and not intended to be framed. It is yet another project revolving around the passage between opposites, asserting an architecture whose rational and emotional aspects are not separate but become portentous propel-lants of surprises and events. Hadid's is an architectural process that explodes all unilaterally constructive and cog-nitive procedures in the face of the invisible and imaginary.

Translated from the Italian by Stephen Sartarelli

IN THE NATURE OF DESIGN MATERIALS: THE INSTRUMENTS OF ZAHA HADID'S VISION

Joseph Giovannini

It is axiomatic that an architect cannot design what she cannot see. But there are little-known corollaries to the rule—that certain drawing and modeling techniques show designs with certain prejudice, that different techniques allow architects to see in different ways, that developing and multiplying these different ways of seeing can generate, drive, and evolve the design itself. Tools are instruments of vision, but the mediums and techniques with which an architect designs can be cultivated so that they take on a life of their own, tending to their own results, becoming integral to a vision they influence, enhance, and even shape. The dancer cannot be separated from the dance; the pencil is instrumental to the drawing.

For a decade before she finally broke ground with her first major building, the Vitra Fire Station (Weil am Rhein, Germany, 1990–94), Zaha Hadid developed her architectural approach through drawing and painting in an office that some critics dismissed as an artist's studio; the office really amounted to an experimental research laboratory in architecture. Pursuing the elusive commission, she remained a paper architect but became visionary.

There was, however, a major, even historic, dividend to the mirage of building. Without the onus of construction, it was, to paraphrase John Milton, like angels making love without their bodies getting in the way. The architecture that Hadid finally built exceeded Vitruvius's admonition that architecture embody firmness, commodity, and delight and achieved, instead, Charles Baudelaire's "luxe, calme et volupté." But the buildings that today distinguish themselves as voluptuaries of a powerful yet refined sensuousness started as an incorporeal vision disembodied from construction. In the most material of the arts, Hadid explored an immaterial vision, and paper proved the correctly groundless ground for constructing the vision.

As Henry-Russell Hitchcock wrote in his book about Frank Lloyd Wright's buildings—*In the Nature of Materials* (1942)—Wright designed according to the capacity and "nature" of construction materials. Louis Kahn asked a brick what it wanted to be. Such modernists anticipated in their designs the physical properties of the materials in which they were building, but Hadid explored the properties of the materials in which she was designing. Instead of asking a brick about its future life in an arch, she asked drawings, models, paper reliefs, and painted tableaux what they wanted a design to be, or how they could force and even precipitate the design. Hadid tested the capacity and nature of a design material so that it would interact with the concept itself, suggesting through its materiality and process different possibilities. She would, for example, walk a drawing over to a photocopier, and drag the image across the glass as the machine copied it to produce a smeared distortion of the drawing. She was proposing to build the same uncanny swish of form that can be found in the paintings of Francis Bacon.

Each art progresses at its own speed, and Hadid accelerated her development by taking architecture to what appeared to be unbuildable extremes in drawing and painting. The rebound from her design process provided a much more immediate response than the feedback usual from the construction process. Her dialogue with design materials, rather than building materials, allowed her artistic control that was not subject to the rationalizing effects of construction, whose many layers of successively practical agreement tend to force compromise and sand off eccentricity. Hadid was striving for nonnormative and even strange qualities, and working experimentally and extensively with design materials, she developed and consolidated her artistic intentions before they could be flattened in conventionalizing construction processes. Early on she refused the inevitability of buildings made common under the banner of practicality.

In Hadid's laboratory, the mediums of design were not tethered to representation but instead encouraged ways of seeing released from convention. The impact of a design material on design often occurred unintentionally—the process of investigation affecting the subject under study inadvertently, as in Heisenberg's uncertainty principle. Through feedback loops, the mediums informed the vision.

Hadid escaped the drafting table, and in acts of interdisciplinarity, she used mediums whose material logic helped her to invent an architecture that the T square and parallel rule no longer controlled. It was not what the brick wanted to be, but what drawing, watercolor, models, reliefs, storyboards, the photocopier, and most recently the computer allowed and encouraged an idea to become. In pursuit of a nonnormative architecture, Hadid avoided the conventional use of conventional architectural tools that were all about rule and measure. She did not design on graph paper. She used mediums so that they were liberating rather than controlling. She tended to the incommensurate.

While working at the Office for Metropolitan Architecture in partnership with Rem Koolhaas and Elia Zenghelis, Hadid sketched a stunning "exploded" axonometric ink drawing of the "Ambulatory and Connection" for the Dutch Parliament Extension (The Hague, 1978–79), showing the parts of the structure separated from each other and suspended within the space of the picture plane in a syntactic relationship resembling a sentence diagram (Fig. 01). Successful as a graphic explanation of parts, it also suggested that the parts of a building could be built suspended in actual space, as fragments of a frozen explosion. Rather than using the medium as a passive explanatory tool, Hadid entered into an inquisitive and interactive relationship with the unusual drawing technique, which in turn pushed to the brink of invention a design thesis about breaking apart the whole. This axonometric drawing anticipated many future consequences for her oeuvre, especially the implication of open rather than closed form. Her buildings would never be contained shapes closed to the outside and opaque to the inside.

The use of drawings to help engender and develop a vision traces to the influence of the Russian avant-garde of the early twentieth century. The DNA of Hadid's work evolves from the art of Kazimir Malevich, who famously sought to escape from the third dimension as he tried to capture an eerie fourth dimension in spectral drawings and paintings of forms floating mysteriously in vaporized space. Though an architect, Malevich was uninterested in constructing on canvas the perspectival space that all architects had invoked since the Renaissance. He sited his forms in indeterminate fogs rather than in the depth of an ordered space that receded to distant vanishing points with measured rationality. Pursuing a spatial mysticism, Malevich posited a vision that seemed unachievable and even antiarchitectural. In illusory tableaux, he introduced notions of transparency, interpenetration, and disappearance, and with the Suprematism he expounded, he proposed a thesis that was as radical in architecture as Cubism was in painting. Air, not ground, was the foundational element. Malevich tried to translate Suprematism into *Architektons*—architectural models that resembled the extruded shafts and profiles of skyscrapers—but did not succeed in capturing the quality and essence of the vision in three-dimensional form. The vision was never built, and the Soviet politics of the 1920s cut short any further experimentation.

In the 1970s, at a time when many architects were looking to history for reference and direction, Hadid, as a student at the Architectural Association in London, turned to the Suprematist precedent, which had seemed so promising. In her now-legendary thesis project, Malevich's Tektonik (London, 1976–77), she simply gave the abstract forms of a Suprematist composition function and scale, transforming an abstract tableau of geometric forms into a mixed-use architectural project, which included a nightclub and hotel perched on Hungerford Bridge over the Thames. It was the start of her effort to revivify Suprematism and carry it forward. Hadid has great intellectual tenacity, coupled with a ferocious visual imagination, and she continued to develop the Suprematist vision after graduation.

Inspired by Malevich's ethereal canvases, she took up the brush as a design tool, adopting forced perspective along with projective drawing techniques, especially axonometric and isometric, which had been used by Suprematists for visualizing their irrational environments. Adding fish-eye perspective to her use of projective geometries and forced perspective, she cultivated distortion in architecture. The fragmentation introduced very early in her career with such tableaux as the Dutch Parliament Extension drawing acquired a binding sense of motion and fluidity.

In such prepossessing tableaux as the the Victoria City Aerial (Berlin, 1988), *The World (89 Degrees)* (1983), and Zollhoff 3 Media Park (Düsseldorf, 1989–93, Fig. 02), Hadid depicted city and buildings from simultaneously divergent views. She multiplied vanishing points and deployed volumes drawn in axonometric projection leaning at various angles, generating a cityscape in constant optical shift. Rather than deferring to an omniscient point of view that locked all the parts in an ordered whole, the collage of viewpoints seemed instead to shift visual gears, precipitating a continuous state of becoming. The order that emerged was controlled, not by a static geometry, but by the sense of space as a force that binds all the matter in it. Curvature and the collective leaning bound the fragments into a force field that was not random but simply ordered in a nonlinear way. Hadid induced through the graphics of her visual physics an Einsteinian vision of form warped by forces in space. The buildings and their contexts did not add up to a Renaissance whole.

Hadid's tableaux anticipated the force fields and sense of vectorial space produced on animation software, but long before the logarithmic intelligence of the computer, there was the photocopier, whose use she subverted by turning it into a drawing tool. A machine acquired the gestural capacity of the hand. Hadid and her studio of architects, including her longtime principal associate, Patrik Schumacher, "smeared" drawings over the glass as the copier rolled across the page. They also "drew" with the machine's one-way sizing feature, at the press of a button stretching or compressing any image, such as a rectangle, in a single direction, transforming it into an isometric projection or a parallelogram. Rotating the rectangle while photocopying produced a curved smear. The copier afforded Hadid and her associates their first opportunity to automate distortion. Of course, with Photoshop and modeling software, the computer would later allow a much greater capacity to breed distortion.

A handful of architects before Hadid had carried over drawing techniques into the built structure. Francesco Borromini, for example, built his famous Galleria in Rome's Palazzo Spada in forced perspective. Hadid, however, grafted several techniques and viewpoints in the same multidimensional tableaux, and the multiplication of viewpoints and forced perspective migrated into her first built structures. In the Vitra Fire Station, she shaped the main volumes in perspectives forced to divergent vanishing points. With slightly curved edges, Hadid seemed to stretch space by attenuating the forms. The curves had migrated into the work through fish-eye perspective, and through the increasing presence of French curves at the drafting table. In the generation of buildings before and after Vitra, including her slender Office Building on Kurfürstendamm 70 in Berlin (1986), the architects always drew with a score of French curves, whose changing radii flattened or deepened the curves. Once a fixture of the Beaux-Arts drafting tables, French curves were banished by straight-lined modernists, but in Hadid's office, the nearly forgotten tools were instrumental in breaking down the domination of the right angle in design. Old tools helped usher Einsteinian curvature into architecture.

With the completion of the Vitra Fire Station, Hadid demonstrated that the vision that was so convincing in drawn form could be realized as a building. She could translate graphic concept into reality without losing the power of the hypnotically strange drawings. A haunting vision that seemed to reside in two-dimensional tableaux could be ushered into a third dimension by applying graphic techniques that further dimensionalized actual three-dimensional form. Especially at night, when the footlights washed its surfaces in gradients of light, the building looked like Hadid's visionary paintings.

Hadid's modus operandi in drawing and painting was not representation (Fig. 03). Instead of re-presenting what existed or what she knew, Hadid was, like a visual fabulist, enhancing and even enchanting reality, aspiring to the spatial ethers of the Suprematists—but without the mysticism. To pursue the painterly issues of transparency, immateriality and above all a strange and intangible spatial otherness, she had to escape the too-predictable, right-angled worlds produced by the T square and parallel rule. Influenced by the liberating visions of artists, she virtually left the drawing boards in the same way Frank Gehry did when—under the influence of Los Angeles's light and space artists—he abandoned the usual drawings to sculpt architectural models with his hands.

During Hadid's speech at the State Hermitage Museum, St. Petersburg, accepting the 2004 Pritzker Architecture Prize, she said, "Studying the revolutionary Russian work, I realized how Modern architecture built upon the breakthrough achieved by abstract art as the conquest of a previously unimaginable realm of creative freedom. Art used to be re-presentation rather than creation. Abstraction opened the possibility of unfettered invention"[1] (Fig. 04).

With the Vitra Fire Station, Hadid already superceded her mentors Malevich and El Lissitzky in realizing what was, effectively, a Suprematist building. In 1992, for her exhibition design of *The Great Utopia: The Russian and Soviet Avant-Garde, 1915–1932* (Figs. 05–06) at the Solomon R. Guggenheim Museum in New York, she literally cited Suprematism's influence by overlaying an abstract Malevich composition over the museum's floor plan, then ushering it through Wright's building and across its rotunda, like an ice flow. She spatialized the graphic so that the forms grew into display cases grafted onto the building, deforming and conforming with its circular geometry. The forms became a spatial field, rising and falling through the building, as the program demanded. The result was a composite structure, Malevich on Wright. In a masterful series of drawings for *The Great Utopia*, Hadid peered into the vortex of a rising energy field, set in motion by Wright's spinning atrium, launching a field of planes into the spiral. She looked at it from the bottom and the top. In these exquisite, but quick, gestural sketches, she posited the notion that space is vectorial.

Hadid makes no apologies about her search and research into space and form, and the paintings were the most conspicuous venues because they doubled as visual manifestoes—the billboards of the practice—during a period when she built little. But her search was intense, taking place in a variety of mediums at a time when the work qualified as pure rather than applied research.

The beauty of the results, both in the studies and the eventual buildings, is deceptive because Hadid and her office do not pursue form simply for the sake of form. Given the amount of work currently in the office, and the accelerating pace, the research is preparatory for expanding the formal repertoire necessary to solve the needs for greater levels of spatial variety and formal complexity in contemporary living conditions. Hadid's radically reinvented forms of organization have resulted in a higher degree of order and information compared to more traditional compositions. She has pursued formal research on the premise that new forms and morphologies and manifesto buildings would in the end facilitate a new functionality. With a contemplative process that abstinence in building affords, there was an increased chance of preparation and innovation.

Most often the paintings and drawings, rather than being illustrations of known facts, were explorations of formal or spatial conjectures. Like a theorist, she established hypotheses that she worked out in drawing, painting, and other mediums. Early on, in 1979–80, she entered a competition for the design of the Irish Prime Minister's Residence in Dublin, and in what have become historic paintings, she posited the notion of collision and fragmentation. A roadway sweeps by a rectangular structure and virtually collides with its form in a body blow that sends fragments exploding into the garden of the walled courtyard, breaking the pure geometric form. Hadid was proposing force, not chaos, as a new kind of order within an energy field that replaced gravity. The syntactic relationship of the parts amounted to the reinvention of the plan. Le Corbusier said the plan was the generator, and it was planimetric in the traditional sense: flat and orthogonal. Hadid's new plan was implicitly sectional because the explosion, her force field, was omnidirectional and therefore radiant and diagonal, not just orthogonal.

The idea of a force field informed many projects, and it surfaced much transformed in a lyrical painting for the interior of Cardiff Bay Opera House (Wales, 1994–96). Reflecting panels and sound baffles fly through the concert hall in an apparently chaotic pattern, simply following a line of force determined by the path of

01 Dutch Parliament Extension, The Hague, 1978–79. Exploded axonometric; drawing

02 Zollhof 3 Media Park, Düsseldorf, 1989–93. Landscape perspective rotation; painting

03 LFOne/Landesgartenschau, Weil am Rhein, Gemany, 1996–99. Drawings

04 Vision for Madrid, 1992. Four paintings

05 *The Great Utopia, The Russian and Soviet Avant-Garde, 1915–1932*, Solomon R. Guggenheim Museum, New York, 1992. *Tektonic*; painting

06 *The Great Utopia, The Russian and Soviet Avant-Garde, 1915–1932*, Solomon R. Guggenheim Museum, New York, 1992. *Tatlin Tower and Tektonic "Worldwind"*; painting

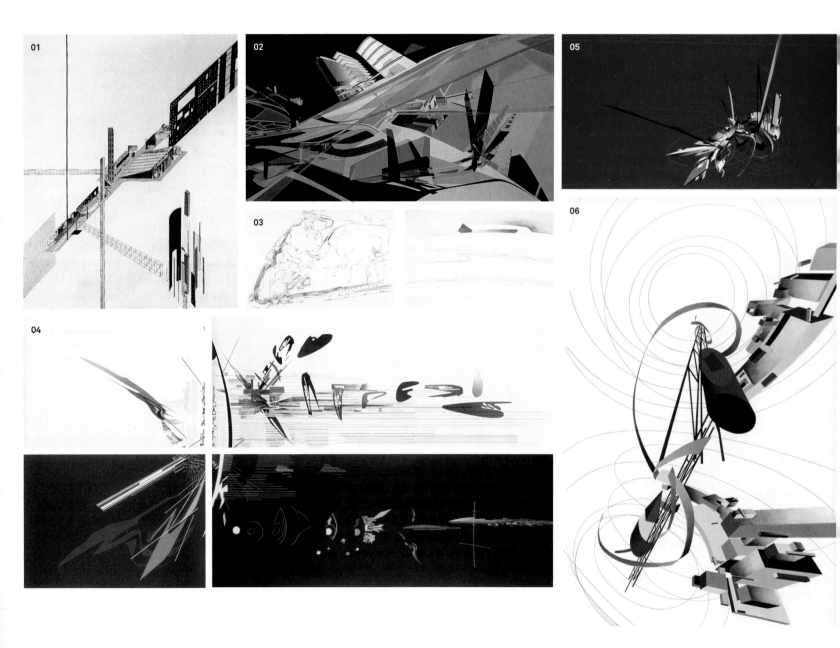

Zaha Hadid, acceptance speech at the formal presentation ceremony
for the Pritzker Architecture Prize 2004 (State Hermitage Museum,
St. Petersburg, May 31, 2004), http://www.pritzkerprize.com/143/
mono2004/Hadid.pdf, p. 21.

Zaha Hadid, quoted in Mohsen Mostafavi, "Landscape as Plan
[a conversation with Zaha Hadid]," in *Zaha Hadid 1983–2001*
(Madrid: El Croquis, 2004), p. 52.

ound. (Another version of the idea was the vortex of plat-forms and vitrines she painted for *The Great Utopia* at the Guggenheim.) Such study paintings come in many forms, from simple sketches to grand tableaux, and the one for Cardiff explores flight and motion in beautiful, succinctly stated visual terms. The idea recently reappeared in the current scheme for the Guangzhou Opera House (China, 2003–ongoing). Despite the apparent formality of distorted planes painted on black paper, the studies are often quickly done, and notional. There may be many variations.

Hadid emerges from her intense search for form and formal organization as a master of space or what R. M. Schindler called "spaceform," an inextricably linked union of form and space. In their radiating quality, Hadid's paint-ings and drawings, like those of the Suprematists, aspire not only to recede into the depth of the space depicted but also to advance out of the picture plane. Lissitzky, conceiv-ing art that projected beyond illusory space into the real space of the viewer, evolved his *Proun* compositions into three-dimensional installations. Hadid adapted this idea by inventing paper reliefs, that is, paper sculpture that breaks free of the picture plane, projecting forward. The distinction is important. Many architects use the frame to compose architectural vignettes, as though the structures were depicted in the perspectival depth of a picture. Their results are cool and distant, as opposed to paintings and buildings that advance into the space of the viewer and engage people with physical immediacy.

Hadid's paper reliefs, like Lissitzky's three-dimensional *Prouns*, jump off the wall and suggest the eventual physi-cal posture and attitude of the building, masses flying for-ward. For the Lois and Richard Rosenthal Center for Contemporary Art in Cincinnati (1997–2003), Hadid did many facade studies in exquisite paper reliefs, simulating the condition of a street wall on which parts of the facade project and recede, breaking free of the virtual frame of the corner site. For the compressed spaces of the interior, these paper reliefs also revealed the spatial impact of planes erupting out of the orthogonal.

In other projects, such as the Cardiff Bay Opera House, Hadid executed reliefs to repre-sent the ground plane, creating a topography that folds, slopes, and shears, giving dimen-sion to a plane normally conceived as flat. She excavated the underground life of buildings in these models, admitting light below while defining precincts above. Though they are analog models rather than pictorial repre-sentations, the reliefs still carry a strong memory of the picture plane and are really hybrids, occupying a tantalizing territory between picture and model, between the second and third dimensions. However, the reliefs—as paper reliefs—use illusionistic techniques borrowed from two-dimensional representation, especially forced perspec-tive. The oldest of the reliefs were studies of the Kurfürstendamm office building, but they became instrumental in the 1990s in the gen-eration of projects, around the time of the Rosenthal Center. These spatial carvings sug-gest that the buildings involve the viewers by projecting forward rather than receding.

Hadid, of course, makes models, from simple maquettes done in construction paper to clear and translucent acrylic models that look like large modernist jewels. In an interview, she told Mohsen Mostafavi, then chairman of the Architectural Association, "With physical models, it is the peculiar nature of the material which affords design opportuni-ties. Because I am always doing the contouring of the site in Plexi, we began to see a similarity between liquid space and rock. Such 'discoveries' can be productive. By the sheer use of the model, almost by total accident, you begin to look at things in different ways." For example, the transparency of the acrylic models that she started to use in studies for the Tomigaya Building (Tokyo, 1987) allowed Hadid to see through the floors of the building, an effect suggesting that the vertical

circulation could shift between floors instead of being stacked. The transparency allowed her to break the usual column of stairs extruded up through floors in favor of a more spatial and exploratory pathway. "This was discovered because we had the different plans overlaid with each other, to construct a way to connect the levels in a new way," she told Mostafavi.[2]

In model making, Hadid is, as always, protean in her inventiveness, sometimes creating hybrids, such as a model growing out of a line drawing. If her paintings can be enigmatic—particularly tableaux with composite views responding to different vanishing points and projec-tive geometries—the models, even in their ambitious complexity, resolve lingering ambiguities as she commits the design to their three-dimensional physicality (Fig. 07). Many subjects that she paints and draws have carried over into models for further development, such as notions of transparency, translucency, interpenetration, and light. Like modernist sculptors of the 1920s and '30s, who broke apart the self-contained object so that space fig-ured within the contours of expanded armatures, Hadid developed forms that separate from each other and involve space within the frame of buildings whose parts open to accept and enfold space within. The idea of maximum porosity within very open forms that reach out at the perimeter into surrounding space is effectively portrayed in models. The space is involving and even inciting rather than cool and distant.

Hadid's buildings tend to be immersive and experiential, and the reliefs and models not only confirm but also develop the ideas first posited in graphic form. In the six-story stairwell of the Rosenthal Center, shifts in the stairways, angling through a vertiginous crevice of space, always change the viewing angles in an interior that, built off the orthogo-nal, shifts itself in constant geometric drift. The experientially rich interior puts into practice the multiperspectivalism Hadid has preached in all her graphic experiments, engaging the perception of visitors and their physical involvement in a building they climb like switchback trails on a mountain. The design invites a participatory engagement, unlike escalators that turn visitors into consumers on a passive ride through space. She has not built an empty shell indifferent to the visitor and to the objects in it, but designed instead an enticement that turns visitors into architectural participants whose senses and curiosity are engaged by a path of discovery. Visitors own this interior because they earn it through a process of peripatetic exploration.

Hadid's heroic manifesto paintings may be the poster images of the office, but just to the left of her desk is a small personal library of sketchbooks that contain the most intimate and seminal of her drawings, done over the better part of three decades. This is the repository of the DNA of her architectural imagination. Notebooks are not rare among architects, but usually the jottings include notes, numbers, written concepts, stray doodles, reminders about going to the laundry. In Hadid's, drawings occupy nearly every page. She visualizes all her ideas, and in a consistently elegant hand.

These sketchbooks (Fig. 08) are a diary of Hadid's most spontaneous design thinking and a history of her evolution as a theorist. The most recent books have page after page of ink sketches to which she adds a wash, enhancing the line drawings graphically so that they are elaborated, nuanced, and more dimensional. In these pages, Hadid is not designing objects or buildings or even details. She is not sketching a vignette from a trip. She is not drawing pretty forms. Despite the fact that everything she and her associates

touch turns to beauty—even study models and drawings—beauty itself is a symptom rather than a root desire of the vision. Hadid develops endless variations of organizational typologies, or conceptual paradigms, in a methodical and perhaps obsessive way. In the sketchbook pages, she proposes and explores, to list a few, striation, fields (as well as fields and object), aggregation, clustering, layering, compression, jigsaw, pixilation, terracing, folding, topography, multiple ground planes, sectional interconnectivity, occupied structure, spatial liquidity, tectonic plates, ravioli curvature, bubbles, amoebas, bundling, and infrastructure (Fig. 09). These are all organizational paradigms, the mappings of a highly organized and spatially inventive mind committed to a search for an order in complexity. Just as the formal explorations are not formalist but organizational, she does not pursue complexity for the sake of complexity: complex forms yield a capacity for much greater organizational accommodation. Always, beyond the search for structuring paradigms is Hadid's enduring attempt to find strangeness, otherness, and difference in the patterns of the page.

Although the drawings have a spatial consequence, and it is tempting to impute a calligraphic aesthetic to the tapering lines, they are basically planimetric patterns with the potential to be teased apart and spatialized. That is, the lines can be injected with space—much as Hadid took the Malevich painting and moved it through Wright's Solomon R. Guggenheim Museum—giving the forms dimension and function. In the most recent sketchbooks, the drawings are essentially plan views, but with three-dimensional potential. They are not object forms but continuously curvilinear matrices open at the edges and porous in the middle. Years ago, the sketches would have been fragmentary and explosive.

As a site of genesis, the sketchbooks constitute an idea bank on which Hadid continues to build her vision, and from which she draws for building strategies. The paradigms become embedded in the collective conscious of the office, and other architects take their own design

initiatives against the background of the seminal ideas that first appear on these pages. Schumacher, her primary associate, has over the last decade taken an increasingly prominent design role in the office, and he also does sketches, though his are more volumetric.

Although Hadid's weightless, dynamic buildings seemed to anticipate abstract, groundless architecture designed using the computer, the advent of computer-aided design in her office presented a potential crisis for an architect whose very process and identity depended on the artisanal approach of crafted models, exquisitely cut paper reliefs, hand-painted panoramas, and the simple sketch. Hadid, one of the most avant-garde architects of her time and a force of change in the field, confronted a paradigm shift that threatened to displace her preeminence at architecture's cutting edge. Just as postmodernism undid many distinguished modernist practices a generation before, marginalizing once eminent architects, the computer threatened to outmode even the deconstructivist architects of the 1980s and '90s, who had displaced the postmodernists.

Hadid's practice anticipated computer-aided design in two important ways. First, her work was already complex and it was within the computer's logarithmic power not only to enable and facilitate such complexity but also to push it into more formidable territory. The computer could deepen the liberations she had already initiated. Second, Hadid's practice anticipated the computer because she had always explored the potential of any medium that could help visualize her design in ways that contributed to its further development. Artistry did not make Hadid a technophobe. She could use the computer as she had all other mediums, as a technologist, plunging into its character and using it as material with which to shape her own vision.

Because Hadid, despite her established design process, opened her practice to the then as yet unknown nature of the computer, her trajectory of innovation accelerated. Computers are the servants of their programs, and waves of software succeeded each other, especially as students coming out of school imported their evolving expertise into Hadid's office. Each generation, every three to four years, brought programs with different capacities, proclivities, and viewpoints, which merged into the evolving process. The open forms that Hadid had long championed paralleled an open design process. Buildings that were permeable to the city and the environment were emblematic of an office that was predicated on change. Hadid welcomed the young architects bearing new tools.

When the computer was first introduced as a design tool in the late 1980s, Hadid's buildings were characterized by the flowing lines enabled by the French curves her architects had used extensively. However, ModelShop, a three-dimensional modeling program that was the first used in her office to shape designs, tended to straighten the curves, even though the rest of the composition remained dynamic. ModelShop effectively stiffened the geometry because it could not easily handle curves of changing radii.

The architects then introduced other programs that were precursors of VectorWorks, which came into the office in the mid-1990s. With its capacity to do splines—a process by which elastic lines can be stretched along curves of variable radii to moveable control points—curves returned to the designs. The concept of splines interpolating between control points comes from shipbuilding, where hulls are built in continuously changing curves that are never arcs but always hyperbolic. With VectorWorks, curves became much easier to draw and integrate than they had ever been with the much more rudimentary French curve. They proliferated.

The computer materially increased the productivity of Hadid's office for competition work in the early design stages. The architects used ModelShop and modeling tools run on the Mac. The programs gave them an ever greater possibility of stretching and distorting form, and while the early programs flattened curves and could not handle distortions in a field, or in what architects call a mesh, they easily handled volumetric compositions and generally accelerated the composition of complex three-dimensional designs.

Because of Hadid's interest in force fields, her office looked for programs that could handle and distort topographies, and for a short period, software like form-Z allowed faceted topographies, but without the possibility of distorting the surfaces in compound curves. Current programs facilitate an elasticized distortion of the mesh, and in some of the office's urban designs, as in town plans for Singapore (One North Masterplan, 2001) and Beijing (Soho City Masterplan, 2003–ongoing), the architects have distorted whole fields, while giving them direction—orienting the plans, for example, to a center, series of centers, or an edge. In a tram transfer station and car park for Strasbourg (Terminus Hoenheim-Nord, 1998–2001), an invisible force derived from a site analysis seems to magnetize the entire project, as though tram shed, parking lot, parking stripes, and lampposts were a field of metal filings. The force in the field, like the impact of the roadway on the proposed guesthouse for the Irish Prime Minister's Residence, gives the project directional coherence. The elements in the field are neither left in a random orientation nor are they mechanically and arbitrarily orthogonal.

Computer-aided design raged through some offices, completely taking over their design logic and even their identity, but Hadid's ongoing approach, with its prescient interest in change and complexity, dovetailed with new software capabilities. The computer did not require her to do an about-face; she could simply harness its powers to further her vision. With some programs that encouraged curvilinear design, architects designed what became known as "blobs," shapeless architectural bubbles that resulted, rather literally, from the instrumentality of the software. Early notions of fragmentation, and the autonomy of the part, however, remained salient in Hadid's philosophy, and with new computer programs encouraging surface and continuity, she resisted blindly following the instrument's leadership. She tensed undulating surfaces by creasing or ripping them, creating corners and edges, giving the handling of the curving meshes characteristics different from those of other offices that followed software dictates to "smooth" differences. Hadid's ongoing, evolving vision always informed the instrument even as the instrument advanced the vision.

The influence of the computer is clearly visible in the Phaeno Science Center (Wolfsburg, Germany, 1999–2005, Figs. 10–11), where the architects started the project by deforming a hypothetical grid, depressing it at points using a 3D Studio Mac program. The strangeness Hadid had achieved by smearing an image through a photocopier was now produced through a more sophisticated, methodical instrument; the distorted grid served simultaneously as envelope and structure. The Phaeno Science Center was conceived essentially as a space frame that, when depressed at points, became stalactites falling to the ground. The Cartesian grid became a living force field as the vortices elasticized a mesh stretching down in what the architects called "worm holes."

From the base, the Phaeno Science Center seems to grow organically from pods into mushrooming columns, which are occupied with stairwells and entrances leading to the exhibition hall in the distorted frame. The several pods guarantee multiplicity, allowing several different points of entry into the structural system, whether for visitors or goods. The pods become objects in a field, establishing the hybridity of the design. The distortions undermine the notion of absolute Cartesian space

07 Philharmonic Hall, Luxembourg, 1997. Model

08 Victoria & Albert Museum, Boilerplate Extension, London, 1996. Sketch

09 MAXXI National Centre of Contemporary Arts, Rome, 1997–ongoing. Presentation model

10 Phaeno Science Center, Wolfsburg, Germany, 1999–2005. Digital rendering

11 Phaeno Science Center, Wolfsburg, Germany, 1999–2005. Photograph

12 University of Connecticut, Storrs. Study model

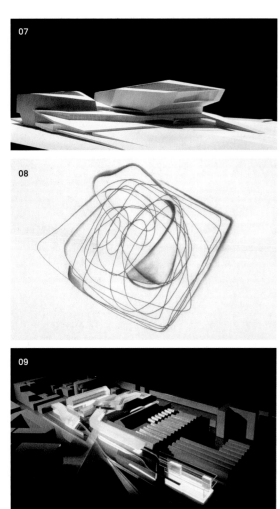

that reigned from the Renaissance through modernist architecture. The building is multilocal, decentralized, and nonlinear rather than Cartesian in its universality and uniformity.

The computer modeled the Phaeno Science Center by absorbing many factors that became sublayers in the composition, absorbing disturbances—apertures, ramps, infrastructure, fenestration—that radiate through the larger system. The space frame, for example, adapts to the trapezoidal outline of the volume with an array of beams fanning in two directions. The distortion places a huge burden on the frame, requiring that each of its cells be unique with respect to size and geometry. The computer easily handled the computational and constructive burden. Sublayers of different building systems influence each other mutually, smoothly reconciling in newly continuous patterns the clashes, discontinuities, and simple juxtapositions that characterized Hadid's work done before the computer. The computer helped to "interarticulate" subsystems in a mutual adaptation so that all points affected others in a relativized field. Disturbances radiate through the design, impacting and inflecting the whole composition, but the disturbances are absorbed into the differentiated continuum of the mesh.

Equipped to think in nonlinear ways, with nonlinear graphics, the computer helped generate a nonlinear, nearly liquid building within an interconnective mesh that would be impossible to design by hand, even with a hundred French curves. The computer was not the generator but the enabler, and at the initial level of design, when the grid was pushed and pulled, modeling on screen proved similar to sketching on a sheet of paper. Computer-aided design helped Hadid's office move beyond conceiving space as a Newtonian void, effectively treating space instead as a warping Einsteinian medium transmitting force. The design, however, was the result of a dynamic relationship between the architect and the program, in an interaction between information and form. Hadid's architects were not passive to the tool but controlling to the extent that they could set off chains of reactions and adaptation on the computer screen.

In 2004, Hadid had a retrospective at the MAK in Vienna (*Zaha Hadid: Architektur*), and although her magisterial tableaux were well represented, along with a wide selection of paper reliefs and impressive models, the centerpiece was the *Ice-Storm*, a large, highly liquid, self-transforming foam sculpture. This spectacular shape—part sculpture, part furniture—completely displaced the paintings on view as manifesto, and signaled a paradigm shift within Hadid's office from the canvas to the screen, from the hand to the digit. She generated the shape, her most liquid form to date, on screen, and the computer transmitted data to a machine that milled blocks of foam, which were then welded together into the solid blue form. The molded blocks acted as an object in the field, but the sculpture was so omnidirectional that it behaved like a flowing field. We are at a point of originality where conventional language fails the object it attempts to define and describe.

As a student of Malevich, air had always been Hadid's medium: she preferred to paint her structures floating against the infinity of a completely white or black background without substance. With the computer, water became equally privileged as a medium in her architectural imagination. The office may still make relief studies and models, but the paintings have mostly stopped, replaced by large digitally produced photographic prints of images lifted from the computer screen. The computer has become the dominant tool used to initiate projects, programmed now with Rhino and Maya, which give a very coherent three-dimensional geometry. Maya especially can set up complex surfaces from and with multiple parameters, which the architects can factor into comprehensive views that absorb all changes simultaneously (Fig. 12).

In an office with an accelerating momentum of work, many recent projects have been designed primarily on the computer, though they are still tenaciously rooted in the principles of change and complexity illustrated in Hadid's sketchbooks. The lyrical pedestrian bridge at Zaragoza, Spain, connecting the town to a 2008 Expo site (2005–ongoing), is based on a computer procedure called "lofting." (Lofting is the continuous morphing of one architectural section into another as the initial shape transforms through the end of its trajectory; the computer can generate this continuous path of non-Euclidean becoming—an echo of the French curves, with continuously changing, nonrepeating radii.) The architects looked at the nineteenth-century Firth of Forth Bridge in Scotland, a complex truss structure with a diamond section that envelops the roadway, and projected that section multiple times, in different forms, across the river. The extrusion of each section intersects with others, morphing as they go along, becoming a highly complex braid. Several continuous corridors serve both as galleries and passages, open to each other and to the outside.

In a competition design for an Islamic wing of the Musée du Louvre (Paris, 2005), Hadid harnessed the visualizing process of another computer operation. In a classic Boolean move that produced a completely hypnotic project, she took two different volumes with different sections and intersected them to get a third shape whose adaptive irregularity allowed breathing room for the facades of one of the Louvre's oldest courtyards, permitting space for light to penetrate into the lower floors. Hadid wrapped the distorted shape, rising in the courtyard like an angular emanation, in a pattern inspired by Islamic geometries. The pattern itself, conforming to the irregular volume like a dress wrapped on the bias around a body, stretched differentially across its surface. The surface distortions resulted from algorithms made along a path from a small square rotated thirty degrees to a larger square. Only two computer operations, the Boolean combining of volumes and a distortion of the pattern in the rotation, created the design, which would have been impracticably difficult to conceive, draw, and dimension by hand. The geometries create a hallucinatory effect that fuses Hadid's underlying desire to "make it strange" and the computer's generative capabilities.

Ever younger architects are introducing the latest software into Hadid's office, influencing designs with these powerful new tools, which are far more agile than the photocopier and French curves had been. The underlying math of the programs establishes an invisible order to the form-finding operations. Most recently, using Rhino, the architects have generated designs based on lines lofted in curves across a site in patterns with different densities. Linking the nodes in this primary two-dimensional matrix, or vector field, generates shells. The "lofted" lines become "nurb" surfaces, or compound curves.

The process is spurring Hadid's office into designing a whole new generation of very recent shell structures, including a street pavilion for public transportation in Innsbruck, Austria, a mediatheque in Pau, France, and the swimming and diving Aquatic Centre, with its wavy roof, for the 2012 Olympics in London (all 2004–ongoing). The undulating, involuted shells in themselves do not mean that the architects have abandoned all their previous concerns in favor of a new silver bullet. The shells, complex in themselves, must accommodate each project's architectural program and its interior demands, and must interact with the ground, interpreted by Hadid as a complex, unfolding topological field. Shell, program, and site are in constant dialogue.

Using advanced, increasingly arcane software requires skill bordering on virtuosity, and the smoothing quality of computer intelligence, which tends to absorb rather than highlight exceptions, implies the liquefaction of an aesthetic that had once featured more overt fragmentation. As in car design, the issue becomes curves evolving into other curves and breaking into countercurves. If, as Mies van der Rohe insisted, God lies in the resolution of the details, the detail here is in the junction of the curves, and in the closure of the figure—how, for example, to end a curve. Once the architects set up the geometries, they have to know how to model the information. The discipline of the discipline shifts to different subjects.

This is where the values and strategies posited in Hadid's sketchbooks play their seminal role, where her ideas and the instrumentality of the computer meet in a Boolean operation, at some indeterminate, unpredictable intersection between two logics. After nearly thirty years of pure and applied research, Hadid heads an office with an oeuvre, both built and unbuilt, which represents a theory of architecture and a methodology of practice. From the time she first learned how to draw, she has used various mediums as vehicles for traveling into uncharted design territory. Always open to their material suggestion, she has never simply been a technician. As in an open, self-diagnostic psychoanalytic process, the computer enables the office to become more itself, to intensify both the vision that is already expressed and the vision that remains latent. Like all the tools she has used, the computer helps Hadid become more Hadid.

THE MODERNITY OF ZAHA HADID

Detlef Mertins

During the heyday of postmodernism in the 1980s, as architects turned to historical styles, urban traditions, and popular culture to rebuild the public support that modernism had lost, Zaha Hadid declared that modernity was an incomplete project that deserved to be continued. This was an inspiring message, and its bold vision was matched by projects such as the competition-winning design for The Peak in Hong Kong (1982–83). Hadid's luminous paintings depicted the city and the hillside above it as a prismatic field in which buildings and landform were amalgamated into the same geological formation of shifting lines, vibrant planes, and shimmering colors, at once tangible and intangible, infused with the transformative energy that Cubist, Futurist, and Expressionist landscapes had sought to capture (Fig. 01). The figure of her building—a hotel—was barely discernible within this field. It was composed of three long prismatic bars—overlapping, rotating, and sliding above one another, as if detaching themselves from the earth or, alternatively, landing from outer space, anchored by vertical staffs, hovering momentarily on terraces cut into the hillside. These images sent ripples of excitement through the architectural world, evidence that modernism was not a dirty word after all. It was alive, larger than life, and totally seductive.

Hadid's was a different modernism than we had become accustomed to, no longer utilitarian, blandly corporate, or aggrandizing of technology. Her vision of Hong Kong offered a powerful wish image, at once futuristic and archaic, geometric and geomorphic. Hadid had tapped into the largely forgotten vein of Russian Constructivism and infused its revolutionary heroics with cosmopolitan urbanity. She rekindled the flame of modernity with this new cocktail of desires.

The word "Constructivism" came into usage in the early 1920s, in art most notably with the Working Group of Constructivists formed in Moscow in 1921, of whom Alexander Rodchenko and Varvava Stepanova became the best known.[1] Yet the term has often been associated with the work of Vladimir Tatlin, whose reliefs, beginning already in 1913, launched a sustained but also diverse field of experimentation into new nonrepresentational modalities of artistic production, for which "Constructivism" has served as an umbrella concept.[2] In the field of architecture, the term was initially associated with the Union of Contemporary Architects, including Moisei Ginzburg and Alexander Vesnin, as well as others such as Konstantin Melnikov. During the late 1920s, a younger generation appeared on the scene, including Ivan Leonidov, whose work on new building and urban types employed the visual language of elemental geometry in a more extreme way than architects had before. At the same time, Yakov Chernikov demonstrated through his teaching that an abstract, graphic (rather than painterly) language of lines, planes, volumes, and color could be employed to generate an extraordinary diversity of things, from machines to engineering works, buildings, and cities.[3]

Though initiated prior to 1917, these lines of research in art and architecture became aligned with the Russian Revolution's radical politics and served as instruments for the reorganization of life after the overthrow of the tsar. Art was enlisted to create festivals in the street, propaganda on railway cars, and didactic programming in theaters and cinemas. Working at times in parallel with the artists and at times independently, Constructivist architects devised new building types that would be commensurate with the forms of social organization desired in the new Communist state. From apartments to social clubs, theaters, and stadiums, they reconceptualized buildings as social condensers, catalysts for new forms of collective living. During the early 1920s, these various trajectories coalesced into the challenge of defining a new paradigm that would unite art and life and transform the world into a new artistic reality.

With their project Exodus, or The Voluntary Prisoners of Architecture (1972, Fig. 02), Rem Koolhaas and Elia Zenghelis with Madelon Vriesendorp and Zoe Zenghelis had already revisited Russian Constructivism at the Architectural Association in London, where Hadid would soon emerge as Koolhaas and Zenghelis's most talented student.[4] This project looked to Leonidov's proposal for a linear infrastructural city of 1930 in attempting to develop an alternative to "the behavioral sink of a city like London."[5] Seeking to operate at the scale of metropolitan reconstruction, the group turned to Constructivism to strike a path between the legacy of CIAM (Congrès Internationaux d'Architecture Moderne), on the one hand, and the more recent artistic urban visions of Superstudio's Continuous Monument (1969), Archizoom's Non-Stop City (1969–72), Archigram's Plug-In City (1962–64), Yona Friedman's Spatial City (1958–59), and Constant's New Babylon (1956–). For Koolhaas, the work of Leonidov became a strategic ingredient in an explosive, ironic mixture that also included the raw vitality of the enclave-city of West Berlin, fantasies of decadence in early twentieth-century Manhattan, Surrealist juxtapositions of incongruous fragments, and the typological delirium of O. M. Ungers.

It was in this context that Hadid rediscovered the Suprematist and Constructivist precursors to the Utopian artist-architects of the 1960s, turning specifically to Kazimir Malevich to find her own way of dreaming the future by deliberately tapping into experiments left incomplete. Where Tatlin and the later Constructivists abandoned the medium of painting in favor of materially based reliefs, assemblages, spatial constructions, stage sets, and even architecture—all of which already occupied the same world as the observer—Malevich launched a "new painterly realism" in 1915, called it Suprematism, and declared it the key to transforming the world.[6] His display of over twenty canvases—with Black Square hung in a corner—at The Last Futurist Exhibition of Paintings: "0.10" in Petrograd (1915, Fig. 03) served to demonstrate both the deductive rigor and generative potential of what he considered a new system of pure painting. Its systemic character lay in the permutation of elemental shapes in black, white, and red—beginning with the square, then the circle, cross, rectangle, trapezium, triangle, ellipse, and combinations of all these. Through the show, Malevich attracted

1 See Maria Gough, *The Artist as Producer: Russian Constructivism in Revolution* (Berkeley: University of California Press, 2005).

2 The term "Constructivism" has also served to subsume diverse formal experiments within the careers of its major figures, such as Naum Gabo, El Lissitzky, László Moholy-Nagy, and Antoine Pevsner.

3 See Catherine Cooke, *Russian Avant-Garde Theories of Art, Architecture, and the City* (London: Academy Editions, 1995); and *The Great Utopia: The Russian and Soviet Avant-Garde, 1915–1932*, exh. cat. (New York: Guggenheim Museum, 1992).

4 By the 1960s, London had already become a major locus of interest in Constructivism among historians, critics, curators, artists, and architects.

5 Martin van Schaik and Otakar Macel, eds., *Exit Utopia: Architectural Provocations 1956–76* (Munich: Prestel, 2005), p. 238.

6 Malevich called this new art "Suprematism" after the Latin word "supremus," which connotes "the highest," "absolute," "excellent," and "ruling." See Larissa A. Zhadova, *Malevich: Suprematism and Revolution in Russian Art 1910–1930* (London: Thames & Hudson, 1982); *Kazimir Malevich 1878–1935*, exh. cat. (Los Angeles: Armand Hammer Museum of Art, 1990); and Matthew Drutt, *Kazimir Malevich: Suprematism*, exh. cat. (Berlin: Deutsche Guggenheim, 2003). See also Malevich's *The Non-Objective World*, trans. Howard Dearstyne (Chicago: Paul Theobald & Co., 1959).

students who joined him in developing Suprematism over the following years, and the style soon incorporated greater diversity, movement, and expression (Figs. 04, 05).

Architect Peter Cook once observed that "Malevich's *Architekton* [Fig. 06] is constantly being erected as the baseline for Zaha's own work."[7] Certainly, presentations of Hadid's oeuvre often, and with biographical inevitability, begin with her graduation project from the Architecture Association—Malevich's Tektonik of 1976–77—for which she transformed Malevich's assemblage of elemental blocks into a hotel on the Hungerford Bridge over the Thames in London. But what kind of origin was this and what kind of repetition did it involve?

Where Malevich considered his *Black Square* of 1915 as the founding origin of Suprematism, the irreducible "degree zero" of painting and seed germ of an entire artistic system, Hadid took up the trajectory of Suprematism already well into its evolution. After five years of developing Suprematism in painting, Malevich and his followers moved from two into three dimensions, from painting into architecture, decorative arts, and even urbanism.[8] More precisely, this constituted a return since it was in his stage sets for the Futurist play *Victory over the Sun* (1913) that he had first discovered the black square. He cast his *Architekton* series in white plaster, each one different, first horizontal and later vertical, and displayed them together in a black room, as if they were creations ex nihilo, floating in the nothingness of space. He even called them satellites and planets. In contrast, Hadid began with an act of appropriation more reminiscent of Marcel Duchamp's *Bicycle Wheel* of 1913 than Malevich's elementarism. She brought Malevich's *Alpha Architekton* (1920) down to earth, anchored it to the Hungerford Bridge, and opened it for business as a hotel. Somewhat too short to span the entire width of the river, somewhat too wide to be contained by the existing bridge, it remained alien and contingent in its new context.

In presenting her project as a painting (rather than as a maquette), Hadid folded Malevich's Suprematist architecture back onto its origins in painting and in the process scrambled the definitions of both mediums. Where Malevich eschewed representation, Hadid's paintings must be considered representational, though not in a naturalistic sense, since what they depict are potential architectures, not physical realities. They represent her vision of an abstract architecture, or in Malevich's terms, a nonobjective reality. Moreover, she sets her projects into specific urban contexts that she portrays abstractly as Suprematist landscapes and cities. Since Suprematism itself did not produce such interpretative abstractions, it is necessary to turn to the paintings of landscapes and cities in Cubism, Futurism, and Expressionism (including Malevich's own, such as Fig. 01) to discern the implications of Hadid's operation. Drawing on Cubist decompositions of landscapes into prismatic fields, Futurist expressions of dynamic energies, and Expressionist renderings of psychic experience, Hadid transformed Suprematism from an art of building complex structures out of elemental geometric shapes into one that seeks to make visible the elemental nature inherent in the world. Where Malevich declared in 1920 that the forms of Suprematism "have nothing in common with the technology of the earth's surface,"[9] Hadid's paintings bring mathematical and geological geometries into greater alignment.

Hadid created Suprematist paintings of Suprematist buildings in Suprematist landscapes and cities, using architectural drawings—plans, sections, and isometrics—in place of pure geometric figures. The plan of the *Architekton*-hotel appears several times in different places on the canvas, in solid red and black and in compositions of mixed colors, so that it is transformed into a series of abstract shapes floating in space. In the bottom left corner, the building is decomposed into its constituent planes of color, bringing the painting even closer to Malevich. Rather than reinforcing the volumetric integrity of the various blocks that make up the *Architekton*, Hadid's application of color decomposes its masses into planes, much as Theo van Doesburg had done for his Maison

Particulière project of 1923. Where modernists such as Malevich sought an origin, or ground, for their work in the autonomous properties of different mediums, Hadid's painting of Suprematist buildings envisions the building of Suprematist paintings.

With such a beginning—a beginning that denies, but then compounds, folds, and twists the modernist idea of origins—we could say that Hadid took seriously Malevich's statement that Suprematism was itself merely the beginning of a new art and that he was merely its initial theoretician.[10] Or we could also say that she gave Malevich a "monstrous child," to borrow the image that Gilles Deleuze gave in describing the relationship of his books to those of philosophers with whom he was in dialogue, such as Bergson, Leibniz, and Spinoza.[11] In "Mediators," an essay from 1985, Deleuze took issue with the return at that time of the modernist problem of origins and insisted instead that creativity was mediated: "Mediators are fundamental. Creation is all about mediators. Without them, nothing happens. They can be people . . . but things as well, even plants or animals. . . . Whether they're real or imaginary, animate or inanimate, one must form one's mediators. It's a series: if you don't belong to a series, even a completely imaginary one, you're lost."[12] Deleuze suggested that, in fact, a change of paradigm was underway, exemplified by the shift in cultural preference from sports of energetic movement, such as running and throwing a javelin, which presume starting points, leverage, effort, and resistance, to sports such as surfing, windsurfing, and hang gliding, which "take the form of entry into an existing wave."[13]

In employing Malevich as mediator, Hadid entered into an existing wave, one that had already gone beyond Malevich and his pursuit of origins, although Malevich remained a presence in it, as did ideas of new beginnings, first principles, and universal elements. Through interlocutors, such as Vasily Kandinsky (Fig. 07), revisionist students such as El Lissitzky, and more distant admirers such as László Moholy-Nagy (Fig. 08), Suprematism had already become a broader, more diverse movement, which

7 Peter Cook, "The Emergence of Zaha Hadid," in *Zaha Hadid: Texts and References* (New York: Rizzoli, 2004), p. 11. For insightful considerations of the relationship between Hadid and Malevich, see Kenneth Frampton, "A Kufic Suprematist: The World Culture of Zaha Hadid," in *Zaha Hadid: Planetary Architecture Two* (London: Architectural Association, 1983); and Gordana Fontana-Giusti, "A Forming Element," in *Zaha Hadid: Texts and References*, pp. 18–39.

8 Malevich encapsulated what he called "the formula of three-dimensional spatial Suprematism" as a black, red, and white cube, and prepared sketches of *Architektons* in color. See Zhadova, *Malevich*, p. 62, n. 71. See also Malevich's *Table No. 3 Spatial Suprematism* (ca. 1920s), which is illustrated in *Kazimir Malevich 1878–1935*, p. 151.

9 Kazimir Malevich, "Suprematism. 34 Drawings, 1920," in Zhadova, *Malevich*, p. 284.

10 See Zhadova, *Malevich*, p. 60.

11 Hugh Tomlinson and Barbara Habberjam cite Deleuze saying, "I imagined myself getting onto the back of an author, and giving him a child, which would be his and which would at the same time be a monster. It was very important that it should be his child, because the author actually had to say everything that I made him say. But it also had to be a monster because it was necessary to go through all kinds of decenterings, slips, break-ins, secret emissions, which I really enjoyed." See Tomlinson and Habberjam, "Translator's Introduction," in Gilles Deleuze, *Bergsonism* (New York: Zone Books, 1991), p. 8.

explored the potential of new mediums and technologies for creating an abstract landscape of dynamic forms and fluid spaces. When Hadid joined the wave, she inflected it further to include conceptual explorations of language, generative process, totality, and openness. Treating each project as an experiment in the laboratory of new beginnings, she replayed the modernist return to origins but without its fundamentalism or teleology.

In translating figures and patterns from two to three dimensions, Hadid qualified the quest for a universal architectonic language by exploiting the diverse formal experiments already undertaken in Suprematist and other abstract painting. Where Malevich had restricted his architecture to the primary language of prismatic blocks, Hadid used each new project to explore the potential of another formal variant developed in painting. Consider, for example, the differences between *The World (89 Degrees)* (1983), A New Barcelona (1989), *London 2066* (1991), Vision for Madrid (1992), the Victoria & Albert Museum, Boilerhouse Extension (London,1996), the New Campus Center, Illinois Institute of Technology (Chicago, 1997–98), and Boulevard der Stars (Berlin, 2004). Today, Hadid's work is at times angular and prismatic (Car Park and Terminus Hoenheim-Nord, Strasbourg, France, 1998–2001), at other times rectilinear (Lois and Richard Rosenthal Center for Contemporary Art, Cincinnati, 1997–2003), sinuous (MAXXI National Centre of Contemporary Arts, Rome, 1997–ongoing), geomorphic (Ordrupgaard Museum Extension, Denmark, 2001–ongoing), plastic (*Ice-Storm* at MAK, Vienna, 2003), and mixed (BMW Plant Central Building, Leipzig, Germany, 2001–05). While these buildings, and even such formally hybrid ones as the Phaeno Science Center in Wolfsburg, Germany (1999–2005)—which is part curvilinear, part angular, part distorted rectangles—draw on modernist research into the possibility of a universal language, they also imply that the language of architecture today is more inclusive, mutable, and personal than it was in the past. Hadid continually distorts, morphs, stretches, and stresses the forms she employs—animating them with energy, direction, variability, and speed.

As opportunities for building her visions gradually arose, Hadid found for architecture the equivalent of the material and sensuous qualities of Suprematist painting—the effects of Malevich's handling of pigment, techniques of fading, and combining of colors. Beginning with the Vitra Fire Station (Weil am Rhein, Germany, 1990–94), she has looked to concrete for its formal malleability, structural flexibility, and expressive capacity. Echoing the monumental plasticity of concrete buildings at mid-century by Marcel Breuer, Oscar Niemeyer, and Eero Saarinen, Hadid has often foregone tectonic expression and used concrete to emphasize form and surface, defy gravity, and evade regularity. For furniture and interiors, she often works in fiberglass and plastic for similar reasons and to similar effect. She prefers to mold and cast than to construct and assemble.

Hadid's way of working married the generative permutations of Suprematism with the step-by-step generative design method devised by Ginzburg and other Constructivist architects. Ginzburg's "functional method" began with the abstract diagramming of given functional requirements and their potential to change over time, and then turned to new industrial materials and methods of construction to "crystallize the social condenser."[14] The resultant spatial form could then be assessed and refined for its ability to "organize perception," since it was understood to be active with respect to the inhabitant rather than passive. By combining generative processes from art and design, Hadid effectively discharged the residual metaphysics of form that limited Malevich. She absorbed his formalism into an ever-expanding repertoire of form-generating techniques—the explosion of matter in space, the bundling of lines and ribbons, the organizing of fields, aggregations, and pixilations, and the warping, bending, twisting, and melting of forms—and put these to work in reorganizing life.

Over the course of her career, Hadid has developed a distinctive calligraphic mode of sketching with which she begins her projects. While her lines at times recall those of Kandinsky or Chernikov, they are more spontaneous and probing. Where Erich Mendelsohn's fluid ink sketches inaugurated the massing and profile of buildings such as his Einstein Tower (near Potsdam, Germany, 1919–21), Hadid's lines explore possible organizations that can gradually be developed into plans, sections, and three-dimensional forms. Likewise, her drawings should not be confused with expressive sketches that seek to manifest the unconscious psyche, such as Coop Himmelblau's drawing with eyes closed for their Open House of 1983 (Malibu, California). Rather, Hadid's drawings capture and reveal the intangible forces, flows, and rhythms already at play in the sites that she is to develop and the building briefs that she is given. Like her paintings of urban sites, they speculate from external givens. Most recently she has refined this kind of diagramming through computer modeling, which is capable of handling vast amounts of information as well as producing complex and mutating geometries. By linking the analytical and generative uses of computing, Hadid demonstrates how powerful a tool it can be for designers eager to participate productively in the evolution of physical environments always and already in motion.

Hadid insists, like Malevich, on seeing art and architecture as a totality, but figures it more concretely as the urbanization of the planet. Her conception of the whole is dynamic, indeterminate, and emergent, rather than static and resolved. In this, she clarifies something

01 Kazimir Malevich, *Morning in the Village after Snowstorm*, 1912. Oil on canvas, 31 3/4 x 31 7/8 inches (80.6 x 81 cm). Solomon R. Guggenheim Museum, New York 52.1327

02 Rem Koolhaas and Elia Zenghelis with Madelon Vriesendorp and Zoe Zenghelis, *Exodus, or The Voluntary Prisoners of Architecture*, London, 1972

03 Installation view of paintings by Kazimir Malevich at *The Last Futurist Exhibition of Paintings: "0.10"*, Galerie Dobychina, Petrograd, 1915

04 Kazimir Malevich, *Suprematism (Supremus No. 56)*, 1916. Oil on canvas, 31 3/4 x 28 inches (80.6 x 71.1 cm). State Russian Museum, St. Petersburg

05 Kazimir Malevich, *Suprematism No. 55 (Spheric Evolution of a Plane)*, 1917. Oil on canvas, 25 7/8 x 19 inches (55.6 x 48.3 cm). Kawamura Memorial Museum of Modern Art, Sakura, Japan

06 Kazimir Malevich, *Alpha Architekton*, 1920 (1925–26). Plaster, 12 3/8 x 31 3/4 x 13 3/8 inches (31.5 x 80.5 x 34 cm). State Russian Museum, St. Petersburg

07 Vasily Kandinsky, *White Cross (Weisses Kreuz)*, January–June, 1922. Oil on canvas, 39 9/16 x 43 9/16 inches (100.5 x 110.6 cm). Peggy Guggenheim Collection, Venice 76.2553.34

08 László Moholy-Nagy, *La Sarraz*, 1930. Gouache, india ink, pencil, and collage on paper, 18 3/4 x 26 11/16 inches (47.6 x 67.8 cm). Solomon R. Guggenheim Museum, New York 48.1155

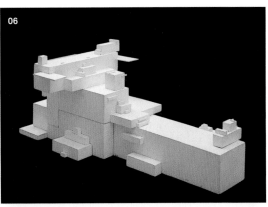

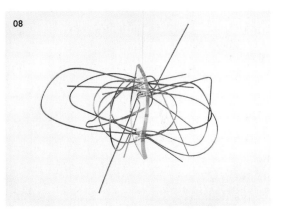

12 Gilles Deleuze, "Mediators," trans. Martin Joughin, in *Zone 6: Incorporations*, ed. Jonathan Crary and Sanford Kwinter (New York: Zone Books, 1992), pp. 281–93.

13 Ibid., p. 281. Deleuze continues, "There is no longer any origin as starting point, but a sort of putting-into-orbit. The basic thing is how to get taken up in the movement of a big wave, a column of rising air, to 'come between' rather than to be the origin of an effort."

14 Moisei Ginzburg, "New Methods of Architectural Thought," in Cooke, *Russian Avant-Garde*, pp. 129–30. See also Cooke's chapter 5, "Constructivism: From Tatlin and Rodchenko to a 'Functional Method' for Building Design," pp. 99–121.

15 Malevich considered Suprematism to be his personal interpretation of creation, referred to himself as a Messiah, and described the *Black Square* as the "image of God as the essence of His perfection on a new path for today's fresh beginning." See Malevich, letter to Mikhail Gershenzon, March 20, 1920, which is cited and translated in Yevgenia Petrova, "Malevich's Suprematism and Religion," in Drutt, *Kazimir Malevich*, p. 91. Petrova points out that in Russian icons, "a white background traditionally symbolizes purity, sanctity, and eternity, while black represents the chasm, hell, and darkness" (p. 91).

16 See Malevich, *The Non-Objective World*, p. 14.

17 See ibid., pp. 81–83, 87. These phrases are in the titles of his work (figs. 76–78, 81).

18 See Umberto Eco, *The Open Work*, trans. Anna Cancogni (Cambridge: Harvard University Press, 1989).

19 Malevich, *The Non-Objective World*, p. 98.

that Malevich himself struggled with. His world-view was theological and transcendental, yet he sought to account for the evolution of art as part of human history.[15] He explained Cubism, Futurism, and Suprematism as adding elements to art from the outside, from the world of modern technology and experience. At first the audience, he recalled, was shocked and dismayed by such abnormalities, but then came to accept them, thereby expanding the horizon of perception, and of the perceptible as such.[16] He considered individual works to be "constructions" that pushed beyond the closed system of art, which was merely "on its way" toward a future system. Later, after Stalin rejected modern art in favor of Socialist Realism, Malevich painted abstract depictions of peasant life, which he still considered to be Suprematist, suggesting just how much he believed Suprematism to be historically contingent. Hadid extended this contingency into the twenty-first century and understands the relationships of part and whole, one and many, past and future, as immanent. The whole is given but elusive. It does not need to be produced through human works, although they participate in its ongoing metamorphosis. For Hadid, the special contribution that an architecture of form—abstract and dynamic—can make is to stand in for that totality, which eludes every effort, every model, and every allegory that seeks to represent it, in science as in philosophy, theology, and art.

Like Piet Mondrian and van Doesburg, Malevich believed in a hierarchical relationship between art and utility. He was indifferent to function, even when it came to architecture. But Malevich spoke of his art producing psychological affects, expressing things like the "sensation of flight," the "sensation of metallic sounds," the "feeling of wireless telegraphy," and "magnetic attraction."[17] In expressing such sensations, he brought the experience of modern technology into art abstractly, without overt representation. He provided an opportunity for the observer to reexperience these feelings directly through perception, which he held to be more capable than the conscious mind of accessing the absolute. As a result, his images are profoundly ambiguous, open to interpretation but also misinterpretation. They have the poetic character of an open work, which, as Umberto Eco has described, rejects definitive and concluded messages and, instead, multiplies possibilities and encourages acts of conscious freedom.[18]

While Malevich gave priority to form over function and material, he recognized that forms could have applications and utility in quotidian life as teapots, decorated china, textile patterns, clothing, and buildings. While his overly geometrized work in these realms was far from convincing, he suggested in his writings a provocative way to rethink the question of use, which was informed by his expressive conception of art: "a chair, bed, and table are not matters of utility but rather, the forms taken by plastic sensations.... [T]he sensations of sitting, standing, or running are, first and foremost, plastic sensations and they are responsible for the development of corresponding 'objects of use' and largely determine their form... We are never in a position for recognizing any real utility in things and ... shall never succeed in constructing a really practical object. We can evidently only feel the essence of absolute utility but, since a feeling is always nonobjective, any attempt to grasp the utility of the objective is Utopian."[19] We are accustomed to objects such as furniture having determined and codified uses, when in fact they can be used in different and unexpected ways. This openness is something that Hadid has pursued in her interiors, from the furniture for her own apartment (originally made for 24 Cathcart Road, London, 1985–86) to her Z-Scape furniture, Iceberg sofa/lounger, and *Ice-Storm* domestic landscape, which beckons one to lie on it, lean on it, climb on it, slide on it, crawl through it, and eat on it, alone or with others.

Certainly the uses of buildings change over time, often radically and unpredictably. In the 1920s, Mies van der Rohe criticized a friend, the organicist functionalist Hugo Haering, for seeking too tight a fit between form and function—optimizing form for only one function when spaces often need to serve many at once and when uses change more rapidly than buildings can. Hadid's buildings, like her furniture, are bigger than their functions, multivalent and multifunctional. They are the infrastructure and support for unexpected events and emergent ways of living as well as programmed scripts. They tease and enable their inhabitants to experiment with other ways of doing things. The subjects of her buildings are both generators of forms and participants in the life and completion of the work over time. It is this combination of attentiveness and openness that defines Hadid's social vision.

Indebted to the catalytic ambitions of Suprematist and Constructivist architecture, Hadid's modernity is fully self-reflexive, aware not only of its devices and the contingency of its dreams, but also the risks it takes. In a world of instability, contrariness, uncertainty, and deception, she produces an architecture that embraces flux and polyvalent mixtures. Urbane, daring, and exuberant, her oeuvre supports a vision of life as an art—lived intensely and expansively, with imagination and style. Like life itself, Hadid's modernity is constitutively unfinished and always surprising.

THE SKYSCRAPER REVITALIZED: DIFFERENTIATION, INTERFACE, NAVIGATION

Patrik Schumacher

Zaha Hadid Architects is entering a new phase of expansion, taking on larger projects and venturing to design towers. The precise (built) implications of this new direction have yet to be seen. Is ZHA going mainstream or is the skyscraper finally succumbing to the pressure of the lessons of the avant-garde? What we currently have on the drawing boards seems to suggest that this encounter is not a losing battle, but the initial mutation of a hitherto ultrastable typology.

Zaha Hadid started by injecting a new level of dynamism into architecture. Her work has been explosive, fluid, and boundless—forcefully questioning the need for urban fortifications in her drive to establish a continuous, active ground-plane. The fragments of her exploded built volumes have drifted across this agitated ground, seemingly defying gravity.

Behind this spatial exuberance lies the real need to organize multiple, dynamic programs within dense urban contexts. This leads to the rejection of closed forms and the adoption of open-ended strategies of networking and layering. The horizontal was always the primary expansive dimension of this new dynamism. The Peak (1982–83)—which metaphorically turned several Hong Kong towers on their sides to generate a horizontal cluster of beams—was the paradigmatic project of this first wave of work. The Vitra Fire Station (Weil am Rhein, Germany, 1990–94), the Zollhof 3 Media Park (Düsseldorf, Germany, 1989–93), and the Cardiff Bay Opera House (Wales, 1994–96) are further well-known early examples.

Coping with complexity

With these early manifesto projects, Hadid contributed to the collective avant-garde effort to forge a new fluid, adaptive language of architecture that responds to increasing levels of social and urban complexity. Contemporary urban life is becoming ever more complex, with diverse, overlapping audiences who have multiple, simultaneous demands. Dense proximity of differences and a new intensity of connections distinguish contemporary life from the modern period of separation and repetition. The task today is to order and articulate this complexity in ways that maintain legibility and orientation.

To meet this challenge a new architectural language is emerging that is inspired by (organic and inorganic) natural systems. This language flourishes via the new digital modeling tools that have augmented the design process with techniques of continuous form-variation. This approach privileges curvilinearity and allows the fusion of multiple trajectories into a coherent texture.[1]

The BMW Plant Central Building (Leipzig, Germany, 2001–05, Fig. 01) and the Phaeno Science Center (Wolfsburg, Germany, 1999–2005) might be cited as the prime built examples of this new architectural language. The MAXXI National Centre of Contemporary Arts (Rome, 1997–ongoing, Fig. 02) and the Napoli-Afragola High-Speed Train Station (Naples, 2003–ongoing) are further examples currently under construction. All these projects follow horizontal trajectories, and most tend to mesh with their context rather than stand apart as clear and distinct objects.

Toppling the modernist tower

Against this story of contemporary social and architectural fluidity stands the stiff, solitary figure of the skyscraper. Once the penultimate architectural symbol of modernism, the skyscraper seems locked in a bygone paradigm of segregating segmentation and serial repetition. The tower typology is the last bastion of Fordism—the system of assembly-line mass production that led to modern mass society—and so far it has consistently resisted the injection of any significant measure of complexity.

Towers are still driven by pure quantity. Their volume is generally generated by pure extrusion and their inner space is nothing but the multiplication of identical floorplates. They are vertical dead-end corridors, usually cut off from the ground-plane by a podium. All this is good for economic reasons, but there are equally valid reasons why it might be time to tackle the tower typology with the concepts and ambitions of our new architectural language.

ZHA resisted the design of towers for a long time. If we had to go high, we much preferred the slab with its lateral extension, which gives more room for spatial manipulation. We experimented with bent slabs (Victoria City Aerial, Berlin, 1988), twisted slabs (Hafenstrasse Office and Residential Development, Hamburg, 1989), clusters of slabs (Zollhof 3 Media Park), and a split slab (Competition for a Hotel and Residential Complex, Abu Dhabi, 1990). In 1995 we finally designed a tower for the first time—for a mixed use development on Manhattan's Forty-second Street (42nd Street Hotel, New York, 1995, Fig. 03). We avoided extrusion, repetition, and hermetic curtain walling and instead proposed a vertical pile of interlocking blocks, differentiated with diverse external textures and interstitial spaces. On the inside we enthusiastically jumped on John Portman's fantastic innovation of an extraordinarily tall atrium surging up the tower. Portman's invention is the only notable innovation concerning the organization of towers in the second half of the twentieth century, and the interior space of his Marriot Marquis Hotel (1972–85) on Times Square remains one of the most inspirational spaces in all of New York.

In retrospect our 42nd Street Hotel tower design seems both prophetic and primitive. It was the first tower design that proposed a radical differentiation of the tower along its vertical axis and did so from both without and within. Portman's idea of the atrium was radicalized into a rhythmically animated navigation-space that gave interest and orientation to the upward journey. But our design was primitive (by current standards) with respect to its collage mode of differentiation by mere juxtaposition. Also, its mode of interfacing with the ground was not developed.

We lost this competition and it was only in the aftermath of 9/11, in the context of speculations about how Ground Zero and Lower Manhattan could be elevated once more, that we made a fresh start in our investigation of the typology of the tower.

1 For an elaborate treatment of how these new digital design techniques have been spurring a new architectural language, see Patrik Schumacher, *Digital Hadid: Landscapes in Motion* (Basel: Birkhäuser, 2004).

2 The idea of a bundle tower was obviously in the air: at the same time that ZHA proposed a bundle tower for Ground Zero, several other architects did as well, including FOA/United Architects and Lars Spuybroek/NOX.

After 9/11: Metropolis beyond the skyscraper?

New York's World Trade Center was designed in the mid-to-late-1960s, at the peak of the era of Fordism. Standardization, grids, series, and the endless repetition of the same was all around. The serial aesthetic of Mies van der Rohe's American period was the most pertinent expression of Fordism in architecture. Minoru Yamasaki's Twin Towers (1966–77) developed this principle to its ultimate symbolic conclusion: even an enormous structure like the great American skyscraper could be subordinated to the principle of repetition as if it were an item for mass production. Today, the tragic destruction of the World Trade Center raises the question of what could replace it. What kind of organizational structure would satisfy contemporary business and life processes, and what kind of formal language would best articulate the new era?

The epoch of the repetitive skyscraper is over, because the skyscraper's organizational structure is too simple and too constricting. A tower only grows in one dimension. The strict linearity of its extension accounts for its characteristic poverty of connectivity. Towers are hermetic units, which are themselves arrays of equally hermetic units (floors). These features of linearity and strict segmentation are antithetical to contemporary business relations as well as to contemporary urban life in general. Much higher levels of complexity are required to spatially order and articulate contemporary social relations. However, the demise of Fordism and of the skyscraper as its urban archetype does not imply a retreat from the large scale or from high density. Both bigness and density are increasing within the contemporary metropolis.

ZHA's sketch design for a new World Trade Center Tower (New York, 2002, Fig. 04) proposed a bundle tower whereby various tubes or fibers emerged from different horizontal trajectories within the site.[2] Thus we conceived a strong compositional device to interface the tower with the complex ground configurations. The filaments of the bundle turned toward the vertical, and their shifting relative size and interplay afforded a mechanism to achieve the continuous differentiation of the tower along its vertical axis. The modulated space between the filaments was exploited as an orienting navigation space. Furthermore, the possibility of mutual stabilization of the tubes meant that the tower could reach a considerable height without imposing a dark and deep interior.

In 2005, we exploited this concept of the bundle once more for our proposal of "Dancing Towers" (Dancing Towers—Business Bay, Dubai, 2005–ongoing, Figs. 05–06), a project that is supposed to mark the center of a series of concentric rings of towers. Here we interpreted the mixed use high-rise development by means of three towers—an office tower, a hotel tower, and a residential tower—that variously converge and diverge, meet and separate, to share a ground-lobby as well as a sky-lobby above the midpoint. The filaments of this bundle spread out in various directions on the ground, generating both additional ground surfaces (for lobbies and retail areas) as well as connections to the surrounding context. One of those horizontal extensions establishes a habitable bridge across the creek.

Compressed complexity and parametric interarticulation

The examples cited above start to demonstrate how ZHA's new architectural language offers a new lease on life for the tower typology. But what is of particular interest to us is also the reverse effect: the disciplining effect of the task of designing a high-rise on the architectural language we are trying to develop and refine. The tower demands high levels of precision and a close-knit integration of all parts and subsystems. It shifts the emphasis of our new architectural language away from freewheeling, expansive layering to a keen sense of compact interarticulation. It also implies tight geometric coordination of all components. If the principles of variation, adaptation, and differentiation are to be upheld, we require a new set of concepts and tools. The geometry of the building has to be conceived as a network of linked parameters and handled with an elaborate parametric model, whose internal subdivision is linked to vary simultaneously with the changing outer shape of the model (e.g., the structure adjusts as the outer shape increases in height). The designs of our towers for Beijing (Soho Forum, Central Business District, 2004), Milan (Fiera di Milano, 2004–ongoing), and Marseille (CMA CGM Head Office, 2004–ongoing, Fig. 07) were generated by means of such parametric models.

Parametric modeling affords a new, concrete understanding of "organic" design as a parametrically controlled interarticulation of the subsystems. As a scripted system of relations, the parametric composition is highly differentiated, yet this differentiation is rule governed. It is based on a systematic set of lawful correlations that are defined between the differentiated elements and subsystems. These correlations integrate and (re-)establish a visible coherence and unity across the differentiated system. It is the sense of law-governed complexity that assimilates this work to the forms we find in (organic as well as in inorganic) natural systems, where all forms are the result of lawfully interacting forces. Just like natural systems, parametric compositions cannot be easily decomposed into independent subsystems. This is a major point of difference in comparison to the modern insistence on clear separation of functional subsystems, like tower and podium, skin and skeleton, post and beam.

A new high-rise paradigm: Three critical agendas

The following presents three manifesto-style slogans that ZHA is promoting as key concerns and ambitions for a new high-rise typology and a new paradigm for the design of towers.

1 Differentiation. The most general slogan and overall headline for a new approach to the design of towers would be: "Injecting complexity." While all the points below may be subsumed under this general headline, it is the differentiation of the mass of the tower that is the most obvious aspect. All of our towers avoid Platonic footprints and extruded volumes. The exterior expression of the tower as a bundle (Dancing Towers—Business Bay), stretched ovoid (Soho City Masterplan, Beijing, 2003–ongoing; NYC 2012 Olympic Village, 2004), wave-shaped tall slab (Zhivopisnaya Tower, Moscow, 2004–ongoing, Fig. 08), stretched prism (CMA CGM Head Office), stretched spiral (Fiera di Milano), or blade (Durango Residential Tower, Spain, 2004–ongoing) gives each project a different recognizable shape. However, it is not so much the icon that we are after as that we are seeking to create an asymmetric, differentiated volume that offers a certain variation of conditions and spaces on the inside, and also affords opportunities for urban contextualizations. We are proposing differentiated volumes that can be oriented laterally within a field, that can be terminated in an interesting way against the sky, that can be worked into the ground in a special way, and so on.

2 Interface. The taller the tower, the more important is its mode of interfacing with the ground-plane. The large amount of traffic coming down from the tower usually occasions special spatial provisions on the ground floor. For instance, in the case of a hotel tower, all additional facilities like lobbies, restaurants, bars, and retail spaces are located on the ground floor or near the ground. Tall residential towers, as well as office towers, also demand ground-level expansion. Usually these additional space requirements are met by means of discrete podium blocks that separate the shaft of the tower from the ground. One of our key ambitions has been to find convincing alternatives to the "tower on podium" typology that avoid the intervention of a discrete third element between the ground-surface and the tower itself.

The simplest concept here is to turn or bend the vertical extension into a horizontal extension. The most successful example of this simple move is perhaps our forty-story apartment tower-slab in Moscow (Zhivopisnaya Tower). The tall slab bends into the horizontal across its full width to produce ample space for a pool, fitness area, restaurant, and retail outlets. The degree to which this horizontal extension is perceived as a direct extension of the body of the tower depends upon the specific continuities of the surface treatment and fenestration patterns. For instance, the great canyon voids in the main facade turn to become linear skylights above the pool. Equally important are the nuances of the volumetric treatment. While the horizontal extension stretches to the riverfront, where it turns into a highly formalized landscape extension, at the opposite (entrance) side the facade pulls inward in a responding countermove. Thus the tower dramatically overhangs the drop-off zone, signaling where to slip into the building.

A similar move characterized our residential towers for Beijing's Soho City Masterplan. As "tails" are pulled out from the tower on one side, the opposite side reacts by pulling the envelope inward, thus clearly articulating the entrance. In this project, we designed a whole swarm of towers. While the higher levels are repeated within each tower and also across towers, the tops have been shaved off according to a global, curved envelope. The tails are all different, adapting to the local context and to each other. The tail-extension gives each tower a clear directionality that facilitates the establishment of the overall swarm logic of coordinated focus and directionality.

Our twin-tower proposal (Soho Forum) for a mixed use tower for Beijing's Central Business District flares out at the bottom (bell-bottom) to accommodate retail space (Fig. 09). The flares of the two towers merge in a grand swoop to enclose even larger retail spaces. Our tower for Milan twists (Fig. 10), continuing the spiraling movement of the shopping mall below. Here, the typical linear atrium that marks the mall typology is continued and reinterpreted in the tower as a split that moves up the height of the tower. This morphological affiliation helps to unify tower and ground extension.

Perhaps the most original and beautiful solution to the problem of how to interface with the ground-plane has been developed in connection with our competition entry for the Olympic Village of New York's 2012 Olympic bid (Fig. 11). Here the tower shaft tightens conically at the bottom, like a pencil, and dips into the "elastic" ground-surface. The ground-surface reacts like a water-surface with a crater and concentric ripples. This crater formation affords ample additional space within its flanks without obstructing or occluding the tower entrance. The tightened footprint of the tower contains nothing but lobby spaces grouped around the vertical circulation shaft (core). Moving between the towers is a pleasure as one's glance wanders up the pencil-tower or down into the craterlike clearing, which contains all the public facilities.

3 Navigation. The idea of explicitly introducing navigation as a key agenda to be considered in the design of towers goes hand in hand with the attempt to inject a certain measure of differentiation and complexity into the vertical trajectory of the tower. The repetition of the same does not require a special design effort to facilitate orientation. Usually the navigation of towers is dead simple: just step into the elevator and select the required floor. As the complexity of the tower increases and public functions start to penetrate the tower, navigation becomes an issue. And by navigation we mean much more than mere mechanical circulation. We mean the conceptual/perceptual penetration of a space. A legibly configured navigation space is called for that affords a certain visual penetration and mental map. Floors are no longer segregated black boxes.

01 BMW Plant Central Building, Leipzig, Germany, 2001–05. Photograph

02 MAXXI National Centre of Contemporary Arts, Rome, 1997–ongoing. Digital rendering

03 42nd Street Hotel, New York, 1995. Isometric painting

04 World Trade Center Tower, New York, 2002. Digital rendering

05 Dancing Towers—Business Bay, Dubai, 2005–ongoing. Model

06 Dancing Towers—Business Bay, Dubai, 2005–ongoing. Digital rendering

07 CMA CGM Head Office, Marseille, 2004–08. Digital rendering

08 Zhivopisnaya Tower, Moscow, 2004–ongoing. Digital rendering

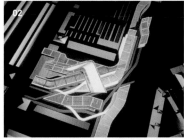

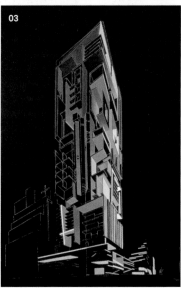

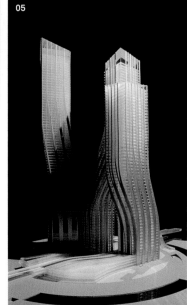

9 Soho Forum, Central Business District, Beijing, 2004.
Digital rendering

10 Fiera di Milano, Milan, 2004–ongoing. Model

11 NYC 2012 Olympic Village, New York, 2004. Model

12 Lois and Richard Rosenthal Center for Contemporary Art
Cincinnati, 1997–2003. Photograph

13 Soho Forum, Central Business District, Beijing, 2004.
Digital rendering

14 Zhivopisnaya Tower, Moscow, 2004–ongoing. Digital rendering

Such a space invites browsing rather than mere destination travel.

We first developed this notion of the navigation space with respect to our more complex museum designs—especially in relation to the Maxxi Centre in Rome. The Lois and Richard Rosenthal Center for Contemporary Art (Cincinnati, 1997–2003, Fig. 12) displays our first vertical navigation space. Here we created a continuous sliver space with a cascade of stair-ramps behind a stack of different gallery volumes. Our concept for a new Guggenheim Museum in Singapore (2005) proposed a tower that was marked by a dramatic internal navigation space with an extraordinarily tall lobby, as well as a tall sky-lobby above the midlevel.

In the case of our Soho Forum twin towers, the flaring of the towers opens up a tent-shaped atrium space on the inside—which indicates the gradient of penetration of the public into the higher floors of the tower—until the void closes to separate off the fully private floors (Fig. 13). The Zhivopisnaya Tower is sliced by three independent navigation spaces (Fig. 14). This tower is designed without corridors; instead it has three independent cores rising up. However, the cores—usually the most solid elements of a tower—are interpreted as canyon-shaped voids that slice all the way through the volume. The elevator walls are transparent glass and the staircases are open instead of closed shafts. The canyon narrows and widens as we move up the building. The arrival at the doorstep of the apartments is a fantastic panoramic journey.

The agendas of differentiation, interface, and navigation combine to articulate a new paradigm for the design of complex towers in urban contexts. On this new basis the tower typology will receive a new lease on life in central metropolitan societies where the desire for connectivity (rather than pure quantity) drives urban density. In the future, even more than now, the high-density tower will be a mixed-use structure, where multiple life processes intersect. These life processes need to be ordered in intricate ways that nevertheless remain legible. More than ever, the task of architectural design will be about the transparent articulation of relations for the sake of orientation and communication. The differentiation, interface, and navigation of spaces constitute a clear agenda that will require a sophisticated and versatile new architectural language if it is to be articulated in all its forms and contexts.

INTERVIEW

Alvin Boyarsky Talks with Zaha Hadid

The following is excerpted from a series of discussions on the occasion of Zaha Hadid's 1987 exhibition of furniture at the Architectural Association (AA), England's oldest school of architecture. Alvin Boyarsky, Chairman of the AA from 1971 to 1990, created a legacy of globalism at the school decades before such ideas as the Internet and multiculturalism were widely considered. Hadid studied at the AA from 1972 to 1977, when she was awarded the Diploma Prize. She returned to the AA to teach and ran her own studio at the school from 1980 until 1987.

October 1987

Alvin Boyarsky: Tell me about the origins of your architectural style, in particular your unusual way of depicting architectural plans.

Zaha Hadid: My work developed out of certain early precedents in modern architecture. My original intention was to inject the ideas of Suprematism into architecture. I was also curious about Rem Koolhaas's bent plan for Mies van der Rohe's Barcelona Pavilion [1928–29]. Another influence was one of Mies's patio houses, the Gericke House [Berlin, 1932]—it's the only one where he bent his plan, and here the energy is not static. If you compare De Stijl to Suprematism, there is a kind of equilibrium in both cases, the former arrived at through total control and the latter through total energy, not unlike a photographic free frame. Mondrian would rework his compositions until they were balanced and frozen. Malevich's compositions were definitive, or finite, but they also functioned as a picture frame—if it could move, it would frame something else. In this way, his work suggests that the whole planet is connected. You might even say that its guiding force is not bound by earthly conditions. The implication is one of liberation. It's from this notion that we arrive at the idea of the liberation of the plan.

The question was how to free the architectural plan in a different way than had been done in the past, how to free it to allow certain elements to operate independently, so that these elements could impose themselves more assertively on the urban condition. What may seem to be frivolous graphics has a special logic of its own. It may not be rational in the European sense, but it is logical in the way it moves people, in the way the building is used.

This logic also has to do with release and compression between the different zones of the plan. Energy is compressed into linear conditions, or it is released in an urban sense, and causes certain forms to flow—in this case, the flow of the people.

It was through observing how Mies did certain things to liberate the plan—how he energized the ground condition, for example—that my work on the Irish Prime Minister's Residence [Dublin, 1979–80] developed. Afterward people said the design was Kandinsky-like. Then the connection with Arab calligraphy struck me. They have the same roots: 1950s architecture was related to Kandinsky's work and Kandinsky's work to Arab calligraphy.

It's my belief that early-twentieth-century abstract painters often turned to primitive, figurative art—generally African—or to Chinese and Arabic calligraphy and geometric design. These were the only abstract forms of art available at the time.

There are various ways of approaching a plan. There are urban conditions and there are points of release. The plan interprets the architectural program—and it can manifest this free-flowing nonlinear form. It's similar to the study of engineering. Most engineers study structure in a linear way and can't deal with it when it's nonlinear. Peter Rice and I had a conversation the other day about an engineer's understanding of the nonlinear condition of architecture. What is very nice about Peter is that he understands it—that's really quite exciting.

AB: What if we were to take a sequence of sketches—any sequence, six, a dozen, fifteen sketches—lay them out like a hand of cards, and discuss their significance?

ZH: The plan develops from a composite of my early sketches. The Peak [Hong Kong, 1982–83], Parc de la Villette [Paris, 1982–83], and the Irish Prime Minister's Residence were each done differently, but there are also many similarities between them. The Residence was done through cutouts; at that point I was opening the space by eliminating elements. The notion of layering the plan and the building came accidentally in the case of La Villette, but deliberately in The Peak. The building was represented in the geological plane of Hong Kong. In the beginning, I didn't know that the building would be dug into the topography of the island. From there I became aware of differences between a linear space that is cellular and a linear space that is fluid.

Every project has certain limitations. The architect's relationship to those limitations is very interesting. You can study these limitations and responses.

AB: Let's say we're planning a document that would lead us to what you're thinking about right now. We would begin by including a few paintings and drawings by other people, and also plans and drawings. We would use Mies, Oscar Niemeyer, and perhaps Le Corbusier. A variety of significant examples could be discussed in terms of the content that interests you; it would tersely but effectively demonstrate your plan. Next to this we would place another, almost parallel sequence of some of your own experiments.

ZH: Fundamentally one has to expose the idea that there is a modern culture and that it never came to full fruition. It's not a matter of borrowing from here and there and blending it all together in a composite. Rather, there's a stream of events, each of which is an experiment. In the end all these projects are a kind of experiment. My own work tests the realm of possibilities. It never stays at the same point.

AB: It's very interesting that you don't use the word "space" at all.

ZH: I always think of a given space—I mean "space" in a broad sense, because you can never perceive small spaces. If you use the term "space," as in public space, you mean a sort of overall concept, like air. You can never perceive the whole if it's only an open space and not on the ground.

AB: But you do use the word "energy" quite a lot. It signals a kind of empathy, the narrow and wide and low. In the 1930s a lot of people, particularly Italians, began to write about the space of architecture as being continuous. They would reverse the plan and make models of the space of a building.

ZH: That's what's interesting about Niemeyer's work. He spoke to us about the lightness of the structure, how you do things to free certain zones.

In the case of Mies's New National Gallery [Berlin, 1962–68], you have an empty space—a place you go to but shouldn't occupy, like a public room. When I go to places like that, I find it staggering that the occupants don't understand this viewing condition. Take the Mies show at New York's Museum of Modern Art [*Mies in Berlin*, 1986]. The exhibition organizers didn't understand that if you have a Mies show, you have to express something of what he taught you. You can't create a space as Mies would have done; that's too difficult to do. But you have to try to give back something, and they couldn't do it.

AB: Unfortunately, I missed that exhibition. What are you working on now, Zaha?

ZH: Right now, my interest is the given ground condition, which has been one of the weakest aspects of modern architecture. The ground condition was never properly resolved, except in New York, where you see lobbies and various ground-floor spaces that resolve the problem, not in a conservative but in a modern way. If you look at all the postwar housing, the CIAM [Congrès Internationaux d'Architecture Moderne] housing, Brasília—it all suffers from this problem of the ground. The ground could be anywhere, but once you establish a ground, you have to operate on it, especially in an urban situation. I think Brasília

[for which Niemeyer was chief architect] operates on two levels. The wings of the plane suffer from the nonresolution on the ground. The reason that the central government buildings operate better than the residential housing on the wings is that they have a ground condition. They have a lobby and two entrances, a grand entrance and a secondary entrance, which implies a datum that is private and operates in all the buildings on the first floor. There is a second datum on the ground and a third below ground. I'm not sure how intentional these things were; they were never declared, and on the wings—the housing—there is this notion that the ground is free. The architecture leaves out the life of the ground.

AB: A small piece of one of the wings of Brasília was landscaped by Burle Marx. It doesn't have the kind of life that you're speaking about, but it does have a kind of articulation. It's the only part of the housing in Brasília that I could feel was reasonable.

ZH: I don't think the wings operate well, and that is the problem with Brasília. If they want to resolve the problem of Brasília, they should begin with this.

AB: But Brasília is interesting as a plan for something. One can see it growing as a sequence of analyses that develops into a thesis. You work in a similar way, with a parallel series of sketches and plans that grow increasingly more intense. But first you need to identify the problem you're trying to resolve. Where do you start? You spoke of Mies. It starts with painting, doesn't it?

ZH: Let me explain how I developed Malevich's Tektonik [London, 1976–77]. There were two layers. First was the program that I developed almost intuitively. A year later I did the plans, but I didn't like them. That's when I started the shipwreck. The shipwreck was very important, because it's my connection to Rem Koolhaas. I did it totally intuitively because I had a nightclub in the Malevich, which was a shipwreck. Rem came to my jury—he wasn't there the first time—and he said, "How odd, I'm also working on a shipwreck." It wasn't designed or published at the time; he was still working on it.

A year later, I was assigned a nightclub as a school project. Here I had a ship literally break through a glass wall. After this, I returned to Malevich's Tektonik with the understanding that the shipwreck had to be done abstractly. I realized that architecture occurs not only on the level of the tectonic, but also on the level of the diagrams. So I began to fragment them. That's how they go from a collision of the nightclub to the twisting of a Mies pavilion.

Then I went on to the Museum of the Nineteenth Century [London, 1977–78], which was also compressed. I realized the thing had to be freed and that it can't be both linear and cellular. The Dutch Parliament Extension [The Hague, 1978–79] was again a thin, compressed slab, but despite the linearity of the slab, certain public areas were much freer. In the Irish Prime Minister's Residence, within the confined walls of the garden, certain things imploded and exploded—all this was indicated in a series of sketches. A pattern links Malevich and all the Russians, Mies, Niemeyer, and even Le Corbusier: through the liberation of the plan they all invent a new kind of space. This realization led me to all kinds of different studies.

AB: Your paintings are beautiful objects. They are beautifully illustrated and succinctly described, but to materialize buildings, you need a series of sketches and plans, which you can focus on one at a time, like a stack of note cards for a lecture. In a way there is very little discussion that goes beyond style in this world. And the motivation to do something is in the end very theoretical, highly speculative, and based on a great deal of observation and digestion.

ZH: Yes, you can experiment when you're younger. But it's difficult to predict what happens if your building is built and occupied by people. How does your idea translate into an urban space or a private house? How do people live in it? If it's office space, how do they operate within it? These are questions that are interesting right now, because these days there is less and less inventiveness. There is no respect for anything visionary. Building is not architecture, and one feels that today there is no interest in architecture.

AB: In the pragmatic world you're describing, architecture becomes applied information, applied allegiances.

ZH: Compare the scenes of 1987 and '75. Back then, so-called thinkers invested time in experiments. It was a respectable line of inquiry. Today, there is no respect for that.

AB: Shall we go back a little and talk about the tradition of the self-determined research project, through which you've made significant contributions to architectural knowledge. It's a very important strand of the English scene in the 1950s and '60s, right up until the early '70s. Think of the input of people like Alison and Peter Smithson, whose work was topographical. Peter was interested in organization devices, and in the organization of the city through its circulation. He worked with Team 10 in opposition to CIAM and its abstract breakdown of things. Then there are people like Cedric Price with his projects of the early '60s—it's almost impossible to believe that the Fun Palace and the Potteries Thinkbelt Project were designed in those years. Nobody paid them; they were actually working out interesting issues. Cedric worked out the issues relating to the flexibility that comes from cybernetics, where things can be controlled and changed according to what's required. Archigram [headed by Peter Cook] was also making a point—you may not like the depth of their research, but they were acting like artists. The reason one thinks of OMA [Office of Metropolitan Architecture] as being part of that glorious tradition is that their early work was fighting the world, making a comment, introducing a whole new criterion. There are a few other people—Bernard Tschumi has opened up a whole new territory of discourse. When it's come time to operate, all of these people have found sufficient funding and done enough research to actually solve the problem that's required. In a sense your work has been in that tradition,

and that's why you're full of contempt for a lot of things, as I would be. But the difficulty right now is that society is in bad shape. It has so little ambition. People rarely expose themselves to the ridicule that goes with theoretical projects.

ZH: I think it's great that there are people with energy and there is economic energy, but unfortunately these two things don't coincide. England operates as a sort of incubator. The AA could never have existed anywhere but London, no matter what style it taught or if there was a different chairman, because London is so miserable. If London was Athens, it wouldn't be the same. You would be on the beach, you wouldn't be sitting and talking. In London, there's space and time for discussion. It's not superficial and there is no pressure or hurry. People don't care so much about money. These conditions are slowly being eradicated. But not the weather. The current generation of young people is more conservative, more interested in making money than anything else. The schools produce great musicians, great TV personalities, great graphics and architecture, but when it comes to backing, there is nothing. There comes a point when a developing artist or architect needs support and that simply doesn't exist here.

AB: Every person I mentioned earlier, whether it's the Smithsons, Cedric Price, Archigram, Rem Koolhaas and Elia Zenghalis [of OMA], Bernard Tschumi—why could none of them get started here? Because of the institutions of society, because of the Protestant work ethic, because of the idea that you don't involve yourself in ostentatious displays, you don't spend money, you don't allow yourself to be seen spending money, you don't get involved in all those curious things like the French, who go overboard for ideas. Here, it's all held back and conservative.

ZH: People either stay here and do I don't know what, or they leave.

England invests a great deal of time, energy, and money in educating people, but it doesn't know how to make use of them. However, the country does make use of people who are second rate. America doesn't have the same problem. The problem in America is that they don't grasp the idea of "an idea." I tried asking some people at Harvard what an idea is, and they didn't understand my question. They are used to appropriating ideas from France and Italy, so why should they bother to waste time developing their own?

Of course, the same can be said of English architects. They haven't always given themselves time to develop their sensibilities, so when it's come time for them to make buildings, they've needed an easy way out. They've simply gone to the nearest source and appropriated from it. I find that disappointing.

AB: What do you think of the notion of worldliness?

ZH: It's very important. Let me give you an example. I ran into a former classmate the other day. He's a Greek citizen and had to return to Greece for military service, but apparently he'd just been dismissed six months early. "That's great," I told him. "It's like being given six months as a present." But when I said this to him, he looked at me as if I was out of my mind.

Yet I know what travel has done for me personally. There comes a point when you have to become worldly. Of course, if you're painting flowers, you can sit in an isolated hut in the middle of nowhere, but if you're an architect you have an obligation to understand how the world operates. A thousand pounds can be made or lost in an instant, but it's always worth the investment. I told this friend that he should go to New York for six months. He's in the third year of architecture school and he still hasn't seen New York. That's a problem.

AB: Yesterday, I was talking with Peter Cook, Ron Herron, David Greene, and a few others about Warren Chalk. We were trying to figure out how to understand his legacy. I reminded them that in 1966 Warren became the first of the Archigram people to see the U.S. I invited him to teach in Chicago for a month and he sent a wire that began, "I'll be touching down

Wednesday." Very English. He didn't say what airline or what time. A total lack of worldliness.

ZH: I think you eliminate a lot of conversation if you haven't seen or experienced things. For a young architect, the Manhattan experience is fundamental. When I first went there as a student, I saw things that I didn't think were possible. The city has to be seen.

AB: It's the great city of the first part of the twentieth century.

ZH: Yes, but it's also very old, almost medieval. Parts of it are like the third world. It's a very layered city, not like anywhere else.

December 1987

AB: We are all very excited that the furniture that you recently designed is going to be exhibited in the Member's Room of the AA. I'm dying to see it.

ZH: You've never seen it?

AB: No, but I've seen the models, sketches, and working drawings. I've also been to the studio apartment that the pieces were originally designed for.

ZH: Now, they're in my apartment. You should come over for a drink to see them. Next year, they'll be reproduced in Italy, so you can always have a little audit over there.

You know, it's extraordinary. Someone said to me yesterday, "If your sofa was twenty centimeters bigger it wouldn't fit into your house." It's true; it misses the wall by that little. It looks like a captured whale, poor thing.

AB: You'll have to get a bigger house.

You designed these for an apartment at 24 Cathcart Road [London, 1985–86]—it's actually a very interesting studio apartment in Chelsea—but I detect that their roots go back beyond the specific requirements of this house. Is that right?

ZH: The furniture developed out of the idea to create an environment. We were given the space, which was like a gallery—very neutral and not the sort of space we would design ourselves. We had to do something with it in a neu-

tral way—without interfering too much. The furniture was purposely built for the house, but it was designed to exist in other conditions as well. The various pieces can act as enclosures and dividers. The challenge was to create a maximum effect with a minimal interjection.

The furniture design relates to the way we organize a plan—this notion of fluid space. The idea was to design furniture that not only fits into this house but into neoplastic forms generally. The shapes and the materials were very important. They had to be light, as if liberated from certain gravitational forces (although they are not). It was interesting to try to design comfortable seating—the idea of comfort is very strange. The furniture is very minimal, and each piece has specific qualities. We always kept in mind the idea that the furniture would be inserted into spaces.

AB: So the pieces had an archetypal quality?

ZH: Yes, we knew that within a given space, there are two ways to release clutter: you can either condense things and bind them into one form, or conversely you can separate them out. The wall unit at 24 Cathcart Road, for example, had three lives: when it's closed, it's just a blank wall; when it's fully open, it disappears; and when parts of it are open, it serves as a partial divider.

When you walk into that space, everything is white, but as it opens, color explodes. The same is true of the furniture, which was supposed to be all off-white. As it turns out, one sofa is white with some gray and black (it also has a black backrest), while the other was injected with a single color—yellow. We didn't use basic yellows and blacks; our yellow was more chartreuse, and our black was mixed with green. These colors all relate to the experiments we conducted while preparing our paintings. The same is true of

the materials. The carpet, which is metal, had to be bronze, but elsewhere, we used unusual materials, including scuba-diving fabric for the back of the sofas. It is interesting how this combination of color and form links to the paintings. In the paintings, we establish color series. We discovered, for example, that there are 200 grays and lots of blacks. These are not simple colors.

AB: It seems that you've detached the horizontal and vertical planes in some of the furniture.

ZH: A lot of the earlier furniture—the tubular furniture in the early part of the century, Le Corbusier's, even 1950s furniture, much of which was very beautiful—never landed properly on the ground. It was really clumsy. The way a piece of furniture lands is very important. Think of how Russian dancers land. These considerations affected the language of our investigation of the plan and the division of space. The yellow sofa is not just a sofa; it also acts as a partition or shield. The seat is not only a seat; it could also be a tray.

AB: What about the materials? You've used an unusual palette of materials for the furniture.

ZH: The sofa seat cover was specially woven because we couldn't find any fabrics for that kind of upholstery. We used synthetic materials like rubber, which is a good material for furniture. We wanted our furniture to fit into its cover like a stocking.

AB: There also seems to have been some need for a few major cantilevers. You've almost involved yourself in a series of engineering structures.

ZH: Yes, we've had to understand the whole notion of how to construct upright, operating structures that won't break or collapse. For instance, the base of the white sofa is supposed to free itself from the actual seating. We had to develop that piece so that it has more than one life. The sofa could be a bench in a lobby; it could be seating in a house; it could seat one person, or two, or ten.

AB: You did a piece for an exhibition in

Milan, didn't you? Was that related to this family?

ZH: In the Milan project, we thought that the twentieth-century notion of comfort, which has to do with tenting and cushioning, could be replaced by a kind of plastic condition and soft materials. This idea is part of a larger reconsideration of the entire notion of comfort—it's related, for example, to the notion of synthetic walls that can be bent. But the Milan project affected the idea of the chaise longue more than the sofa.

AB: Would you trace some of the pieces back to your brother's house, 59 Eaton Place [London, 1981–82]?

ZH: One of the first times I did a limp curved seat was for my brother. It was never designed, but it still implied a curve on the floor as a diagram. I was always interested in the notion of anticorner seating. Corners don't need to be right angles; they can be much more fluid, like curves. These ideas developed from the language of The Peak, and after that our project in Berlin [Office Building on Kurfürstendamm 70, 1986], where we expanded on the whole notion of the curve, creating a very shallow curve, like a boomerang.

AB: But in 59 Eaton Place, the furniture was treated as equipment in the room, which is what these new pieces are.

ZH: They were seen as architectures, not as buildings. It was as if one were to take an interior as a landscape. This furniture would operate as elements in that landscape, each with its own life. At the same time, they would ultimately help to organize the plan.

AB: It's quite an ambitious project to essentially rework the interior of the house through the arrangement of furniture. The pieces constitute the stations of the cross, so to speak, delineating where people go, the interior's activity centers, and so on.

ZH: Yes, but the house was basically done when we accepted this job.

It's very expensive to produce furniture in England. We should have approached manufacturers right at the beginning, but we found that they either do things in an old-fashioned, traditional way, and create very conserva-

tive furniture, or they make pieces that collide together and have a rough appearance, which is fashionable now—for instance, Nigel Coates's stuff, or Tom Dixon's, or André Dubreuil's. We wanted to do something different—furniture that was modern, but also very well made. With modern buildings, as with modern furniture, a great deal of detail and attention is required to make it look like there is no detail. I don't understand the preoccupation with detailing in the European sense; it's an overobsessive idea. On the other hand, if you want to do a really good building, a good modern building, then the work has to be very well detailed. After making the furniture, I realized that just as I had to invent a new language for drawing and painting, I also had to reinvent certain detailing methods—to make it seem as if there was no detail.

AB: The scheme for Berlin—the curved wall—depends enormously on the range of furniture in it because there is a momentum to the space that normal office furniture would destroy. Did you have a range of furniture in mind?

ZH: We came across this problem when we were doing 24 Cathcart Road. The apartment had a very strange, wiggly glass wall. We couldn't find a piece of furniture that would fit the wall as well as the entire space. It's important to establish our pieces of furniture so that they can either sit against a wall or float freely in space. Their backs are very important, since they can be viewed from all sides.

AB: What about the cost of the pieces? They were one-off and carefully made and probably were extremely expensive for that reason.

ZH: Well, it's not really how much each piece costs. The real expense is the time at the office. Our time in the end is more expensive than the furniture. After we did those pieces, we realized that we couldn't do others in the same way. There's no way—also the clients were extremely meticulous and very fussy, but not worldly.

AB: That intrigues me. Obviously you have

sketchbooks filled with ideas, but how did you approach these clients, who seem to be fairly ordinary people?

ZH: They came to us.

AB: You showed drawings?

ZH: We made models. Michael Wolfson and I did some sketches and someone in the office made models. Everything was adjusted. The dining room table went through many sessions. First it was done very crudely, then I sketched it, then it changed again. The sperm-shaped table was based on a squiggle I drew. It was very simple and we put glass on it.

AB: Do you still have those sketches?

ZH: Some of them, but this furniture was really done through the models.

AB: In a catalogue essay Ken Frampton wrote some time ago, he said that a lot of your furniture seems to go back to the Arabic script we discussed last time.

ZH: Yes, that does seem right, but only in hindsight.

I was explaining to Charles Jencks the other day that there are problems with this upcoming show at MOMA in New York [*Deconstructivist Architecture*, Museum of Modern Art, 1988]. The show suggests that the architects on display read some Derrida and then invented a wholly new style of architecture. Not only is this wrong, but it trivializes Derrida. In fact, deconstructivist architecture has nothing to do with Derrida's philosophical deconstruction. It originates from a very optimistic view and has to do with energy and with an understanding of abstraction, not with taking something and dissolving it. Deconstructivist architecture goes back to a whole series of people operating in Europe in the 1960s and '70s, who were concerned with shattering and breaking—and before that to the beginning of the twentieth century, when certain abstract movements in art were looking at figurative art, and also certain geometric abstractions, as well as Arabic and Chinese calligraphy. I'm absolutely sure the Russians—Malevich, in particular—looked at those scripts. Kandinsky's art also has to do with script. The person who first observed this connection was Rem Koolhaas. He noticed that only the Arab and Persian architecture students were able to make certain curved gestures. He thought it had to do with calligraphy.

The calligraphy you see in architectural plans today has to do with the notion of fragmentation in space. Plastic form is indirectly related to calligraphy. The 1950s were affected by Kandinsky, and Kandinsky, in turn, by calligraphy. That's how we've arrived at deconstructivist architecture.

AB: Going back to Charles Jencks and his quest to find out all about Derrida and deconstruction, I said more or less the same thing as you. Charles interviewed me and wanted to know why I was interested in Derrida.

ZH: I explained to him that you should contribute an essay to the MOMA catalogue, because ultimately these tendencies started here at the AA, and this has to be acknowledged. The Americans appropriated from us. I don't want to sound arrogant, but I told Philip Johnson that I knew where it started. I'm not saying I invented it, but I remember when it started. I was in my fourth or fifth year with Rem and Elia [at OMA]. Rem was trying to expand on Mies's bending. In his plan for the Gericke House , Mies experimented with the notion of bending, but he was too Germanic to develop this concept fully. Now, when others use these ideas, they're appropriating.

AB: And now, of course, it's become quite common.

As a result of this MOMA exhibition, a new style will develop in the U.S., but it will be derivative, because the initial experiments have already been made. I like your furniture very much. It has a style of its own, a quality of made pieces. There is a level of sophistication in terms of materials and scale, as well as this new discovery of floating lines and so on. The trouble is what to contribute to the exhibition.

ZH: I'm in a difficult situation. I have sincere reservations about some people in the show, though they are all friends of mine. I happen to think much of the work is derivative, but at least I understand it. But Coop Himmelblau is a different situation—I simply do not comprehend what they're doing. There's no connection between them and anyone else in the exhibition. It would be more appropriate to have Rem and Bernard Tschumi, because they're part of the Peter Cook and Peter Salter school.

The biggest compliment I had from people who've seen my furniture is that it really looks like the drawings, which they didn't think was possible. The pieces were not outrageous, but they are the nearest thing to the drawings, and this was very exciting for me. When people see my drawings, they always ask, "But can you make it?" I think it could be done better, but really those pieces are much nicer than models, paintings, or photographs.

AB: I want to ask about a small exhibition you did in Kyoto [*Kyoto Installations*, 1985], which unfortunately I didn't see.

ZH: We showed a house in plan. In the middle we had a wall without services. It was curved. The apartment at 24 Cathcart Road had a straight wall in the middle—it's very similar. Except we had partitions everywhere, because the space is supposed to feel electronic. We tried to have these walls open and close. The table can pivot and so can the chairs. We wanted to capture the movement in the drawings—the way these things operate. They always have two conditions: they either sit still or begin to move. When the pieces move, they become something else.

AB: Did you furnish the house at Halkin Place [London, 1985]?

ZH: Very minimally. Then we did the studies for the interiors at Melbury Court [London, 1985]. One was a penthouse with very specific pieces—for example, a wall that acts as a divider but also a closet or shelving.

AB: Would you be able to take those out of drawings and realize them materially?

ZH: These residences all begin to link together. Apart from 59 Eaton Place, they were all done in the same year, 1985— Halkin Place, Melbury Court, the installation for Kyoto 24 Cathcart Road. That's how the furniture started.

AB: I think it would be a good idea to find a way to show all those interiors in some sort of sequence, to begin to build a story. Those plans have never been published?

ZH: They were never drawn properly so we never released them. We were going to make them into a series of prototypes, an investigation of London. Two were penthouses, one was built from scratch, one was a renovation. They would make a very nice arrangement of prototype interiors.

AB: What happened?

ZH: The owner of 24 Cathcart Road is leaving London. He's planning to sell the house.

AB: So having put all that effort into it, you simply got all the furniture back?

ZH: There were several problems. First, they wanted us to make adjustments at our own expense, which we were not prepared to do. Second, they wanted the sole rights to use the pieces, even though I spent two years designing them. Third, his mother didn't like the furniture. So I said, "Fine, I'll take it back."

This client was very interesting. He's very young and courageous, but he has mixed feelings about his courage. I finally understood this the other day. Some friends were hanging out at my place, but rather than sitting on the sofa, they were standing in the kitchen. "What are you doing in here?" I asked. "We were too scared to sit on it," they answered, pointing at the sofa. And that's how this client was—too scared to use it.

AB: That's very interesting. Do you think it was because of the materials you used?

ZH: No, I think it was because it cost so much money. When we got the pieces back, they were covered in wine spots. But he had a very good offer for the house.

AB: Well, he must be remarkable to have bought that house in the first place and invited you to do the furniture. It's a pity it wasn't in use for longer.

ZH: And it's a pity we didn't do all the pieces, but that's partly our fault—we were inexperienced in furniture design. The people we hired to make it were also inexperienced. We should have gone with a manufacturer.

AB: But you are now going to do it....

ZH: A very small company approached us about doing the sofas, and we want to sell the other pieces to other manufacturers—do a line of sperm-shaped furniture.

AB: Would you use different materials, different scales?

ZH: No, the manufacturer thinks the sofas are perfect and should not be made any smaller.

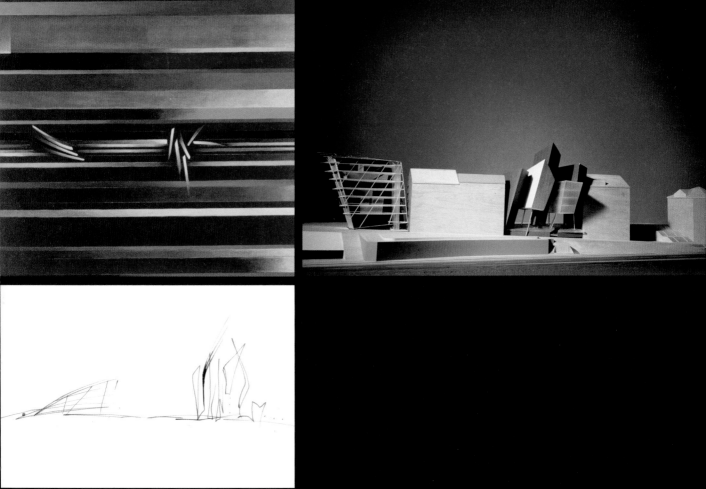

Zollhof 3 Media Park
Düsseldorf, 1989–93
01 Aerial perspective; painting
02 Block rotation; painting
03 Agency core rotation; painting
04 View through Vierendeel
   toward street; painting

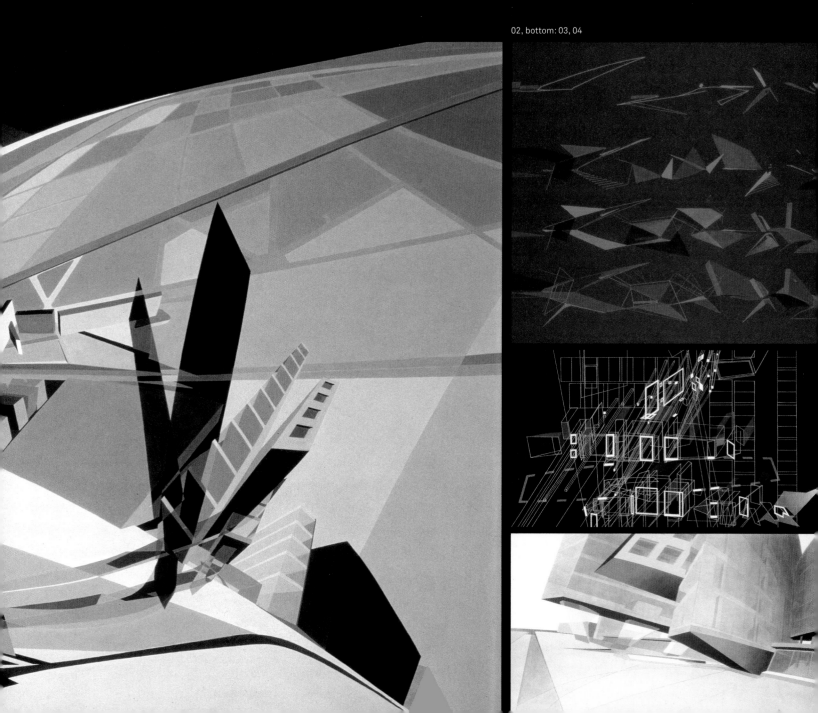

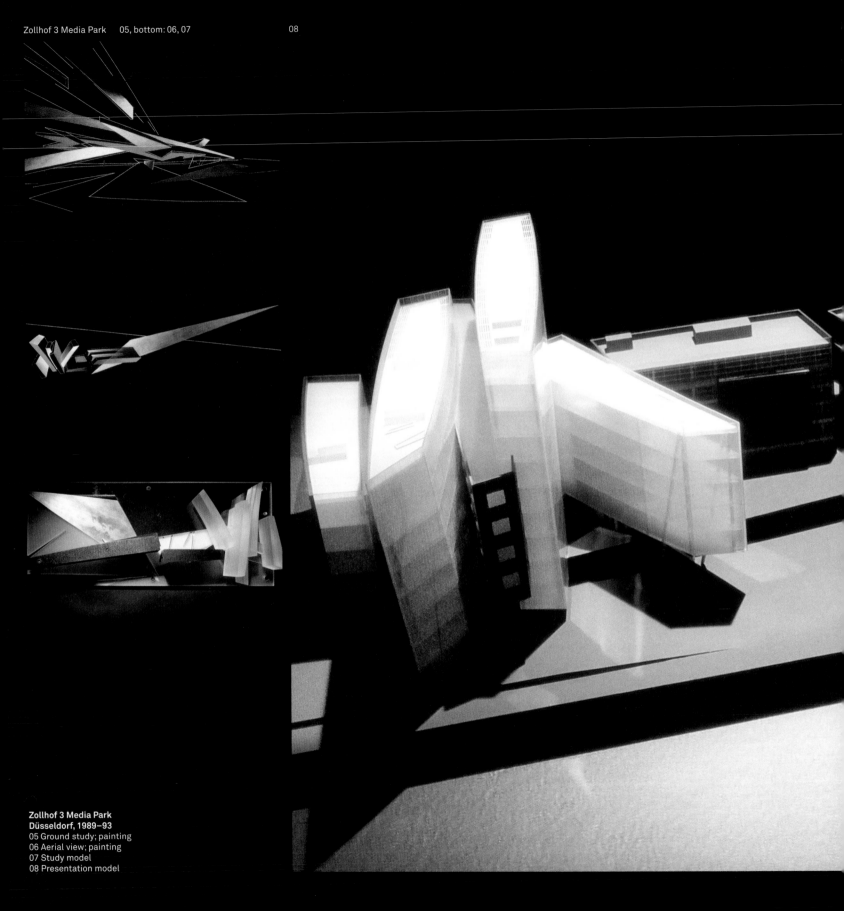

Zollhof 3 Media Park
Düsseldorf, 1989–93
05 Ground study; painting
06 Aerial view; painting
07 Study model
08 Presentation model

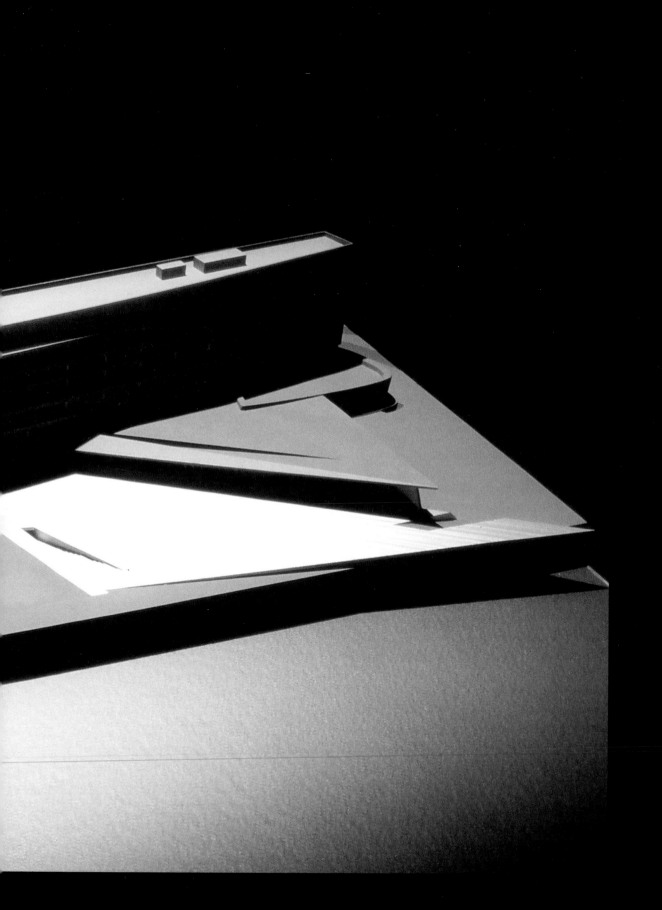

01

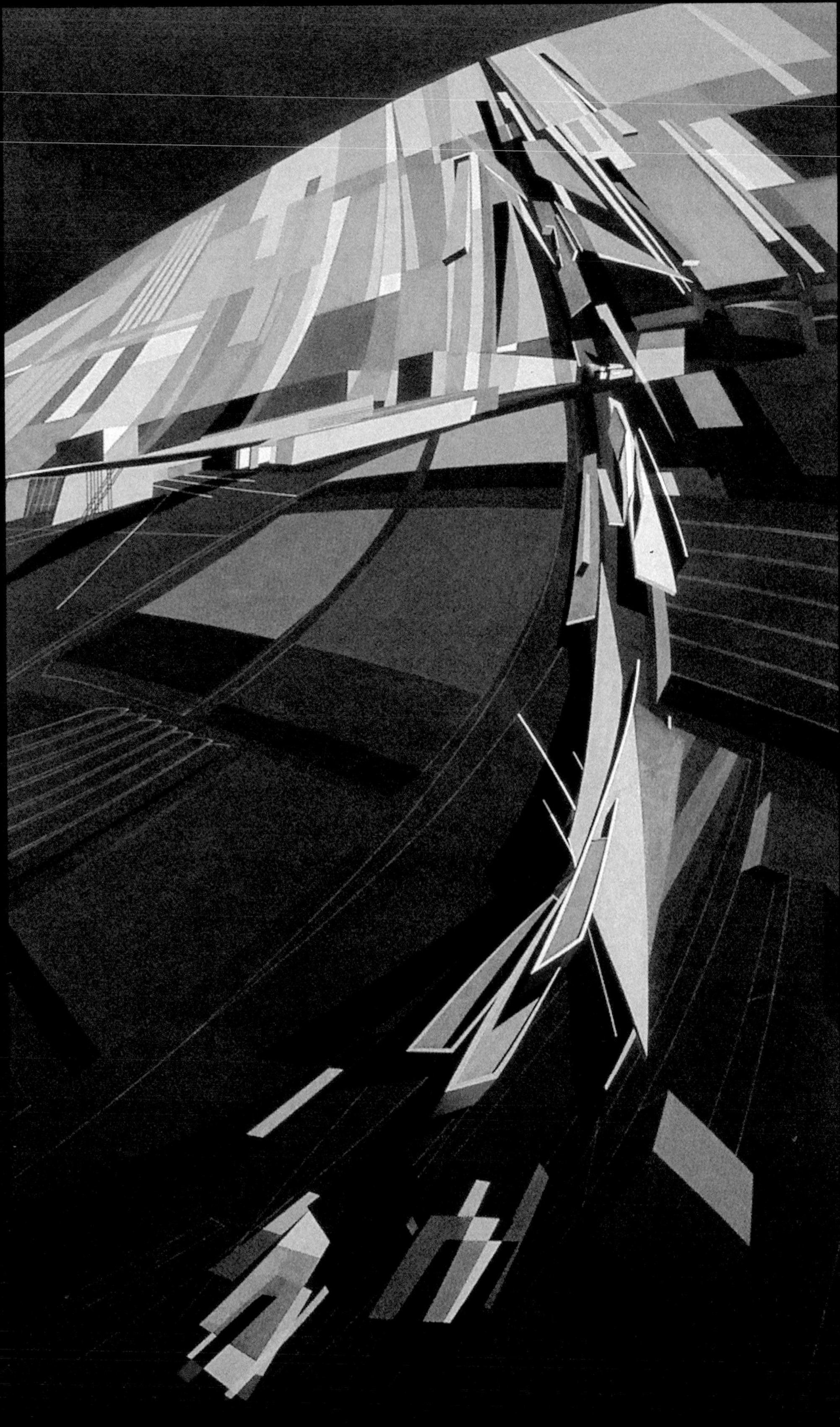

02, bottom: 03

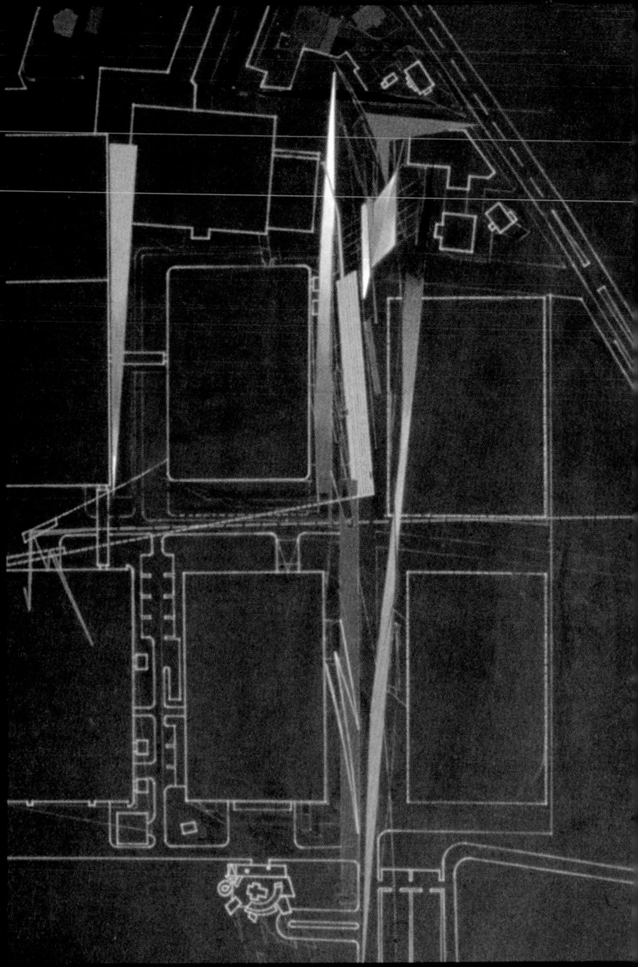

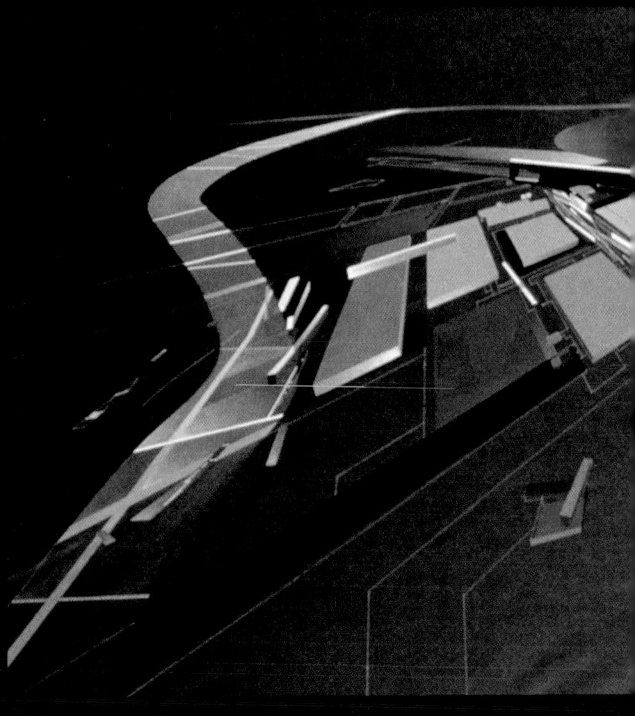

Vitra Fire Station
Weil am Rhein, Germany,
1990–94
01 Painting
02 Abstract plan; painting
03 Aerial site plan; painting
04 Corridor; painting

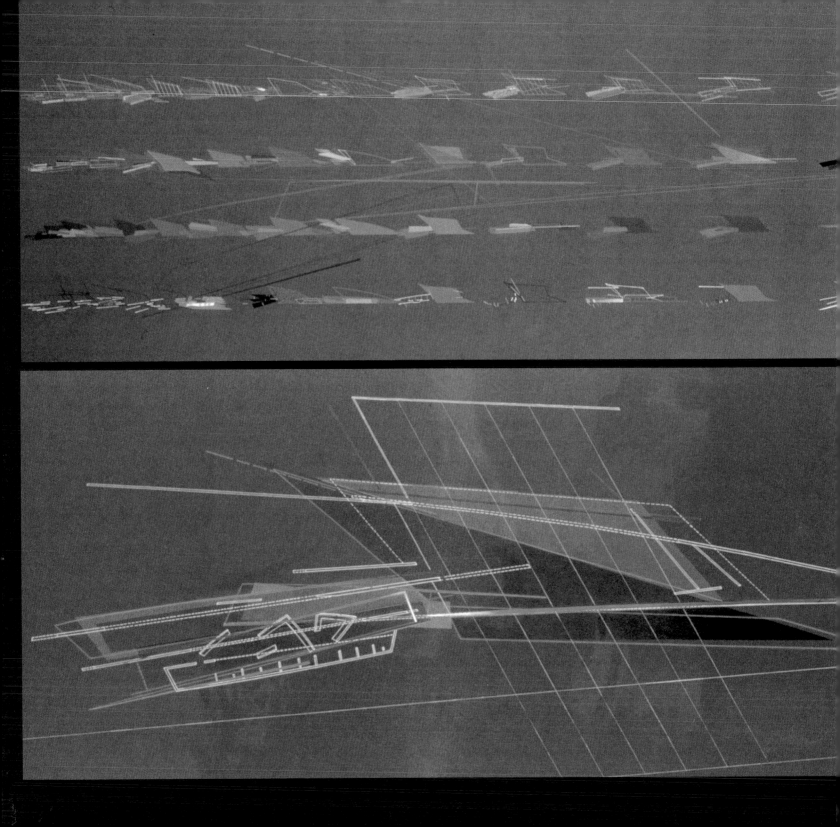

Vitra Fire Station
Weil am Rhein, Germany,
1990-94
05 Plan variations; painting
06 Composite plan; painting

Vitra Fire Station
Weil am Rhein, Germany,
1990-94
07 Relief model (perspective)
08 Relief model (perspective)
09 Photograph

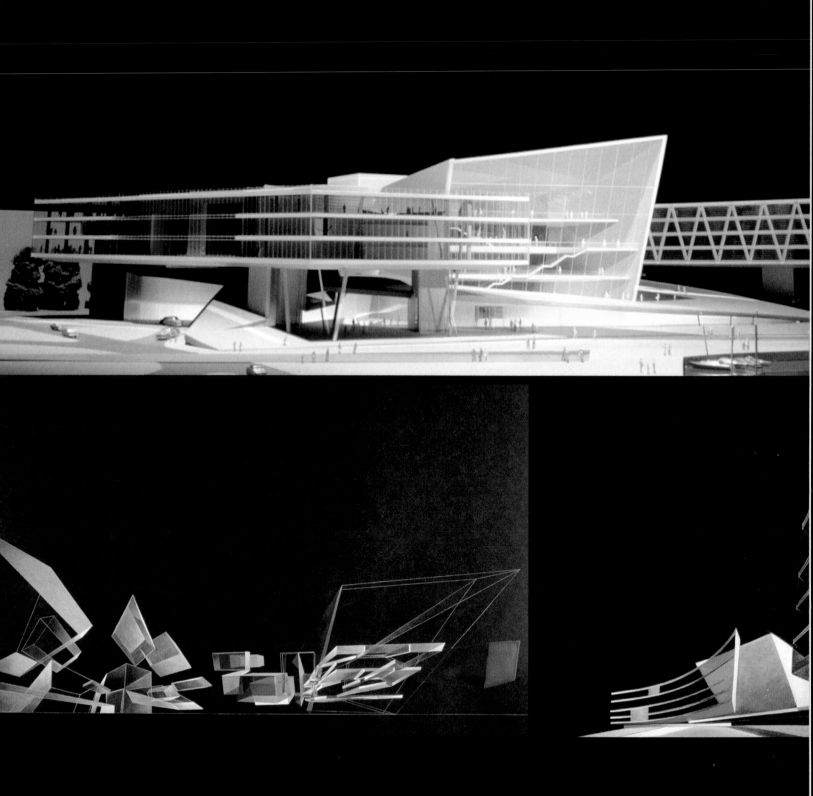

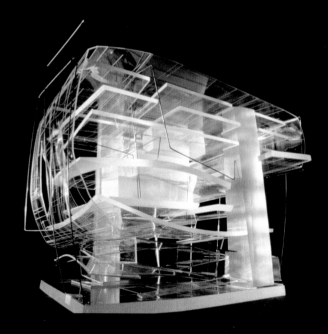

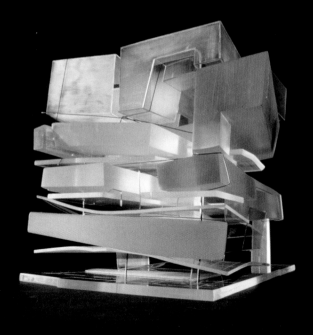

**Cardiff Bay Opera House
Wales, 1994–96**
01 Final presentation model
02 *Jewels*; painting
03 Perspective from Pierhead
    Street; painting

**Victoria & Albert Museum,
Boilerhouse Extension
London, 1996**
01 Study model
02 Study model

LFOne/Landesgartenschau
Weil am Rhein, Germany,
1996–99
01 Model
02 Model
03 Photograph

FOne/Landesgartenschau
Weil am Rhein, Germany,
1996–99
04 Photograph

Mind Zone
Millennium Dome, London,
1998–2000
01 Working model
02 Photograph

is and Richard Rosenthal
enter for Contemporary Art
ncinnati, 1997–2003
Early study model
Photograph

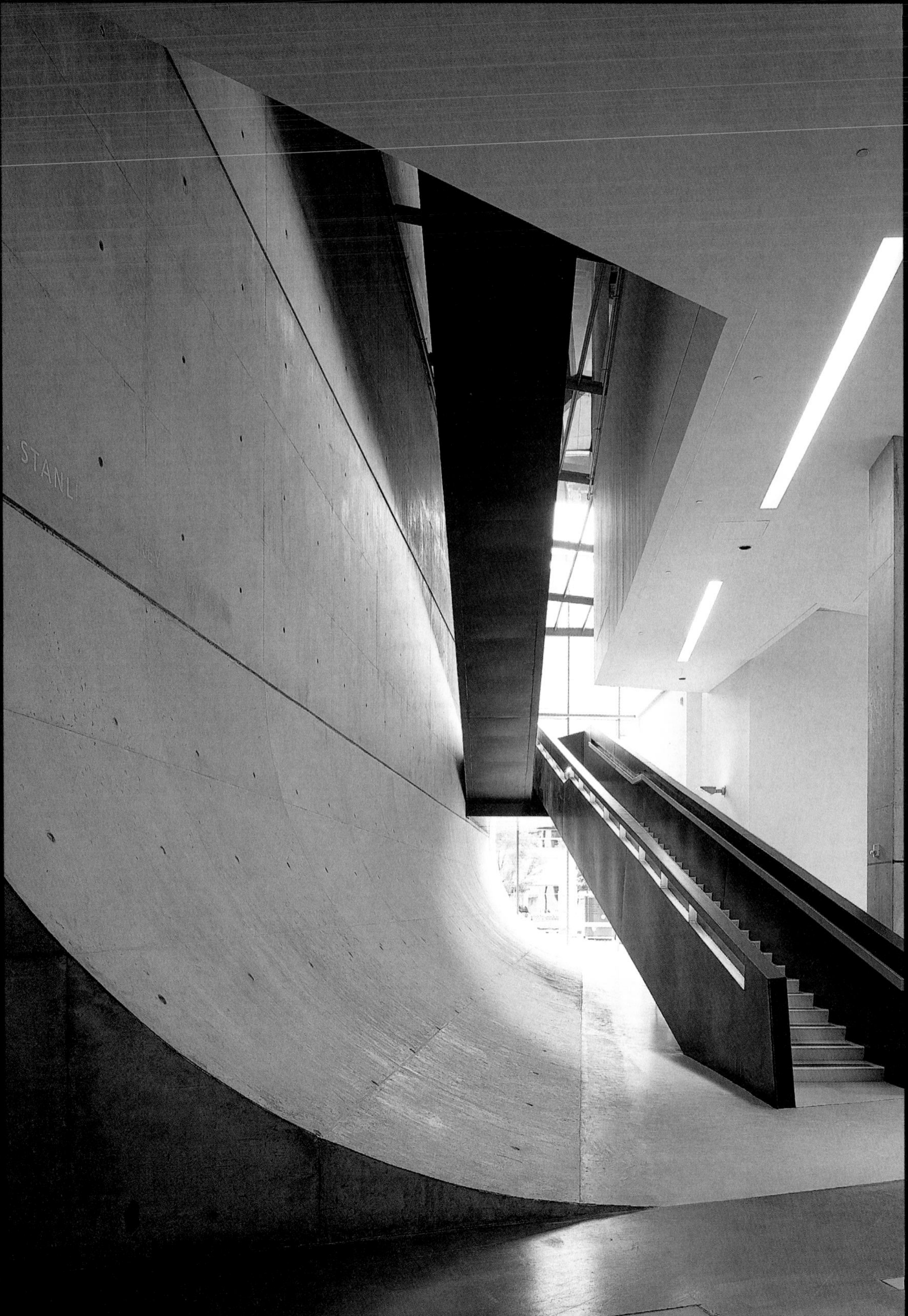

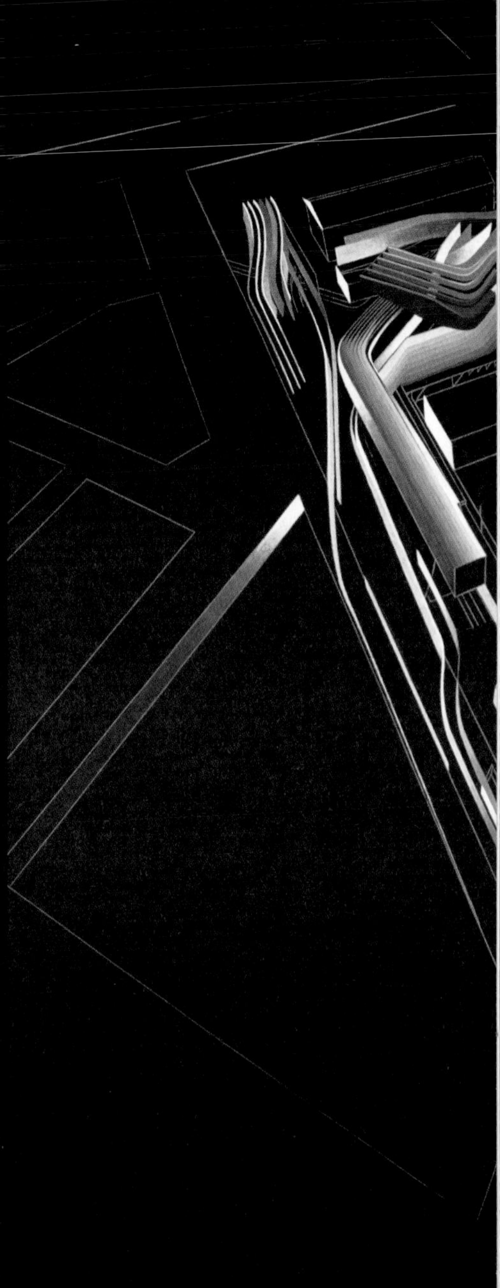

Lois and Richard Rosenthal
Center for Contemporary Art
Cincinnati, 1997–2003
07 Photograph

MAXXI National Centre of
Contemporary Arts
Rome, 1997–ongoing
01 Aerial view; painting
02 Painting

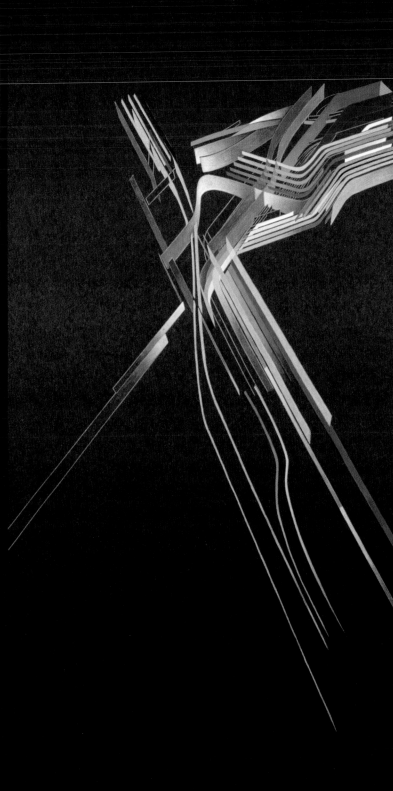

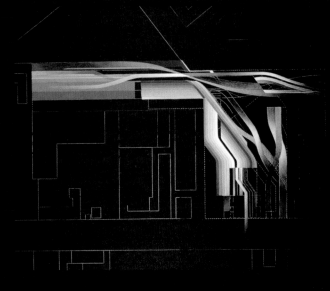

**MAXXI National Centre of
Contemporary Arts
Rome, 1997–ongoing**
03 Model
04 Painting
05 Painting
06 Scale model 1:500
    with lightbox

MAXXI National Centre of Contemporary Arts 07

Car Park and Terminus Hoenheim-Nord 01, bottom: 02

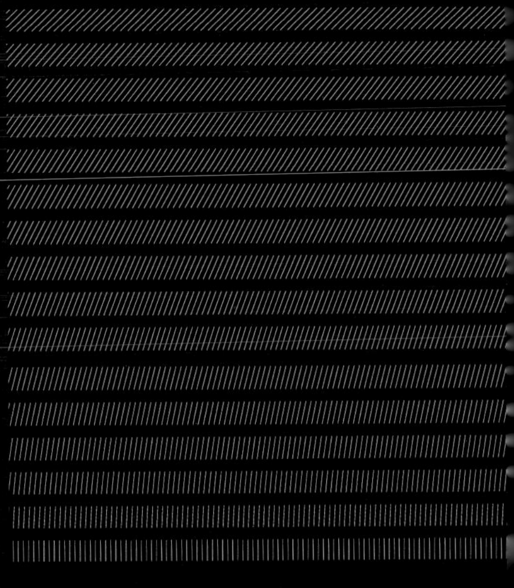

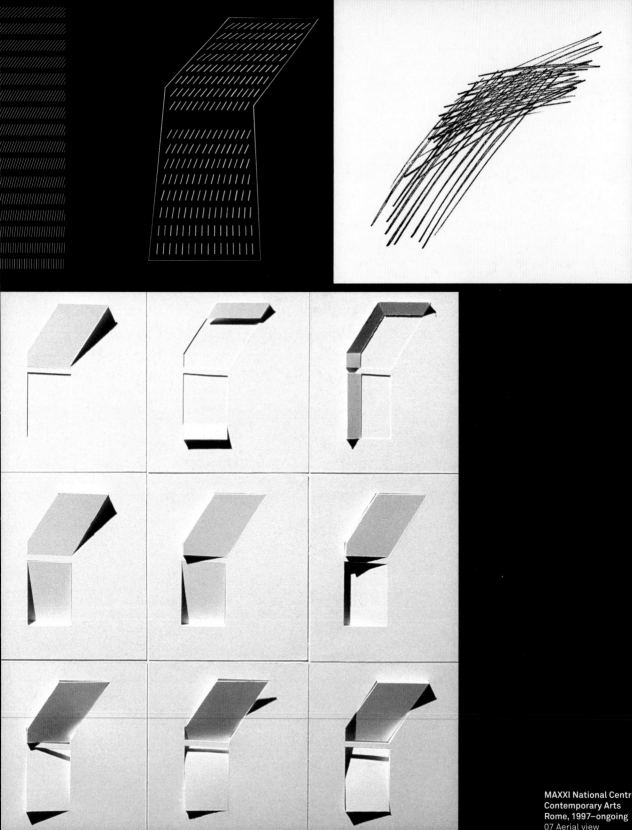

MAXXI National Centre
Contemporary Arts
Rome, 1997–ongoing
07 Aerial view

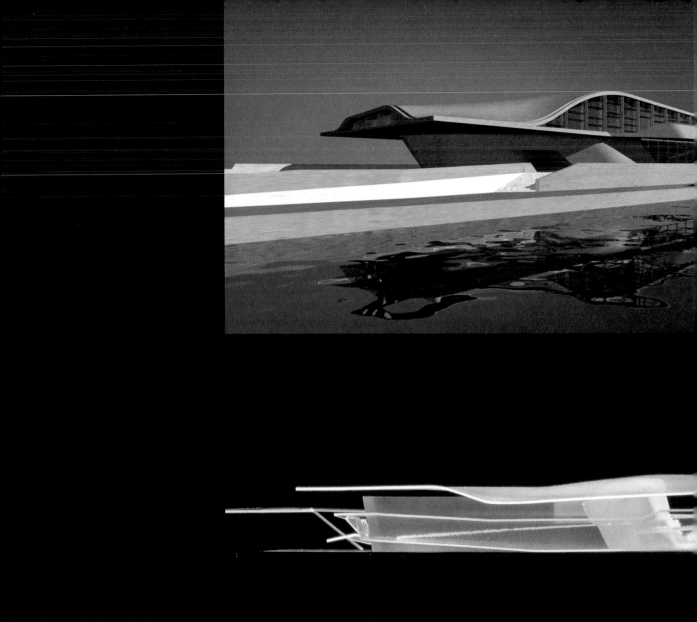

Bergisel Ski Jump
Innsbruck, Austria, 1999–2002
02 Photograph
03 Photograph

Phaeno Science Center
Wolfsburg, Germany, 1999–2005
01 Study model

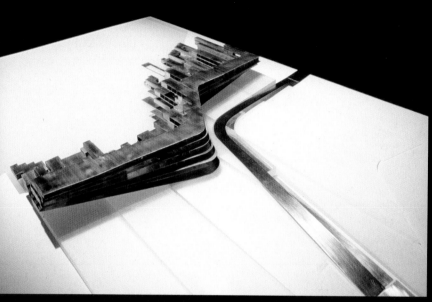

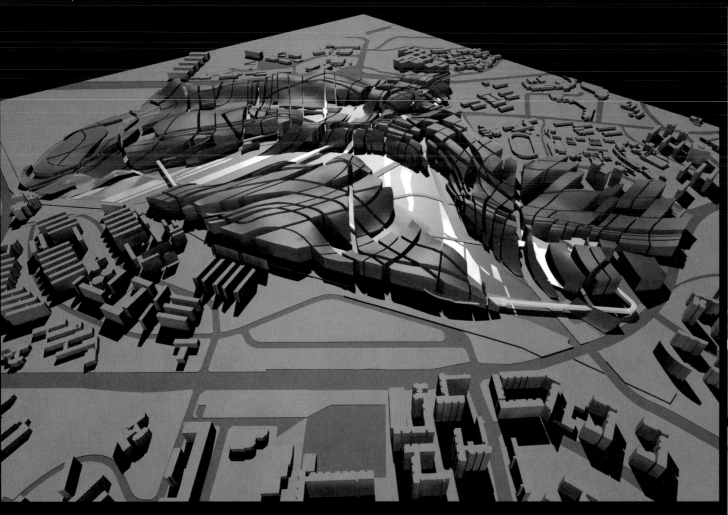

One North Masterplan
Singapore, 2001–ongoing
01 Aerial view rotation
02 Aerial view rotation;
   two paintings

Ordrupgaard Museum Extension
Denmark, 2001–05
01 Model
02 Photograph
03 Photograph
04 Photograph

Nelson Secondary 2
Maths

Nelson

Thomas Nelson and Sons Ltd
Nelson House Mayfield Road
Walton-on-Thames Surrey
KT12 5PL UK

Thomas Nelson Australia
102 Dodds Street
South Melbourne
Victoria 3205 Australia

Nelson Canada
1120 Birchmount Road
Scarborough Ontario
MIK 5G4 Canada

© Jim Noonan, Paula Barker, Terry Bevis, Gay Cain, Brian Martin, Christine Mitchell, Robert Powell, Gwen Wood 1996

First published by Thomas Nelson and Sons Ltd 1996
I(T)P Thomas Nelson is an International Thomson Publishing Company
I(T)P is used under licence

ISBN 0-17-431454-X
NPN 9 8 7 6 5 4 3 2 1

Printed in Spain

Nelson Secondary Maths 2 is written by:

Jim Noonan (Series Coordinator)
Paula Barker
Terry Bevis
Gay Cain
Brian Martin
Christine Mitchell
Robert Powell
Gwen Wood

The authors are grateful to the schools in Avon, Birmingham, Cornwall, Cumbria, Essex, Gloucestershire, Gwent, Hampshire, Hereford & Worcester, Nottingham, Salford, South Glamorgan, Tyneside and Wiltshire involved in trials of material for this book.

Contents

Preface

This book forms part of the Nelson Secondary Maths series, designed to cover the Programme of Study for Key Stages 3 and 4 of the National Curriculum in England and Wales. The Scottish 5–14 Guidelines and Northern Ireland Curriculum are also referenced.

Starting points at the beginning of each chapter give an indication of the background knowledge and skills needed to tackle the chapter content. Assignments covering all aspects of 'Using and Applying Mathematics' occur as separate tasks and as parts of many exercises. These exercises give plenty of opportunity for consolidation and practice of work in Number; Algebra; Shape, Space and Measures and Handling Data. Each chapter ends with a review of the work covered.

The material is designed to support you in acquiring skills and knowledge on the pathway to gaining a better understanding of mathematics.

Ordering numbers about

In this chapter you will learn:

→ more about the four operations $+$ $-$ $\times$ $\div$
→ more about using a calculator
→ how to use number facts to check answers
→ how to use brackets
→ some ways to solve problems
→ the correct order for operations

Starting points

Before starting this chapter you will need to:

- be able to carry out simple calculations

- understand each of the four operations $+$ $-$ $\times$ $\div$

- know what a factor is.

Exercise 1

1 (a) $342 + 98$

(b) $72 + 48 + 53$

(c) $248 + 133 + 82$

2 Copy these calculations and complete them.

(a)
```
    2 ☐ 4
 + ☐ 8 2
 ───────
   6 1 6
```

(b)
```
   1 9 ☐
 + ☐ 4 5
 ───────
   4 ☐ 1
```

(c)
```
   4 ☐ 6
 +   9 9
 ───────
   5 5 ☐
```

(d)
```
   7 3 8
 - 1 ☐ ☐
 ───────
   5 5 6
```

(e)
```
   ☐ 0 6
 - 1 ☐ 7
 ───────
   2 8 ☐
```

3 (a) 168×7 (b) 324×14

   (c) $133 \div 7$ (d) $546 \div 13$

4 Copy these calculations and complete them.

(a)
$$\begin{array}{r} \square\ 7\ 6 \\ \times\ \ \ \ 4 \\ \hline 1\ 1\ \square\ \square \end{array}$$

(b)
$$\begin{array}{r} 9\ 2 \\ \times\ \square\ 3 \\ \hline 9\ 2\ 0 \\ \square\ \square\ \square \\ \square\ \square\ \square\ \square \end{array}$$

(c)
$$\begin{array}{r} \square\ \square\ \text{r}\ \square \\ 5\overline{)\ 8\ 3} \end{array}$$

(d)
$$\begin{array}{r} \square\ \square\ \square \\ 11\overline{)\ 2\ 3\ 8\ 7} \end{array}$$

5 List the factors of each of these numbers.

   (a) 21   (b) 12   (c) 25   (d) 30   (e) 44   (f) 75

6 There are 134 pupils in Year 7, 209 in Year 8 and 173 in Year 9.

   (a) How many pupils are there altogether?

   (b) If the total number of pupils in the school is 1350, how many pupils are there in the other years?

7 A man bought 35 metres of fabric to refurbish a room. There are three chairs to be covered, and four curtains to be made.
Each chair will need 4.5 m of fabric. Each curtain will need 4 m.
Any fabric left over is to be used for making cushions.
How much fabric is left for the cushions?

Addition and subtraction

Addition

Think about this problem.

$$6 + 1 + 3 + 9 + 2 + 8 + 7 + 4$$

Would you use a calculator to help you solve this problem?

It would probably be quicker **not** to use one. Suppose you pair off numbers which add to give 10. For example,

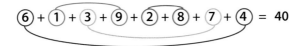 = 40

> Numbers do not have to be added in the order they are written.

Check that this is correct.

We can often make a problem easier by looking at the **whole** sum carefully. Look for groups of numbers which add to give 10.

Here is another example.

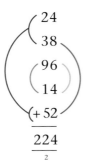

$$\begin{array}{r} 24 \\ 38 \\ 96 \\ 14 \\ + 52 \\ \hline 224 \\ \hline \scriptstyle 2 \end{array}$$

Exercise 2

Solve these problems by grouping numbers which add to give 10.

1. $3 + 3 + 5 + 7 + 5 + 6$

2. $8 + 6 + 4 + 9 + 2 + 3 + 5 + 1 + 1$

3. $12 + 19 + 38 + 41 + 72$

4. $38 + 42 + 15 + 18 + 35$

5. $128 + 432 + 385 + 772 + 645$

When do you need to add?

Always check that you need to add to solve a problem. Look for **word clues**, as the plus symbol (+) may not always be there.

All these words and signs can mean you need to **add**.

| Assignment 1 | Total one hundred |

- Find the total of the first 5 numbers.
  Is it divisible by 5?

- Find the total of the first 6 numbers.
  Is it divisible by 6 or by 3?

- Find the total of the first 10 numbers.
  Is it divisible by 10 or by 5?

- Find the total of the first 20 numbers.
  Is it divisible by 20 or by 10?

- Can you spot a pattern?

- Find the total of the first 100 numbers.

> It helps to try with easy examples first, e.g.
>
> 1
> 1 + 2
> 1 + 2 + 3
> 1 + 2 + 3 + 4
> etc.

Key fact

A digital root of a number is the single digit found by adding all the digits.

Digital roots

Look at the number 1349.

To find its digital root, add its digits together:

$1 + 3 + 4 + 9 = 17$

And again:

$1 + 7 = 8$

So the digital root of 1349 is 8.

Assignment 2   Digital root patterns

Here is a multiplication grid which uses the digital root for each answer.

For example, look at the entry for 3×4.

We write 3 instead of 12 because 3 is the digital root of 12.

$$3 \times 4 = 12 \rightarrow 1 + 2 = 3$$

×	1	2	3	4	5	6	7	8
1								
2								
3								
4			3					
5								
6								
7								
8								

> Do not write 12.
> Write 3 because
> $1 + 2 = 3$

- Now copy and complete the grid.

  Remember to use the digital root for each answer.

- What patterns do you notice in the grid?

- How can these patterns help you to complete the grid more quickly?

- Try to find other patterns in the grid by investigating further.

  Describe any patterns that you find.

- Compare what you have found with a friend.

- Which rows of the grid use all of the digits, 1 to 8?

Assignment 3　　The root of the problem

Investigate the digital roots involved in some addition problems.

Look, for example, at this sum

$32 + 48 + 15 = 95$

The digital roots of 32, 48 and 15 are 5, 3 and 6

$32 \rightarrow 3 + 2 = 5$

$48 \rightarrow 4 + 8 = 12 \rightarrow 1 + 2 = 3$

$15 \rightarrow 1 + 5 = 6$

The digital root of their sum is $5 + 3 + 6 = 14 \rightarrow 1 + 4 = 5$

The digital root of 95 is also 5.

$95 \rightarrow 9 + 5 = 14 \rightarrow 1 + 4 = 5$

- Check some other addition problems.

- What conclusions can you make about digital roots and addition problems?

- What happens with subtraction problems?

Exercise 3

Use the digital roots method to check these totals. If you find any mistakes, correct them.

1　$318 + 445 + 129 = 892$

2　$2239 + 8476 = 10\,715$

3　$7745 + 832 + 9370 = 16\,947$

4　$234 + 345 + 456 = 935$

5　$7468 + 11\,345 = 18\,713$

6　$825 + 485 + 829 = 2139$

7　$49\,504 + 86\,114 = 135\,618$

8　$73\,664 + 28\,490 = 102\,144$

Subtraction

When you are subtracting you need to take more care than when you are adding.

This is because the order of the numbers **does** matter.

$$72 - 38 \quad \text{is not the same as} \quad 38 - 72$$

However, there are still quick ways of doing these problems.

Here is one quick method, which actually uses adding.

Start with 38, and add enough to reach 72.

38

40 $+ 2$

72 $+ 32$

> **Always check your calculations.**

Altogether **34** is added. So $72 - 38 = 34$.

Subtracting is the **inverse** of adding which explains why this method works.

Use addition for a final check

$$38 + 34 = 72$$

or check using digital roots so that you are sure about your answer.

$$38 \rightarrow 3 + 8 = 11 \rightarrow 1 + 1 = 2$$

$$34 \rightarrow 3 + 4 = 7$$

$$72 \rightarrow 7 + 2 = 9$$

$$2 + 7 = 9$$

Exercise 4

Use the adding on method for these subtractions.

1 $39 - 23$ **2** $48 - 24$

3 $90 - 46$ **4** $83 - 58$

5 $123 - 70$ **6** $148 - 115$

7 $342 - 198$ **8** $223 - 159$

When do you need to subtract?

Always check that you need to subtract to solve a problem. Look for **word clues**, as the subtraction symbol (–) may not always be there.

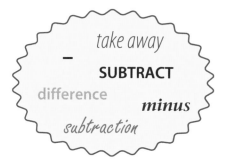

All these words and signs can mean you need to **subtract**.

Assignment 4	Mind reader

- Try this using a 3-digit number.

  Write down the number: 123

  Reverse it: 321

  Find the difference: 321 – 123 = 198

- Try other 3-digit numbers and see what difference you get each time.

  Look at the first digit.

  Can you predict the difference?

- Test your theory on a partner.

- Reverse one of your differences.

  Then add your number and its reverse.

  >   198
  >
  >   891
  >   ─────
  >   1089

  Try this with your other differences. Write down what you notice.

- Investigate 4-digit numbers.

Combining addition and subtraction

Look at this problem.

$$4 + 3 - 9 + 2 - 6 - 1 + 8 = ?$$

One way to solve it is to separate out the parts that are to be **added** and those that need to be **subtracted**.

Add first

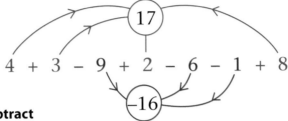

Then **subtract**

So: $17 - 16 = 1$

There is another way to solve it. Pair up opposites like this:

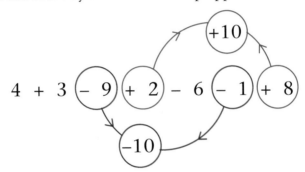

This leaves: $7 - 6 = 1$

Often these methods can be quicker than using a calculator.

<h3>Exercise 5</h3>

Solve these, without using a calculator.

1 $3 + 2 - 8 + 4 + 6 - 2 + 7 - 5$

2 $6 - 8 + 6 - 4 + 5 - 2 + 4 - 7$

3 $3 - 4 + 8 + 7 - 9$

4 $5 - 2 + 4 + 8 + 3 - 9 - 4 + 5$

5 $1 - 9 + 5 + 7 - 4 + 6 + 7 - 3 - 2$

6 $12 + 6 - 4 + 3 - 14 + 8 - 10$

7 $27 - 15 + 36 - 42$

8 $3 + 6 - 9 + 4 + 8 - 4 + 11 - 2$

Multiplication and division

When do you need to multiply?

Always check that you need to multiply to solve a problem. Look for **word clues**, as the multiplication symbol (×) may not always be there.

All these words and signs can mean you need to **multiply**.

The order of multiplying

Numbers need not be multiplied in the order that they are written. A different order can make a calculation easier for you.

Look at this example. Multiplying by 2 is easy, just double so you can leave this till last!

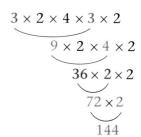

Always check your working.

*   Is your answer about the right size?

You would expect the answer of 318×42 to be about $300 \times 40 = 12\,000$.

*   Is the last digit what you would expect it to be?

The last digit must be 6 because $8 \times 2 = 16$.

Assignment 5	Multiplication patterns

*   Explore these patterns. Can you predict the answers?

    (a) 1089×1 (b) 1×1 (c) $1 \times 8 + 1$

    1089×2 11×11 $12 \times 8 + 2$

    1089×3 111×111 $123 \times 8 + 3$

    and so on ...

*   Try to explain why these results occur.

When you need to divide

Always check that you need to divide to solve a problem.
Look for **word clues**, as the divide symbol (÷) may not always be there.

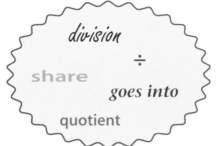

All these words and signs can mean you need to divide.

Dividing in order

Numbers must be divided in the order they are written.

48 ÷ 12   is **not** the same as   12 ÷ 48.

> **Check this with a calculator.**

Dividing can produce a **remainder**, but how should this be recorded?

Here are three possible methods.

Look at the division 25 ÷ 8.

$$\frac{3}{8 \overline{)\ 2\ \ 5^1}}\quad \text{r } 1$$

With this first method, you just write the answer as 3 r1.
r is short for remainder.

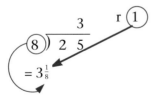

This second method includes the remainder, written as a **fraction.**

$$\frac{3\quad .\quad 1\ 2\ 5}{8 \overline{)\ 2\ \ 5^1\ .\ \ 0^2\ 0^4\ 0}}$$

The third method uses the decimal system. You just keep on dividing.
Calculators always use this method.

The method you choose depends on the question.
What are you trying to divide? Can it be cut into fractions?
Or must some whole amounts be left unshared?

Exercise 6

1 Answer each of these using all three methods of recording remainders.

(a) $74 \div 5$ (b) $83 \div 4$ (c) $234 \div 8$

(d) $321 \div 6$ (e) $112 \div 3$ (f) $112 \div 9$

2 Answer these questions using whichever method of recording you think best suits the problem.

(a) At a Christmas party, 350 chocolate coins are to be shared. 12 children are to be given the same number of coins each. How many should each receive? How many will be left over?

(b) A shop donates 76 metres of fabric to help with furnishing a day centre.
Eight couches need recovering.
How much fabric would be allowed for each?

(c) Seven people form a group for a lottery.
They decide to share any winnings equally.
They win £8452. How much should each receive?

(d) The number 38 557 492 is divided by 27. What is the remainder? You may use your calculator to help you solve this, but explain your reasoning carefully.

Common factors

Key fact

A factor is a number which divides into another number exactly.

Some divisions can be simplified by recognising common factors.

For example, 1440 and 36 both have a factor of 2 (they are **even**) so we can **halve** them both.

$$1440 \div 36 = 720 \div 18$$

And halving again:

$$720 \div 18 = 360 \div 9$$

It is easier to see the answer now!

$$360 \div 9 = 40$$

Check with a calculator.

Checking: $40 \times 36 = 1440$

We can check in this way because multiplying is the **inverse** of dividing.

We can also write divisions like this:

$$\frac{1440}{36}$$

$\frac{1440}{36}$ means

$1440 \div 36$

Key fact

Dividing by common factors is known as simplifying.

So another way of solving a problem is to consider the **common factors** of the two numbers:

$$\frac{1440}{36} = \frac{144 \times 10}{12 \times 3}$$

$$= \frac{12 \times 12 \times 10}{12 \times 3}$$

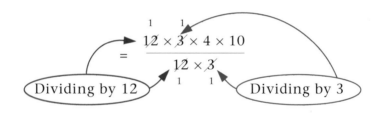

$$= \frac{4 \times 10}{1} = 40$$

$\frac{40}{1}$ is the same as 40

For this next exercise you will need to divide by common factors to solve the problems.

Exercise 7

1 $72 \div 18$ 2 $210 \div 30$

3 $192 \div 24$ 4 $126 \div 14$

5 $105 \div 21$ 6 $342 \div 18$

7 $336 \div 28$ 8 $1344 \div 24$

9 $504 \div 36$ 10 $1170 \div 78$

Assignment 6   Friendly numbers

Friendly numbers are pairs of numbers where all the factors of one number, except itself, add to give the other number, and vice versa.

- Check that 220 and 284 are friendly numbers.

  Add all the factors of 220 to see if the sum is 284.

  Add all the factors of 284 to see if the sum is 220.

- Find the friends of these numbers.

  1184

  17 296

A number which is a friend to itself is called **perfect**.

- Check that 6 is a perfect number.

- Find the next two perfect numbers.

Assignment 7   Calculators and conventions

Without using a calculator:

- Choose five different starting numbers.

- Follow the flow chart from top to bottom.

- Record each starting number with its result.

With a calculator:

- Use the same five starting numbers.

- Follow the flow chart from top to bottom.

- Record each starting number with its result.

Are your results the same?

If not, try to explain why not.

Compare your results with someone else.

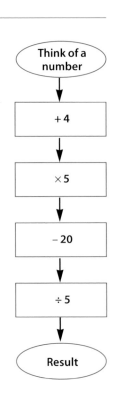

Order of operations

Here the flow chart in Assignment 7 is written as a problem:

$$\boxed{?} \; + \; 4 \; \times \; 5 \; - \; 20 \; \div \; 5 \; = \; \boxed{??}$$

$\boxed{?}$ is the starting number and $\boxed{??}$ is the result.

You should work from left to right, but multiplying and dividing first.

So
$$\boxed{?} \; + \; 4 \; \times \; 5 \; - \; 20 \; \div \; 5 \; = \; \boxed{??}$$
$$\boxed{?} \; + \; 20 \; - \; 4 \; = \; \boxed{??}$$

Then you should add and subtract.

$$\boxed{?} \; + \; 16 \; = \; \boxed{??}$$

So, the result is to add 16 to each starting number.

Look at this calculation.

$$15 \; - \; 6 \; \times \; 2 \; + \; 9 \; \div \; 3$$
$$= \; 15 \; - \; 12 \; + \; 3$$
$$= \; 6$$

Exercise 8

Solve these, working them out in the correct order.

1. $13 - 3 \times 2 + 5$
2. $8 \times 6 - 4 \times 5 - 5 \times 3$
3. $40 + 2 \times 6 \div 3 - 5$
4. $15 - 6 \times 2 + 8 \div 2$
5. $12 \div 4 + 7 \times 2 - 3$
6. $24 \div 6 + 5 \times 4 - 7$
7. $45 \div 9 + 6 \times 3 + 9$
8. $189 \div 9 + 3 \times 4 - 1 \times 5$
9. $15 \times 6 - 2 \times 8 - 5$
10. $12 \times 4 \times 7 - 2 \times 3$
11. $6 \times 5 + 4 \times 7 - 24$
12. $40 \div 2 + 6 \times 3 - 5$

Adding before multiplying

Look at this problem.

> A pupil travels to school by bus.
>
> Each day the pupil makes the whole journey by bus in the morning, but walks part of the way home with a friend.
>
> The morning fare is 50p, but the afternoon fare is 40p.
>
> How much is the pupil's weekly bus fare?

There are two stages to this problem – add and multiply – and two ways of solving it.

(1)   Either add and then multiply:

Daily fare: 50p + 40p = 90p

Weekly total: 90p × 5 = 450p

(2)   Or multiply and then add:

Morning fares are 50p × 5 = 250p

Afternoon fares are 40p × 5 = 200p

Weekly total: 250p + 200p = 450p

The first method looks much shorter, but both methods are correct.

The second method is easy to record:

$$50 \times 5 + 40 \times 5 = 450$$

But you cannot record the first method so easily:

$$50 + 40 \times 5$$

Written like this, you must multiply before adding. You would not get the correct amount.

When you need to + or – before × or ÷ use brackets.

To show you need to add before multiplying you use **brackets**.

$$(50 + 40) \times 5$$

This shows the correct order needed to solve the problem.

Exercise 9

1 Calculate these.

(a) $(7 + 4) \times (5 + 2)$ (b) $15 + 6 \times 2 - 9$

(c) $4 \times (6 + 8) - 9$ (d) $15 \div (2 + 3)$

(e) $9 \times 8 \div (4 + 2)$ (f) $(9 + 8) - (4 \times 2)$

(g) $7 \times 8 - (4 \times 3)$ (h) $5 \times 3 - 4 \times 2$

(i) $6 \times 9 - 5 \times 4$ (j) $9 \times 5 \div (5 - 2)$

(k) $(7 + 8) \times (5 - 3)$ (l) $(6 + 8) \times 5 + 9$

2 Use brackets, if necessary, to make sense of these calculations.

(a) $6 + 3 \times 2 + 4 = 16$

(b) $6 + 3 \times 2 + 4 = 22$

(c) $6 + 3 \times 2 + 4 = 24$

(d) $6 + 3 \times 2 + 4 = 54$

3 By using brackets, write these expressions in four different ways, giving the result of each calculation.

(a) $5 + 3 \times 7 - 4$

(b) $8 + 2 \times 6 - 3$

(c) $9 + 3 \times 2 - 1$

(d) $7 + 2 \times 6 - 3$

4 Fill in the missing digits in the following calculations. (You may find a calculator helpful.)

(a) $(78 + \square\square) \times (5 + 3) = 816$

(b) $(128 - 7\square) \div (\square 2 - 4) = 7$

(c) $\square \times 9 \times \square 1 \times 13 = 9\square\square 9$

5 (a) Make up five questions like those in Question 4.

(b) Swap your questions with a friend.

(c) Compare your answers.

Looking at brackets more closely

$3(4 + 5)$ means the same as $3 \times (4 + 5)$

You do not need to write $\times$ when multiplying a bracketed term like $(4 + 5)$ by another number, like 3.

Without using a calculator, you can write:

$$3 \times (4 + 5) \qquad\qquad \text{or} \qquad\qquad 3(4 + 5)$$
$$= \ 3 \times 4 + 3 \times 5 \qquad\qquad\qquad = \ 3(9)$$
$$= \ 12 + 15 \qquad\qquad\qquad\qquad = \ 3 \times 9$$
$$= \ 27 \qquad\qquad\qquad\qquad\qquad = \ 27$$

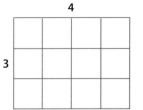
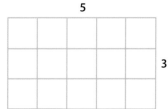

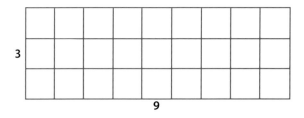

Using a calculator, you can enter:

If you enter:

you get the same result: 27.

Pressing = here ensures adding is done first.

Exercise 10

Do these calculations, using a calculator.

1 $15(72 + 43) + 38(172 - 39)$

2 $21(138 + 92) - 18(15 + 73)$

3 $16(9 + 28) + 19(31 + 24) - 15(72 - 15)$

4 $(48 + 64 - 32) \times (94 + 15 + 24)$

5 $(542 + 981) \div (24 + 32 + 94)$

6 $84[92(43 + 62) - 75(13 - 4)]$

Estimate to check that the answer is sensible.

Assignment 8   Making numbers

- Write down the digits in your date of birth. For example, if your birthday is 15th September 1982, write this as 15/9/82.

- Using **all** of these digits once **and once only**, together with any mathematical symbols (e.g. ×, +, −, ÷) try to write calculations to make the first twenty counting numbers.

  For example, using 15/9/82 the digits can be used to make 10:

$$10 = (8 + 2) \div 5 + 9 - 1$$

- Copy and complete this table using your own birthdate:

My birthdate:	
1 =	11 =
2 =	12=
3 =	13 =
4 =	14 =
5 =	15 =
6 =	16 =
7 =	17 =
8 =	18 =
9 =	19 =
10 =	20 =

Calculators

Using your memory

You can use the memory button on your calculator to help with ordering calculations.

Usually you will find:

 for adding to memory

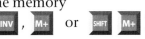 for subtracting from the memory
(you may have to use 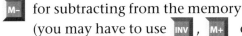)

 for memory recall

> M displayed on the calculator means there is already something in the memory.

Using the memory buttons lets you see and record answers to parts of the calculation, as well as the final result.

Look at this calculation.

$$12 \times 34 + 62 \times 3 - 24 \times 14$$

> Always clear the memory before starting a new calculation.

Enter: Display:

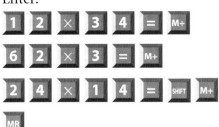

We can record the calculation as:

$12 \times 34 + 62 \times 3 - 24 \times 14$

$= 408 + 186 - 336$

$= 258$

Exercise 11

1 Try using the memory key on your calculator for these calculations. Record each stage of the answer.

(a) $72 \times 3 + 94 \times 18 - 38 \times 15$

(b) $184 \times 2 + 13 \times 14 \times 15 + 112 \times 13$

(c) $54 \times 12 - 34 \times 5 + 45 \times 6$

(d) $174 \times 7 + 38 \times 27 - 23 \times 12 - 14 \times 15$

Don't forget to clear the memory before starting each question.

2 On a copy of this bill, complete the totals.

ITEM	Number ordered	Price per item	Total cost of item
PENCILS	100	24p	
RULERS	250	19p	
ERASERS	45	43p	
PENS	75	£1.39	
		TOTAL	

3 How would you use your calculator to solve these?

(a) $\dfrac{4 \times 3 \times 2}{6}$

(b) $\dfrac{14 \times 9 \times 4}{21}$

(c) $\dfrac{14 \times 9 \times 4}{21 \times 2}$

(d) $\dfrac{32 \times 49}{56 \times 4}$

Calculator constants

Another useful function of most calculators is a feature known as a **constant**. If this feature is working then a K is displayed.

Assignment 9   Keeping constant

Explore the constant feature of your calculator by entering:

- What happens when you continue to press ▢ ?
- What happens when you press 3 2 ▢ ?
- Explore other operations.

Solving number problems

Key fact

The agreed order of operations is:

B brackets

O of (meaning multiply)

D division

M multiply

A add

S subtract

      BODMAS

Whenever you are working out or recording calculations, remember to keep to the conventions, so that what you want to say is understood by everyone.

- Read the problem through carefully, at least twice.
- Check that you understand it and what you need to do.
- Plan your work; order it carefully and break it into small stages.
- Trial solutions, check, and improve.
- Use patterns with smaller numbers to help to solve problems with larger numbers.
- Test any patterns or rules you spot.
- Try to give reasons as to why the pattern works.

Exercise 12

Here are some problems. Try to solve them.

1 We are odd numbers less than 100 but bigger than 9. One of our digits is twice the other. What two numbers are we?

2 My three digits add to 18 and their product gives a square. I am the same backwards. What number number am I?

3 I am a 3-digit number, less than 200. All my digits are odd. I equal the sum of my digits cubed. What number am I?

4 The difference between two numbers is 37 and their sum is 215. What are the two numbers?

5 A book is lying open. The product of the two page numbers showing is 5550. What are the page numbers?

6 Two pupils are thinking about their pets. They have cats and birds. The pets have 10 heads in all and 34 feet. How many of each pet do the pupils have?

7 One famous mathematician who lived in the nineteenth century noticed that his age squared was the year of his birthday! When was he born?

8 Three football teams were comparing their results. Rangers won three times as many matches as County. County won only a quarter of the number of United wins. United won three more matches than Rangers. Which team won 12 matches?

Review Exercise

1 Calculate these without using a calculator.

(a) $12 + 25 + 98 + 73 + 15$ (b) $72 - 48$

(c) $13 + 4 - 12 + 6 + 9 - 14$ (d) $194 \div 13$

2 For each of these operations write down two words that can replace the symbol.

(a) $+$ (b) $-$ (c) $\times$ (d) $\div$

3 Find the sum of the first nine numbers.

4 Fill in the missing blanks to make these equations correct.

(a) $198 + 72 + 8 \square + 15 = \square \square 5$

(b) $(15 + 2 \square) \times (\square 8 - 11) = 1053$

5 Use brackets to make these calculations correct.

(a) $7 + 4 \times 8 - 2 = 31$

(b) $26 - 14 \times 5 - 3 = 24$

6 Make a sum using the same digit five times to make 14.

7 Calculate these.

(a) $78 - 5 \times 4 + 15 \div 5 - 8 \times 5$

(b) $158 - (34 + 16) \div 5 + 36 \times 12 - 98$

8 Find the total cost of buying five rose plants at £2.89 each, seven dahlia plants at £2.65 each and a dozen trays of bedding plants at £1.79 a tray.

9 A pupil gave the answer to:

$(172 + 13) \times 4 - 152$

as 72.

By estimating, decide whether you think this answer is right or wrong. Explain your reasoning.

How would you use the calculator to give you the correct answer?

10 In a bag of marbles, there are less than 100 but more than 50. When shared among eight people 5 are left over; but when shared among nine people 4 are left over. How many marbles are in the bag?

11 What is the smallest number of strawberries that could be put into punnets containing 9, 15, 20 or 24 fruits with no spares left?

12 A new ball holds 13.5 m of string. I use 2 m, 30 cm, 1.8 m, 95 cm and 2.37 m of the string. The remainder is divided into lengths of 32 cm. How many lengths will there be?

13 Write down any 4-digit number. Reverse it and add the two numbers together. The result is always divisible by a certain number. What is the number? Explain why this happens.

Assignment 10 **Max product**

Partitions of 12 are numbers which add to 12.

For example **2, 3, 3, 4** is a partition of 12

because **2 + 3 + 3 + 4 = 12** .

Here are some more:

2, 3, 7

1, 11

1, 3, 5, 3

• Which partition gives the largest product?

• Explore partitions of numbers other than 12

CHAPTER 2

Organising data

In this chapter you will learn:

→ how to calculate the mean and range of a set of data
→ how to use different types of average
→ how to read information from line graphs
→ how to read information from simple pie charts
→ how to draw simple pie charts

Starting points

Before starting this chapter you will need to know how to:

• record information as tally charts, bar charts, line graphs and pictograms

• extract information from tally charts, bar charts, bar line graphs, pictograms, tables and lists

• calculate the mode and the median.

Exercise 1

1 Roll a dice 25 times.

> The modal value in a set of data is the most common value.

(a) Record your results using a tally chart.

(b) Draw a bar graph of the results.

(c) What is the modal result?

(d) What is the median result?

> The median is the middle value when the values are placed in order of size.

2 A survey of the ages of pupils carried out at a school disco provided the following data.

Year group	Tally	Frequency
7	ⅻ ⅻ ⅻ ⅻ ‖	
8	ⅻ ⅻ ⅻ ⅻ ⅻ ⅻ ‖‖	
9	ⅻ ⅻ ⅻ ⅻ ⅻ ⅻ ⅻ ‖	
10	ⅻ ⅻ ⅻ ⅻ ⅻ ⅻ ⅻ ⅻ ⅻ ⅻ ⅻ ⅻ ⅻ ‖‖	
11	ⅻ ⅻ ⅻ ⅻ ⅻ ⅻ ⅻ ⅻ ⅻ ⅻ ⅻ ‖‖	
		Total

(a) What is the number of pupils from each year attending the disco?

(b) What is the total attendance?

(c) Which is the modal age group?

(d) How old is the pupil who represents the median value?

(e) Record this information using a pictogram.

> Your pictogram will need a key.

3 Calculate the mode and median values of each of the following sets of numbers.

(a) 2   3   7   4   2

(b) 15   14   16   14   17

(c) 2   4   5   6   3   5   3   7   5

(d) 1.5   2.5   2.05   1.05   2.0   1.0   1.05

(e) 205   208   245   232   216   209   223

(f) 0.3   0.4   0.8   0.6   0.4   0.7

(g) 2   4   6   8   4   1   7   9

(h) 8   12   15   16   17   14   23

> The median is the middle value in an ordered list, or the average of the middle two values.

4 1889 was the first year of the football league. These are the results of the matches played by the ten top teams on 30 December 1889.

Derby County	5	Aston Villa	0
Blackburn Rovers	2	Everton	4
Stoke on Trent	1	Accrington Stanley	2
Bolton Wanderers	6	Burnley	3
West Bromwich Albion	1	Wolverhampton Wanderers	1

(a) What is the modal number of goals per team for these matches.

(b) What is the median of the number of goals scored per team.

5 (a) Find the football results from recent Premier Division matches.

(b) Calculate the modal and median scores for these matches.

(c) Using your results for this question and question 4, write a few sentences explaining whether football was better in 1889 than it is today.

Mean and range

The mean is calculated by adding all the values in the data and dividing by the number of items of data.

Example

Burton's netball team scored the following number of goals in their last eight matches: **14, 11, 12, 8, 14, 17, 11, 13**

$$\frac{14 + 11 + 12 + 8 + 14 + 17 + 11 + 13}{8} = \frac{100}{8} = 12.5$$

Total number of goals

Number of games

The **mean** is 12.5.

The **range** of the data shows how the data is spread.

The highest number of goals is 17; the lowest is 8.

The range is given by the difference between these numbers.

$17 - 8 = 9$

The **range** is 9.

Exercise 2

1 Calculate the mean values and the range for each of the following sets of data.

(a) 12   14   15   13   16

(b) 1   37   8   18   6

(c) 1   3   2   4   2   4   2   3   4   2   1   4   5   3   5   3

(d) 12   14   15   12   16   17   14   12

(e) 3.5   5.5   4.8   7.2   3.6   4.4   9.3   7.3   1.7   8.9

(f) 15.5   42.8   17.3   32.6   14.4   91.7   71.5   14.2

2 Two batsmen in a local cricket league scored the following numbers of runs.

Set 1	26	35	3	17	42	63
Set 2	28	42	30	37	44	29

(a) Find the average (mean) score for each batsman.

(b) Which has the highest average?

(c) Calculate the range of scores for each batsman.

(d) Use your data to decide which is the best batsman.

3 At an athletics meeting the times (in seconds) for the 200-m sprint are:
26.3   27.2   28.1   27.4   26.7   26.9   26.4   27.8

(a) What was the mean time for the race?

(b) What is the difference between the average time and the fastest time?

(c) What is the range of the times taken to complete 200 m?

4 A dice is rolled 12 times giving these results:

6   5   3   1   2   4   3   3   1   1   5   2

(a) Calculate the average score.

(b) Write the range of the scores.

5 The heights of eight people (in metres) are
1.93, 2.01, 1.72, 1.62, 1.67, 1.87, 1.74 and 1.84.

(a) Calculate the average height of this group.

(b) Two more people join the group.

Their heights are 1.93 m and 1.97 m.

Calculate the new mean.

(c) What is the range of the original people's heights?

(d) Why is the range including the new people the same as the range in (c)?

6 Here are the prices charged for 1 kg of apples in seven different shops.

Shop	1	2	3	4	5	6	7
Price per kilo	72p	80p	64p	84p	79p	76p	98p

(a) Calculate the average cost of 1 kg of apples.

(b) In a different shop apples are 63 p per kg.
Calculate the new average cost.

(c) What is the range of the prices in the eight shops?

Assignment 1   Dice games

• Roll a dice 30 times and record the results in a tally chart.

• Write the modal result.

• Calculate the mean score.

• Roll two dice 30 times.
Add their results.
Record the results in a frequency table.

• Calculate the mean of the data you have collected.

Assignment 2 **A mean activity**

The mean and the median for the set of numbers 5, 6, 7 are both 6.

- Find another two sets of three or more numbers less than 10 with a mean and median of 6.

- Find three sets of numbers whose mean is 6 and whose range is 8.

- Find a set of three numbers whose mean is 6, with a median of 6.5 and a range of 5.5.

Which average?

Exercise 3

1 Look at these three sets of data.

(a) Shoe size in a Year 8 class:

    3   3   4   4   5   5   6   7   8   11

(b) The ages of five people getting married:

    16   20   24   26   79

(c) The number of people in vehicles arriving at school:

    2   3   4   53   2

For each set of data:

(i) Calculate the mean, median and mode.

(ii) Choose mean, median or mode to describe the average.

(iii) Give the reasons for the choice you have made.

2 The following data gives the number of merit marks received by a class last term.

0 0 0 0 0 0 0 0 0 0 0 0 1 5 6 6 7 8 9 10 12 15 18 19

(a) Calculate the mean, median and mode.

(b) Give one reason for, and one reason against, using each of these to describe the average number of merits achieved by this class.

3 Two groups of five people go on a ride at a theme park.

The ages of the people are:

Group A	16	18	14	17	15
Group B	42	16	15	20	7

(a) Why is the mode not suitable to describe the average for each of these groups?

(b) Calculate the median value for each group.

Explain why the median is not a good representative of the average age in group B.

(c) Calculate the mean age of the people in each group.

Why does this give you a different result for each group?

(d) Calculate the range for each group.

How does this help you to make the data clearer to understand?

4 These are the numbers of pupils in five Maths groups in Year 8:

Group	Number of pupils
1	37
2	40
3	29
4	27
5	22

(a) There is no modal value here. Explain why.

(b) Calculate the mean class size.

(c) Calculate the median class size.

(d) What is the range?

(e) If the average class size is over 30 pupils, a new group will be created.

Explain whether the mean or median would help to show this.

Types of data

The way in which numerical data is recorded depends on the type of data being collected.

Data that can only take exact values is called **discrete** data.

For example, recording the different makes of car in a car park will result in discrete data.

Data gathered by measuring to a certain degree of accuracy is called **continuous** data.

For example, recording the heights of pupils in a class will result in continuous data.

Key fact

Discrete data is gathered by counting. Continuous data is gathered by measuring.

Exercise 4

1 Decide which of these are discrete data and which are continuous data.

(a) the scores on a dice

(b) the time taken to run 100 metres

(c) the number of sisters each person in a class has

(d) the number of books in your bag

(e) the temperature in your classroom

(f) the length of the arms of the people in your class

(g) the shoe sizes of the people in your class

(h) the number of people in each year in your school

(i) the weight of a group of people

(j) the number of each type of pet recorded in a survey

Grouping continuous data

When continuous data is grouped, the upper measurement in each group interval is not included in that interval.

Example

In a javelin competition the following results (in metres) are recorded.

77.6 51.6 55.4 61.5 67.6 69.4 57.6
67.2 71.4 53.8 72.6 69.0 64.6 58.2

If 5-m intervals are used starting at 45 m, then 50 m starts the second interval, 55 m starts the next, and so on. The first interval is called '45–50' metres although results of 50 m fall into the next interval.

Exercise 5

1 Using the data above, copy and complete this table.

Length of throw (m)	Tally	Frequency
45–50		
50–55		
55–60		
60–65		
65–70		
70–75		
75–80		
Total		

> The end value of each interval is not included in the interval.
> 50 m would be placed in the second group.

2 The weight in kilograms of 50 pupils is given in the following list.

43 37 29 28 36 38 41 50 46 42

27 36 42 35 37 33 40 32 30 33

30 38 34 29 34 42 31 30 41 28

25 35 39 41 39 41 40 50 51 40

42 37 26 43 29 27 39 43 49 54

Complete a grouped frequency tally using class intervals of 5 kg.

Bar charts of discrete and continuous data

This bar chart shows discrete data, recorded by counting. The labels are put at the centres of the columns. Notice the gap between each bar.

This bar chart shows continuous data, recorded by measuring. It is also called a **histogram**. The labels are put at the left of each column, and there is no gap between the bars.

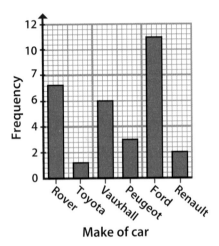

Make of car

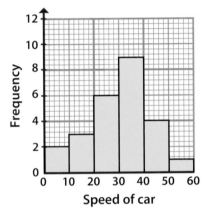

Speed of car

Exercise 6

1 On a copy of these axes, draw a bar chart of the data from the tally chart you completed in question 1 of Exercise 5. (This bar chart is a histogram.)

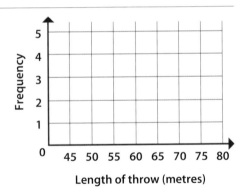

Length of throw (metres)

2 Here are the heights (in metres) of 30 pupils in Year 8.

1.68   1.75   1.88   1.62   1.67   1.58   1.75   1.73   1.81   1.54
1.65   1.51   1.73   1.78   1.80   1.82   1.72   1.73   1.75   1.62
1.58   1.79   1.68   1.69   1.78   1.66   1.73   1.86   1.58   1.67

(a) Choose suitable class intervals and tally this data.

(b) Draw a bar chart to show this information.
    (The data is continuous so your barchart is a histogram.)

Assignment 3   **Kids like us**

- Measure the heights of the people in your class.

- Choose suitable group intervals and tally your results as continuous data.

- Draw a bar chart to illustrate this data.

Line graphs

A line graph should only be drawn between points plotted for items of data when values between those plotted could exist.

This means line graphs are only drawn for continuous data.

Example

You could draw a line graph of the temperature of a car engine during a journey. Values between the points when the temperature was measured make sense.

Line graphs should not be drawn to represent discrete data.

Example

It would make no sense to draw a line graph for the colours of cars in this car park.

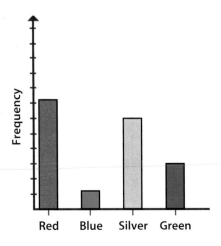

1 Which of the following would it be sensible to record using a line graph?

(a) the make of the cars on the car park

(b) the temperature during the day

(c) the primary schools from which the people in your class came

(d) the height of the tide at the seaside

(e) the number of pets you have

(f) the distance you have travelled on a walk

Explain your answers.

Reading from line graphs

Example

This graph records a pupil's height and age.
At what age was the pupil 1.5 metres tall?

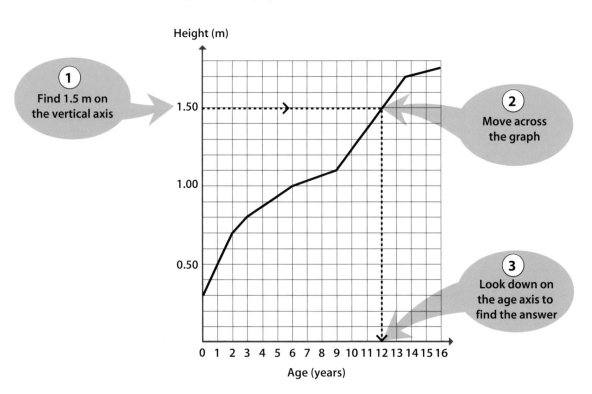

1 Find 1.5 m on the vertical axis

2 Move across the graph

3 Look down on the age axis to find the answer

Exercise 8

1 This graph shows the temperature recorded in a classroom.

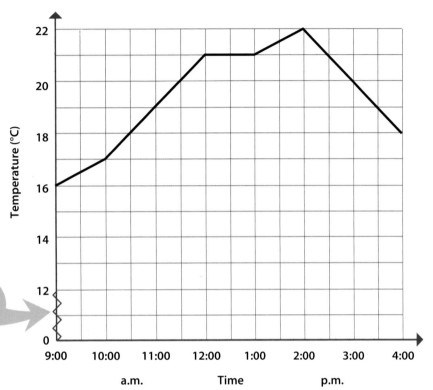

If the scale is different at the start of the axis, show it like this.

(a) At what time does the graph start?

(b) What is the temperature at that time?

(c) What is the temperature at 10:00 a.m.?

(d) At what times does the temperature reach 19°C?

(e) What happens to the temperature between 12:00 noon and 1:00 p.m.?

(f) What is the highest temperature recorded during the day?

(g) When is the temperature at its highest?

(h) When is the temperature rising fastest?

(i) What is the temperature at 3:00 p.m.?
At what other time was the temperature the same?

2 This graph shows the journey made by a group of friends.

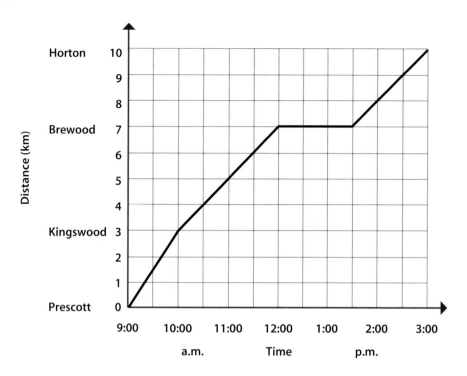

(a) Where does the journey begin?

(b) At what time did the journey begin?

(c) At what time did the group of friends reach the village of Kingswood?

(d) At what time did they reach the village of Brewood?

(e) How far is it (in kilometres) between the two villages of Kingswood and Brewood?

(f) Describe what you think happened at 12:00 noon.

(g) At what time did the friends leave the village of Brewood?

(h) Where did the journey finish?

(i) How far had the friends travelled altogether?

Give your answer in kilometres.

(j) What can you say about the speed between 10:00 a.m. and 12:00 noon, and the speed between 1:30 p.m. and 3:00 p.m.?

3 Imagine that you make the journey shown in this graph.

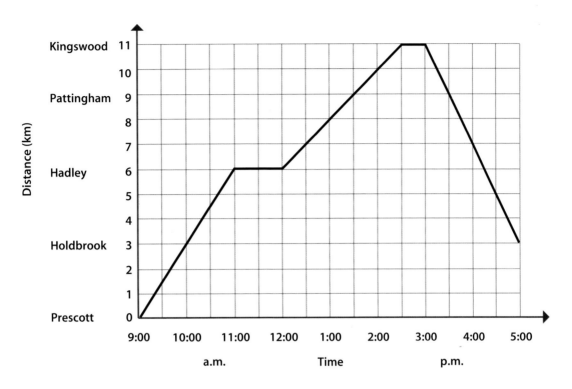

(a) Where does your journey begin?

(b) At what time does your journey begin?

(c) At what time do you reach the town of Holdbrook?

(d) Where is the first stop?

(e) At what time do you make the first stop?

(f) How long is this stop?

(g) At what time do you reach the town of Pattingham?

(h) How far is it between the towns of Pattingham and Kingswood?

(i) How long do you stay in Kingswood before setting off on the return journey?

(j) Where does the journey finish at 5:00 p.m.?

(k) At 5.00 p.m., how far away from Prescott are you?

(l) Which is the fastest part of the journey?

(m) At what speed was the fastest part of the journey?

4 This line graph shows the number of pupils in the school canteen during the lunch break. Break starts at 12 noon.

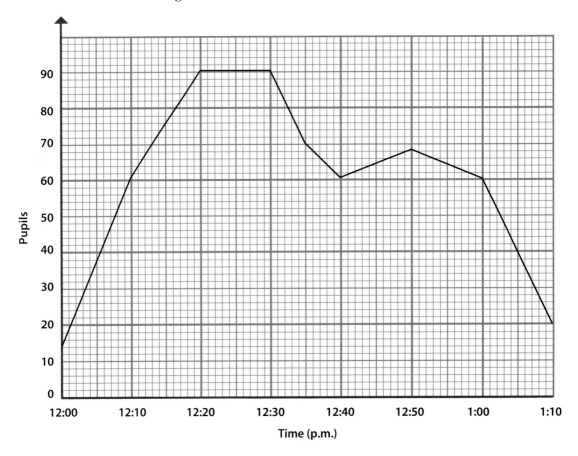

(a) How many pupils were there in the canteen at the start of break?

(b) How many pupils were in the canteen at 12:10 p.m.?

(c) At 12:30 p.m. the number of pupils in the canteen began to fall. At what time did it start to rise again?

(d) Between which two times was the number of pupils in the canteen going up fastest?

(e) Between which two times was the number of pupils in the canteen going down fastest?

(f) What was the maximum number of people in the canteen at any one time?

Drawing line graphs

Exercise 9

1 The number of shoppers in a superstore was recorded at 15-minute intervals during a morning.

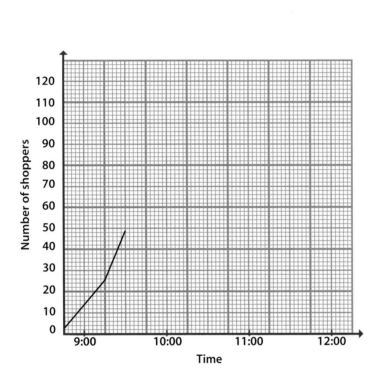

Time	Shoppers
8:45	3
9:00	14
9:15	25
9:30	48
9:45	?
10:00	56
10:15	48
10:30	60
10:45	?
11:00	90
11:15	113
11:30	87
11:45	72
12:00	65

(a) Copy these axes and plot the number of shoppers at the given times. Join them with a line graph.

The first three values have been plotted for you.

(b) No record was made for 9:45 a.m. or 10:45 a.m. Use your graph to estimate the number of people in the store at these two times.

(c) At approximately what time did the number of people in the shop reach 100?

2 The number of people attending a concert was recorded.

(a) Copy these axes and plot the values in the table.

Time	People
7:00	0
7:15	20
7:30	40
7:45	60
8:00	90
8:15	14
8:30	17
8:45	17
9:00	180

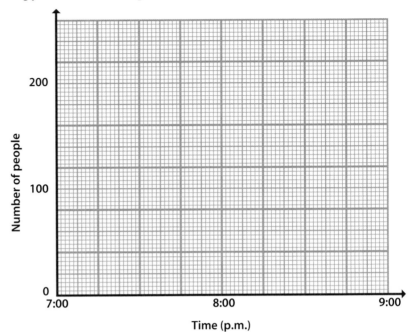

(b) Between which two times did the most people arrive at the concert?

(c) Between which two times did no more people go into the concert?

(d) How many people were in the concert by 9:00 p.m.?

3 During an experiment in Science, the temperature of a liquid was measured at 1-minute intervals. The measurement at 6 minutes was missed.

(a) Draw a set of axes and plot the temperatures at the given times. Join them with a line graph.

(b) What was the temperature after 3 minutes?

(c) When did the temperature drop below 50°C?

(d) Estimate the temperature after 6 minutes.

Time from start (minutes)	Temperature (°C)
1	100
2	84
3	68
4	56
5	46
6	–
7	26
8	24
9	22
10	20

Pie charts

A pie chart uses sectors of a circle to represent data.
Each sector represents a share of the total.

Example

This pie chart shows the number of pupils in Years 7 to 11.

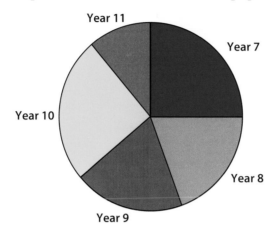

Pupils' year groups	Frequency
7	9
8	7
9	7
10	9
11	4
Total	36

Exercise 10

1 This pie chart shows the favourite subjects of the pupils in a class.

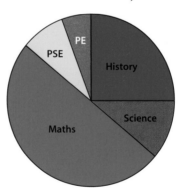

Use it to answer these questions.

(a) Which is the least popular subject?

(b) Which is the second most popular subject?

(c) Which subject was twice as popular as PSE (personal social education)?

(d) Which subject is twice as popular as history?

2 This pie chart shows the number of cars in a car park. There are 10 red cars in the car park. Half the cars are blue.

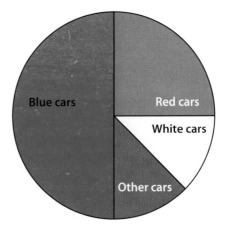

(a) How many cars are blue?

(b) How many cars are white?

(c) What is the total number of cars?

(d) What angle represents the red cars?

(e) What angles represent cars of the other colours?

> There are 360°
> in a complete
> turn.

3 This pie chart shows the number of pupils who eat baked potatoes, rice, chips or salad at lunch time.

The school canteen serves salads to 200 pupils a day.

This is a quarter of its pupils.

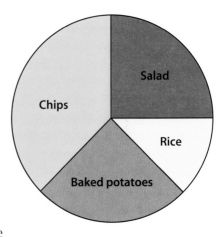

(a) How many pupils are represented by the whole pie chart?

(b) How many baked potatoes are served each day?

(c) Twice as many people have salads as rice. How many have rice each day?

(d) How many pupils choose chips?

(e) Write down the angles that represent each of the four sectors.

4 A survey was carried out to see which fruits are chosen by 120 pupils. The results are shown in this pie chart.

(a) How many pupils chose oranges?

(b) How many chose apples?

(c) How many chose bananas?

(d) How many did not choose oranges, apples or bananas?

(e) What angle in the pie chart would this represent?

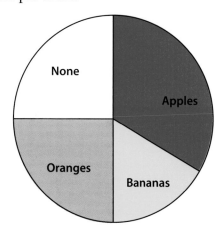

5 The year groups of pupils in a school were recorded in this pie chart.

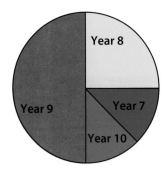

(a) Copy this table. Fill in the missing values.

Year	Number of pupils	Pie chart angle
7	30	45°
8		
9		
10		
Total		

(b) What angle of the pie chart represents Year 8?

(c) How many pupils are in Year 8?

(d) How many pupils are represented by the whole pie chart?

Sharing out the pie

Imagine that you have done a survey of 180 pupils present in the dining hall at a particular time.

To calculate the angle 'per pupil' you should divide the number of degrees at the centre of the circle by the number of pupils in the survey.

Example: $360° ÷ 180 = 2°$ per pupil.

Exercise 11

1 Copy and complete this table of angles which represents each Year group present in the dining hall at a particular time.

Year	Number of pupils	Angle
7	36 ×2° ⟹	72°
8	45	90°
9	72	
10	18	
11	9	
Total	180	360°

Assignment 4   Drawing a pie chart

You are going to draw a pie chart using your results from Exercise 11.

- Draw a circle.

- Mark the starting point for your pie chart (usually at the top of the circle).

- Measure the first angle (72°).

- Measure the next angle (90°) starting at the end of the last.

- Carry on to complete the pie chart.

- When you have measured all your angles, check that the sectors fill the whole circle.

- Label the sectors Year 7, Year 8 and so on.

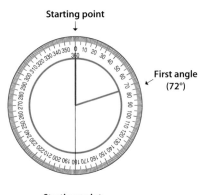

Starting point

First angle (72°)

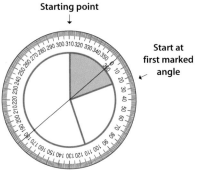

Starting point

Start at first marked angle

Exercise 12

1. This table shows the number of pupils in the dining hall at a particular time.

   (a) Calculate the angle per pupil.

   (b) Use this to copy and complete an angle table.

   (c) Draw a pie chart to illustrate this data.

Year	Number of pupils	Angle
7	48	
8	36	
9	18	
10	6	
11	12	
12	0	
Total		

2. (a) Copy and complete an angle table for these results.

Year	Number of pupils	Angle
7	18	
8	27	
9	27	
10	9	
11	9	
Total		

   (b) Draw a pie chart to illustrate this data.

3. (a) Copy and complete this angle table.

Year	Number of pupils	Angle
7	6	
8	8	
9	12	
10	10	
11	12	
Total		

   (b) Draw a pie chart to illustrate this data.

Assignment 5   Favourite lessons

Carry out a survey of the favourite lessons of 30 pupils.

- Record your results in a table.

- Use the information in the table to help you to decide how to draw a pie chart to show this data. Draw your pie chart.

- You may wish to record your data on a computer spreadsheet and to produce a pie chart on the computer.

Review Exercise

1 Calculate the mean, median, mode and range for the following data.

  (a) 3   6   10   5   3   (b) 26   24   24   26   24

  (c) 101   117   135   125   101   126   142   113

2 The pupils from a school travel home on five different school buses. The numbers of pupils on each bus on one day are shown in this table.

Bus	Number of pupils
Lilleshall	41
Edgemond	39
Horton	49
Donnington	52
Tibberton	30
Total	

  (a) Find the median number of pupils on these buses.

  (b) Find the mean number of pupils on these buses.

  (c) Explain why there is no modal value.

  (d) What is the range of pupils on the buses?

  (e) The bus company says the average number of pupils on the buses is less than 42.

     (i) Which average have they used?

     (ii) Which average would you use to prove this is not true?

     (iii) Explain the difference.

3 The Maths marks of two pupils are to be compared.

Pupil A	59	66	85	81	64
Pupil B	67	81	70	68	65

(a) Calculate the mean and range for each of these sets of marks.

(b) Which pupil has the most consistent marks?

(c) Does the mean or the range give you the better idea of which pupil is better at Maths?

4 A biscuit weighs 80 grams. This pie chart shows the ingredients used. There are 20 grams of chocolate in the biscuit.

(a) How many grams of the biscuit are butter?

(b) How many grams are flour?

(c) How many grams are oats?

(d) The remainder of the biscuit is syrup. How many grams of syrup is this?

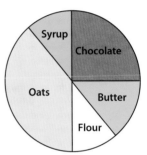

5 A survey recorded the colours of 72 cars in a car park.

(a) Calculate the angle per car.

(b) Copy the table and complete it.

(c) Draw a pie chart to represent this data.

Colour	Number of cars	Pie chart angle
blue	16	80°
red	9	
white	12	
green	5	
other		
Total	72	360°

Assignment 6   Traffic survey

- Carry out a survey of 120 vehicles of different types, e.g. car, lorries, etc.

- Record your results in a table.

- Draw a pie chart to illustrate this information.

- You could record this data on a computer spreadsheet, and produce a pie chart on the computer.

Simplifying and substituting

In this chapter you will learn:

→ **how to use simple formulae expressed in words**
→ **how to find inverse operations**
→ **how to simplify diagrams**
→ **how to express situations symbolically**

Starting points

Before starting this chapter you will need to know how to use letters to represent numbers.

Exercise 1

1 Four pupils buy the following equipment from the school shop.

(a)

(b)

(c)

(d)

 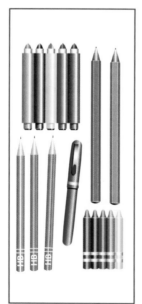  

(i)   Make a list of the equipment each pupil has bought.

(ii) Show how you could record this data more quickly.

2 (a) This is a list of the things the shop sells on one particular day.

black pen	ruler	red pen	ink pen	ink pen
red pen	blue pen	calculator	black pen	felt pen
red pen	blue pen	ink pen	ink pen	black pen
red pen	calculator	ruler	blue pen	set square
rubber	felt pen	ruler	compass	sharpener
black pen	ruler	red pen	ink pen	ink pen
red pen	blue pen	calculator	black pen	felt pen
red pen	blue pen	ink pen	ink pen	black pen
red pen	calculator	ruler	blue pen	set square
rubber	felt pen	ruler	compass	sharpener
black pen	ruler	red pen	ink pen	ink pen
red pen	blue pen	calculator	black pen	felt pen
red pen	blue pen	ink pen	ink pen	black pen
red pen	calculator	ruler	blue pen	set square
rubber	felt pen	ruler	compass	sharpener

Record this data using a tally. Explain why tallying the data in this list is a good way to record this data.

(b) Use a tally to record the items in each of the following lists.

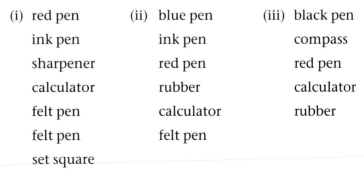

(i) red pen
   ink pen
   sharpener
   calculator
   felt pen
   felt pen
   set square

(ii) blue pen
   ink pen
   red pen
   rubber
   calculator
   felt pen

(iii) black pen
   compass
   red pen
   calculator
   rubber

Explain why tallying the data in these three lists is *not* a good way to record this data.

Using shorthand

An alternative way to record data is to use a single letter to represent an item.

Example

You can use *i* for each ink pen, *p* for pencil and *s* for set square in the list.

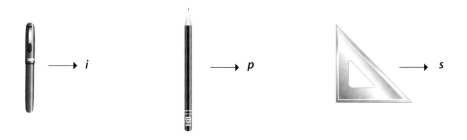

If 6 felt pens, 5 rulers, 1 calculator and 3 more felt pens are sold you can use this code:

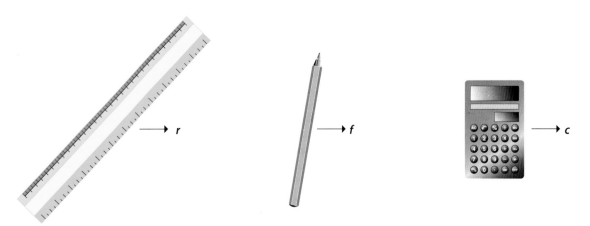

and this can then be recorded as:

$$f, f, f, f, f, f, r, r, r, r, r, c, f, f, f$$

This can be simplified to:

$$6f + 5r + c + 3f$$

Then *6f* and *3f* can be added giving:

$$9f + 5r + c$$

> *f + f + f + f + f + f* is usually written as *6f*. The multiplication sign is left out.
> *1c* is written as *c*.

Exercise 2

1 Copy this list of items for sale and choose for each item its own single letter code.

ITEM	CODE	ITEM	CODE
black pen		ruler	
red pen		set square	
blue pen		rubber	
ink pen		compasses	
felt pens		sharpener	
pencils		calculator	
crayons		notepad	

No two things should have the same code.

2 Record what is in each of the following boxes using the codes you chose in question 1 to represent each of the different items.

(a)  (b)  (c) 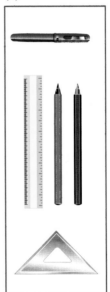 (d)

3 Write these shopping lists again as simply as you can.

(a) $f + f$

(b) $s + s + s + s$

(c) $b + b + k + k + k$

(d) $s + s + s + s + c$

(e) $s + s + s + c + c$

(f) $r + r + s + r + s$

(g) $s + s + r + c + r + c + c$

(h) $b + r + b + c + r + b + b$

Key fact

Putting algebraic terms together is called simplifying.

4 Simplify these lists.

(a) $2f + 3f + 4r$

(b) $5r + 2s + 3r$

(c) $7f + 3r + 6r$

(d) $2c + 4f + c + 3f$

(e) $5r + 2r + r + f$

(f) $12f + r + 3f + 6r$

(g) $2s + 4r + c + r + 3f$

(h) $3s + 2c + 6c + 2s + 2f$

(i) $4r + r$

(j) $7f + f + 9r + 5r$

(k) $4f + 3f + 2f$

(l) $12c + 6c + 3s + 2s$

(m) $12f + 3r + 4f + 2r + 2s + s$

(n) $13f + 9r + 3r + 8f + 2s + 4c + c$

5 Write each of these algebraic expressions in its simplest form.

(a) $a + a + a + a$

(b) $b + b + b + a + a$

(c) $x + x + x$

(d) $2p + 2p$

(e) $7a + 3b + a + 2b$

(f) $5n + 5m + 6n + m$

(g) $p + r + 3r + 4r + 3p + 2r$

(h) $7f + 9e + e + 2f$

(i) $3c + c - 2c$

(j) $2x + 5y + y$

(k) $4a + 3a - 2a$

(l) $4m - m$

(m) $2c + 6c + 3d + 4d$

(n) $x + y + 5y$

6 If there were 6 felt pens to start with and then 2 felt pens were sold, this could be written

$6f - 2f$

Because $6f - 2f = 4f$ we know there are 4 felt pens still in stock.

Copy and simplify these expressions to see how much is still in stock.

(a) $4f - 2f$

(b) $8r - 3r$

(c) $2s - s$

(d) $5c + 2c - 3c$

(e) $7s + 3r - 2s - r$

(f) $5r - 3r + 6c - 4c$

(g) $8f - 5f + f + 9c - 6c$

(h) $7s - 5s - s + 9r - 6r + r$

Using letters for unknown values

Letters can be used to represent any value that can change or that you do not know.

Example

There are three different length strips, coloured
red, green and yellow. These could be coded *r*, *g* and *y*.

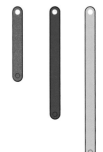

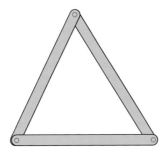

This shape has been made with
three yellow coloured strips. The correct
name of the shape is 'equilateral triangle'.
The strips used to make this triangle could be
coded *y* + *y* + *y*. This can be written simply as 3*y*.

Exercise 3

1 (a) Write down the correct name for each of these shapes.

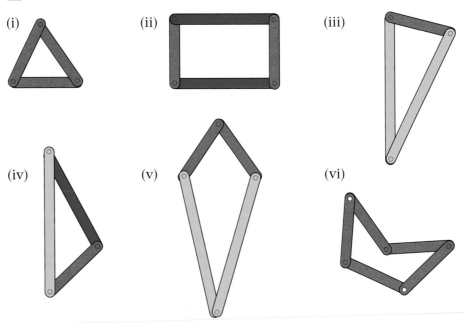

(i)

(ii)

(iii)

(iv)

(v)

(vi)

(b) Write down a simplified code for the strips used to make each
of these shapes.

2 These are the codes for making other shapes using the coloured strips.

(i) $g + g + g$ (ii) $y + y + g$ (iii) $g + r + g$

(iv) $g + r + y$ (v) $r + r + r + r$ (vi) $y + r + y + r$

(vii) $r + r + y + y$ (viii) $r + r + r + r + r + r$

(a) Each of the shapes has at least one name.
Write down the correct names for each of them.

(b) Simplify each of these codes.

Assignment 1   Shape codes

• Using nine coloured strips, three of each colour, investigate the number of different triangles that can be made. You can use the same colour more than once.

• Record each triangle using a suitable code.

• Simplify your code if you can.

Letters for numbers

We now use letters to represent a length.

Exercise 4

1 Write down the length of the perimeter of each of these shapes, in its simplest from, using the codes shown.

The perimeter is the distance around the outside of a shape.

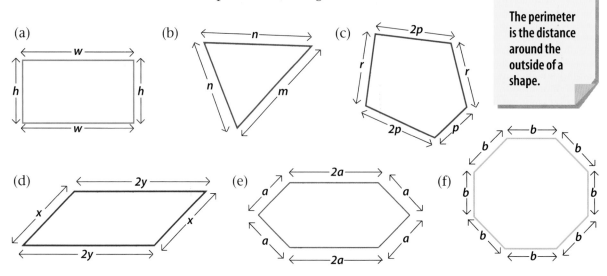

Putting in numbers

If you use the letter to represent the cost of each item, you can work out the total cost by substituting the price of each item into your expression.

Example

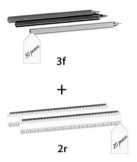

3f

+

2r

PRICE LIST

Felt pens	30p
Rulers	20p
Compasses	50p
Sharpeners	25p

$$\begin{aligned}
\text{Total cost} &= (3 \times 30\text{p}) + (2 \times 20\text{p}) \\
&= 90\text{p} + 40\text{p} \\
&= 130\text{p} \\
&= £1.30
\end{aligned}$$

Exercise 5

1 In a shop, the price list is as given in the example above. If you buy felt pens *(f)*, rulers *(r)*, compasses *(c)* and sharpeners *(s)*, what will be the total cost for each of the following lists?

(a) $f + r + c$ (b) $2f + 3r$ (c) $2f + 4r$ (d) $5r + 2s$

(e) $7f + 3r$ (f) $2c + 4f$ (g) $5r + s + f$ (h) $12f + 6r$

(i) $2s + 4r + 3f$ (j) $3s + 6c + 2f$ (k) $3r + 4f + s$ (l) $3f + r + 2s + 4c$

(m) $4f + 2r$ (n) $4r + f$ (o) $2c + 3s$ (p) $7f + 2r + 3s$

2 Write down a simplified expression for the following orders and calculate the cost of each order.

BURGER BAR MENU

Tea	£0.50
Cola	£0.90
Milkshake	£0.90
Burger	£1.50
Fries	£1.10
Doughnut	£0.60

(a) A burger and fries.

(b) Tea, cola and a milkshake.

(c) Two burgers, two fries and a cola.

(d) Two teas, a burger, two fries and a doughnut.

(e) A burger, fries, doughnut and a milkshake each for two people.

Assignment 2   **Coding quadrilaterals**

Here are five different length strips.

The red strips are length 3.

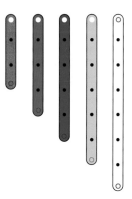

Using four strips you can make a number of quadrilaterals with a given perimeter.

With 2 red and 2 yellow strips you can make these shapes, both with perimeter 18.

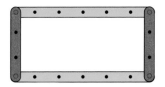

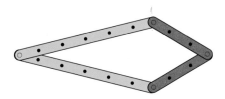

Rectangle: Kite
$r + y + r + y = 2r + 2y$ $r + r + y + y = 2r + 2y$

Perimeter is $(2 \times 3) + (2 \times 6) = 18$ Perimeter is $(2 \times 3) + (2 \times 6) = 18$

> For some perimeters it is possible to have more than one code.

- Investigate what shapes you can make if you use any number of strips but:

  - only two colours
  - only three colours
  - only four colours.

- What is the smallest perimeter that can be made using four coloured strips?

- What is the largest perimeter that can be made?

- How many different perimeters can you make using the coloured strips? Show clearly the code for each perimeter.

Key fact
Values that can change are called variables.

Substitution

Often letters are used to represent a value, like length, that can change. These are called variables. If an expression contains a variable, substituting the variable with a value gives a value for the expression.

Example

What is the value of $2x + 3$ if $x = 5$?

Replace the x by 5:

$2x + 3 = (2 \times 5) + 3 = 13$

> Remember to multiply before you add.

Exercise 6

1 What is the value of each of the following expressions if $x = 4$?

(a) $x + 6$ (b) $x - 2$ (c) $16 - x$ (d) $3x$

(e) $4x$ (f) $\frac{1}{2}x$ (g) $2x + 1$ (h) $3x - 1$

Assignment 3   A spider's web

• Copy this diagram and fill in each of the missing numbers using the value of x in the centre.

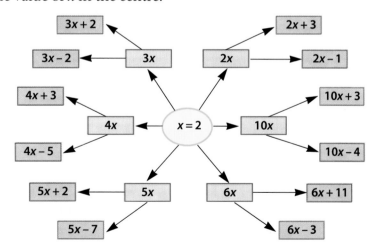

If you start with $x = 2$ then $3x + 2 = 8$ and $4x = 8$.
Find other sets of expressions which give the same results when $x = 2$.

• Copy the diagram again and substitute another value for x, e.g. 3 or 4. Investigate which expressions have the same values.

Number loops

In these number loops, each value in a circle is produced by starting with the given value and filling in the missing values.

Example

If $n = 2$ then $n + 2 = 4$, so the next circle (going clockwise) becomes 4.
If you carry on around the circle, the end circle holds 2, which matches the starting value.

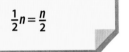

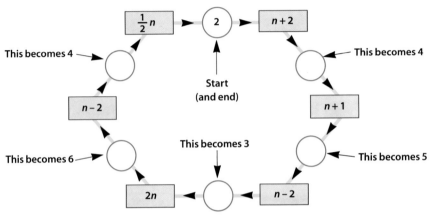

Exercise 7

1 (a) Copy the loop from the example above leaving the circles blank.

  (b) Put 3 into the starting circle. Calculate the values for the other circles. Does this form a complete loop?

2 (a) Copy and complete this loop.

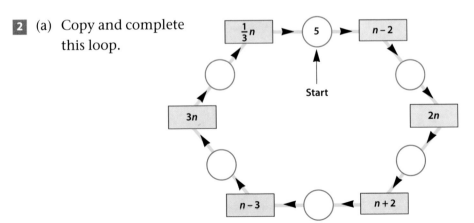

  (b) Put 8 into the starting circle. Does this form a complete loop?

3 (a) Try your own starting values in the loop in Question 2.

(b) Is it possible to form a loop with these chains starting in a different position?

4 Find five different starting values that will make this number chain into a loop.

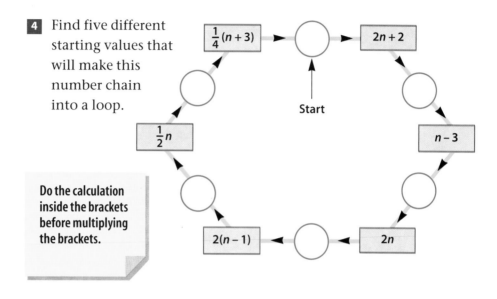

Start

Do the calculation inside the brackets before multiplying the brackets.

Assignment 4   Round and round

• Start with 3 and complete this number loop.

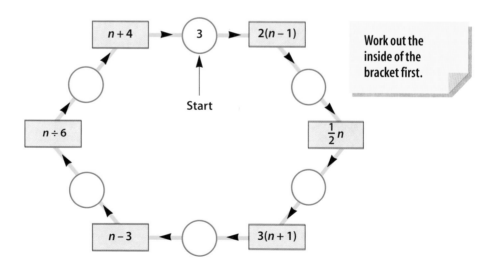

Start

Work out the inside of the bracket first.

• Does your answer return to 3?

• Investigate which starting values will work in this loop. There is a solution less than 10.

Forming expressions

Example

Start with a number, multiply by 2 and then add 3.

If you start with the number 4, the result is 11.

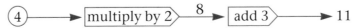

Exercise 8

1 What is the result of substituting the given values into each of these? Show your working.

(a) Start with a number, multiply by 3, add 3.

    (i) 2   (ii) 3   (iii) 4

(b) Start with a number, multiply by 2, take away 3.

    (i) 3   (ii) 4   (iii) 8

(c) Start with a number, multiply by 4 and then add 3.

    (i) 2   (ii) 3   (iii) 4

(d) Start with a number, add 3, multiply by 4.

    (i) 2   (ii) 3   (iii) 4

2 Why are the answers to parts (c) and (d) of question 1 different?

Assignment 5   Letters for numbers

A code changes these numbers to letters.

- These statements are all true.

$$a + d = b + c \qquad\qquad e \times b = e$$
$$e - a = c - b \qquad\qquad e \div a = a$$

- Work out the value of each letter.

Using flowcharts

Instead of using words, you can use flowcharts to describe sequences of operations. Then you can substitute variables into the flowchart.

Example

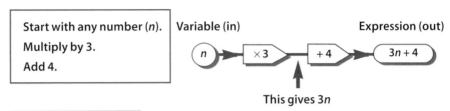

| Start with any number (*n*). | Variable (in) | | | | | | Expression (out) |

Start with any number (*n*).
Multiply by 3.
Add 4.

Variable (in)

n ▸ $\times 3$ ▸ $+ 4$ ▸ $3n + 4$

Expression (out)

This gives $3n$

1 Copy these flowcharts and complete the expressions which come out of them.

(a) Start with any number.
Add 4.

n ▸ $+ 4$ ▸ ⬭

(b) Start with any number.
Take away 3.

n ▸ $- 3$ ▸ ⬭

(c) Start with any number.
Multiply by 2.
Add 4.

n ▸ $\times 2$ ▸ $+ 4$ ▸ ⬭

(d) Start with any number.
Multiply by 3.
Take away 2.

n ▸ $\times 3$ ▸ $- 2$ ▸ ⬭

(e) Start with any number.
Multiply by 4.
Take away 3.

n ▸ $\times 4$ ▸ $- 3$ ▸ ⬭

(f) Start with any number.
Multiply by $\frac{1}{2}$.
Add 1.

n ▸ $\times \frac{1}{2}$ ▸ $+ 1$ ▸ ⬭

(g) Start with any number.
Multiply by 2.

n ▸ $\times 2$ ▸ $+ 4$ ▸ ⬭

Unknown numbers

You have already replaced words with letters in this chapter.

In this section you will replace unknown numbers with a letter.

Example

'A number plus 4' could be written as $n + 4$.

Exercise 10

1 Write each of the following in words.

(a) $n + 3$ (b) $n - 2$

(c) $2n$ (d) $\frac{1}{2}n$

(e) $2n + 3$ (f) $3n - 1$

(g) $10 - 2n$ (h) $2(n - 1)$

2 Write the following statements symbolically (using letters and numbers).

(a) a number add three

(b) a number minus five

(c) two different numbers added together

(d) a number taken away from another number

(e) a number times five

(f) a number subtracted from another number

(g) a number multiplied by 2

(h) two less than a number

(i) a number times 2 plus 6

(j) a number add 3 then the result multiplied by 5

(k) a number take away 4 then the result multiplied by 2

(l) a number multiplied by 3 then the result subtracted from 10

Using substitution

1 The school library charges a fine (*f*) if books are returned late. The fine, in pence, is based on the number of days (*d*) they are overdue.

$f = 10 + 2d$

Find the charge (*f*) when:

(a) $d = 1$ (b) $d = 3$ (c) $d = 12$

2 The cost (*c*) in pence of hiring a taxi depends on the number (*n*) of miles travelled. The cost is given by the formula:

$c = 90 + 50n$

Find the cost when:

(a) $n = 4$ (b) $n = 8$ (c) $n = 12$

3 The time (*t*) in minutes taken for a runner to run a distance (*u*) in kilometres up a hill and the distance (*d*) in kilometres down is given by:

$t = 10u + 5d$

Find the value of *t* for these values of *u* and *d*.

(a) $u = 3, d = 4$ (b) $u = 5, d = 8$ (c) $u = 4, d = 3$

4 The perimeter (*p*) in centimetres of a rectangle is given by the equation:

$p = 2l + 2w$

Calculate the perimeter for these measurements of the length (*l*) and the width (*w*).

(a) $l = 5\,\text{cm}, w = 6\,\text{cm}$

(b) $l = 10$ inches, $w = 8$ inches

(c) $l = 15\,\text{m}, w = 20\,\text{m}$

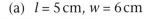

Brackets

When the brackets in the expression $2(x - 1)$ are opened this is the result.

$2(x - 1) = 2x - 2$

Assignment 6	**Brackets**

- Look at this grid.

- $2(x - 1)$ and $2x - 2$ have been shaded because they are equivalent expressions.

- Find eight more pairs of squares which contain equal expressions when the brackets are opened.

$2x + 4$	$2(x - 1)$	$2x + 2$	$3(x - 3)$	$2x + 3$
$3(x - 2)$	$3(x + 1)$	$4x + 8$	$2x - 2$	$\frac{1}{2}(x + 4)$
$2(x + 3)$	$\frac{1}{2}x + 2$	$\frac{1}{2}x + 4$	$3x - 9$	$3x + 3$
$3x - 6$	$3(x - 1)$	$2(x + 2)$	$4(x + 2)$	$2x + 6$
$3x - 2$	$3x + 1$	$4(x + 8)$	$x + 3$	$3x - 3$

Exercise 12

1 (a) Copy this diagram and substitute $x = 4$ in each expression.

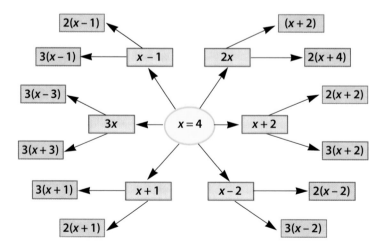

(b) Which expressions are equal?

Review Exercise

1 Look at each of these shapes and then write down its perimeter in its simplest possible form.

(a)

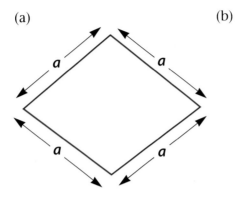

(b)

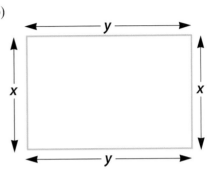

(c)

(d)

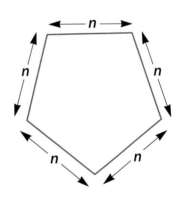

2 Simplify these expressions.

(a) $3a + 4a + a$

(b) $5f + 4f - 2f$

(c) $7x + 3z + 3x + z$

(d) $a + 3a + 4b + 3b$

(e) $2c + c + b + 4b - b$

(f) $9s + 7s + u + 5s - u - 2s$

3 Find the values of the following if $x = 2$, $y = 3$ and $z = 5$.

(a) $z + y$

(b) $y + z - x$

(c) $7x + 3z + 3x + z$

(d) $x + 3x + 4y + 3y$

(e) $2z + x + 3y$

(f) $9z + 7x - 2y$

4 (a) Using 2 in the start circle of this number chain, write down the value produced in each circle, working clockwise.

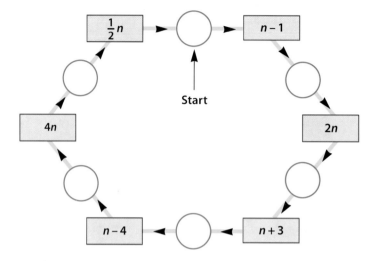

(b) Do any other values between 1 and 10 make this number chain into a loop? Show your working.

5 Write these statements using symbols.

(a) a number add six

(b) a number take away two

(c) two take away a number

(d) a number multiplied by three, then take away one from the result

6 The cost (c) in dollars of hiring a car on holiday is made up of a deposit of $30 plus $25 a day.

(a) Write down an expression to show this, starting: $c = \ldots$

(b) What is the cost of hiring the car for:
(i) 2 days?   (ii) 5 days?   (iii) 14 days?

7 Substitute these values for n into each expression in the grid and find as many pairs of equal expressions as you can.

(a) 2   (b) 3   (c) 4

$n + 3$	$2n$	$3(n + 1)$
$3n - 2$	$2n + 1$	$2(5 - n)$
$2(2n + 1)$	$2(10 - n)$	$2n + 3$

Working without a calculator

In this chapter you will learn:

→ some quick calculation methods
→ how to multiply a 3-digit number by a 2-digit number
→ how to estimate answers to problems
→ how to use knowledge of number patterns to check answers
→ about some historical calculating methods

Starting points

Before starting this chapter you will need to know:

• how to carry out simple calculations using + − × ÷

• how to multiply whole numbers by 10, 100 or 1000 without using a calculator

• some simple multiplication patterns.

Exercise 1

 1 Do these calculations. Show all your working.

(a)   65
     + 32
     ─────

(b)   325
      + 42
     ─────

(c) 543 + 154

(d)   37
     + 25
     ─────

(e)   572
     + 146
     ─────

(f) 875 + 157

(g)   65
     − 43
     ─────

(h)   647
     − 132
     ─────

(i) 265 − 122

(j)   65
     − 39
     ─────

(k)   934
     − 281
     ─────

(l) 143 − 64

2 Do these calculations. Do not use a calculator.

(a) 5×10 (b) 10×7 (c) 32×10

(d) 65×100 (e) 372×10 (f) 100×42

(g) $60 \div 10$ (h) $750 \div 10$ (i) $8300 \div 100$

3 Copy and complete these calculations.

(a)
$$\begin{array}{r} 2\ 7 \\ \times\ 7 \\ \hline 1\ 8\ \square \end{array}$$

(b)
$$\begin{array}{r} 6\ 3 \\ \times\ 2 \\ \hline 1\ 2\ \square \end{array}$$

(c)
$$\begin{array}{r} 5\ 4 \\ \times\ 6 \\ \hline 3\ 2\ \square \end{array}$$

(d)
$$\begin{array}{r} 2\ \square \\ \times\ 7 \\ \hline 1\ 4\ 7 \end{array}$$

(e)
$$\begin{array}{r} 6\ \square \\ \times\ 8 \\ \hline 5\ 2\ 0 \end{array}$$

(f)
$$\begin{array}{r} 4\ \square \\ \times\ 3 \\ \hline 1\ 4\ 1 \end{array}$$

(g)
$$\begin{array}{r} 5\ 4 \\ \times\ \square \\ \hline 1\ 0\ 8 \end{array}$$

(h)
$$\begin{array}{r} 8\ 3 \\ \times\ \square \\ \hline 4\ 1\ 5 \end{array}$$

(i)
$$\begin{array}{r} 7\ 3 \\ \times\ \square \\ \hline 6\ 5\ 7 \end{array}$$

4 Do these calculations. Show your working.

(a)
$$\begin{array}{r} 23 \\ \times\ 5 \\ \hline \end{array}$$

(b)
$$\begin{array}{r} 271 \\ \times\ 7 \\ \hline \end{array}$$

(c) 39×6

(d) $2\overline{)86}$ (e) $3\overline{)963}$ (f) $844 \div 4$

(g) $4\overline{)68}$ (h) $5\overline{)425}$ (i) $678 \div 6$

5 At their new school 85 pupils are divided equally into five classes. How many pupils will go into each class?

6 A pack of drinks contains 6 tins of cola. How many tins of cola are there altogether in 15 packs?

7 In Year 7 there are 215 pupils. In Year 8 there are 187.

(a) How many pupils are there altogether in Years 7 and 8?

(b) How many more pupils are there in Year 7 than in Year 8?

Looking at addition

This diagram shows that
$3 + 4$ is the same as $4 + 3$.

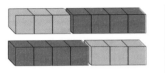

An addition sum can be done in any order.

It can also be shown that
$200 + 176$ is the same as $176 + 200$,
and $1276 + 13 + 76 = 76 + 13 + 1276$.

Sometimes an addition is made easier if you alter the order of the numbers to be added.

Example

The addition sum $21 + 46 + 9$

can also be written $21 + 9 + 46$

$$= 30 + 46$$

$$= 76$$

Exercise 2

1 Work out these additions as easily as possible. Do not use a calculator. Show the order in which you decide to add the numbers.

(a) $31 + 53 + 9$

(b) $7 + 87 + 33$

(c) $25 + 42 + 5 + 8$

(d) $6 + 53 + 7 + 14$

(e) $138 + 24 + 30 + 2 + 6$

(f) $5 + 77 + 50 + 3 + 95$

(g) $17 + 36 + 13$

(h) $82 + 49 + 18$

(i) $152 + 69 + 48$

(j) $88 + 25 + 12 + 70 + 5$

2 Calculate the perimeter of this shape.

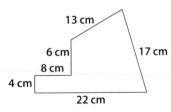

13 cm

6 cm   17 cm

8 cm

4 cm

22 cm

Key fact

A process in which the numbers can be taken in any order is called commutative.

3 Is subtraction commutative? Give three examples to show your answer.

Looking at multiplication

This diagram show that
2×5 is the same as 5×2.

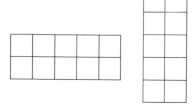

Similarly, 300×7 is the same as 7×300.

Like addition, multiplication can be made easier if you alter the order of the numbers to be multiplied.

Example

The multiplication
can also be written

$$5 \times 14 \times 2$$
$$5 \times 2 \times 14$$
$$= 10 \times 14$$
$$= 140$$

Exercise 3

1 Work out these multiplications as easily as possible. Do not use a calculator. Show the order in which you decide to multiply the numbers.

(a) $2 \times 8 \times 5$ (b) $5 \times 23 \times 2$

(c) $50 \times 19 \times 2$ (d) $25 \times 12 \times 4$

(e) $18 \times 2 \times 5$ (f) $20 \times 5 \times 11$

(g) $4 \times 375 \times 25$ (h) $5 \times 13 \times 2 \times 10$

(i) $2 \times 18 \times 5 \times 5 \times 2$ (j) $25 \times 32 \times 5 \times 4 \times 20$

2 A jumbo jet has 4 seats in each of its 58 rows.

The airline has 25 jumbo jets.

What is the total number of seats available?

3 Is division commutative? Give three examples to show your answer.

Multiplying a 2-digit number by a 2-digit number

There are several ways to multiply two numbers together.
Here are two examples for 23×54.

Example A

	50	4
20	1000	80
3	150	12

$1000 + 80 + 150 + 12$
$= 1242$

Example B

$23 \times 54 = 23 \times (50 + 4)$

$$
\begin{array}{cc}
23 & 23 \\
\times 50 & \times 4 \\
\hline
1150 & + \quad 92 \\
\end{array}
$$

so, $23 \times 54 = 1242$

Exercise 4

1 (a) 5×30 (b) 4×70

    (c) 16×20 (d) 24×80

2 (a) 7×32 (b) 5×65

    (c) 6×48 (d) 9×53

> After you have worked out your answers, check them using a calculator.

3 (a) 23×31 (b) 43×15

    (c) 52×27 (d) 83×35

    (e) 73×77 (f) 85×54

    (g) 99×99 (h) 67×89

4 A carpet costs £18 per square metre. How much will it cost to carpet a room with a floor area of 21 square metres?

5 A bus can carry 54 passengers. How many passengers can be carried by a fleet of 24 buses?

6 A boy has a part-time job. He is paid £28 per week. He manages to save half the money he earns. How much will he save in one year?

Assignment 1   Napier's bones

Many people have tried to devise aids to make mathematical calculations easier. In 1617, a Scotsman named John Napier made a device for multiplication. He etched a pattern of numbers onto some animal bones, and this aid to calculation is called Napier's bones.

- Ask your teacher for a Napier's bones workcard.

- Cut out your strips of card like those below.

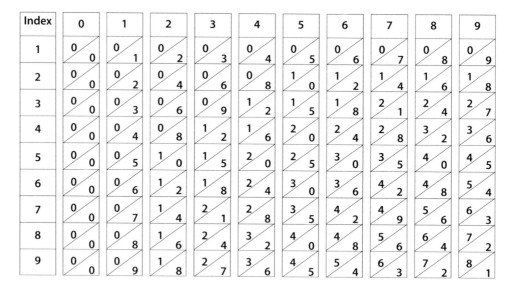

- Can you see the pattern of numbers that make up the 'bones'? If so, describe it.

- This diagram shows the 'bones' set for the multiplication 3×47.

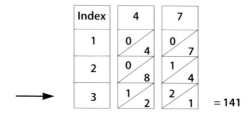

$$3 \times 47 = 141$$

- Can you see how the answer is obtained? If so, explain it. If not, ask your teacher for help.

Exercise 5

1 Use your Napier's bones for these calculations.

(a) 3×23 (b) 5×57

(c) 4×64 (d) 9×79

(e) 3×247 (f) 8×456

2 Now try these. Hint for (a): 23 = 20 + 3.

(a) 23×34 (b) 37×48

(c) 42×64 (d) 73×52

(e) 42×234 (f) 79×864

3 Now try these. Hint for (a): 153 = 100 + 50 + 3.

(a) 153×235 (b) 243×346

(c) 425×479 (d) 738×697

4 It is impossible to multiply 5 by 77 in this order with a set of Napier's bones.

(a) Why is this so? How could you overcome this problem?

(b) Use your answer to (a) to obtain the answer to 5×77.

(c) What is 634×757?

Multiplying a 3-digit number by a 2-digit number

The method for multiplying a 2-digit number by a 2-digit number can be extended to multiplying larger numbers.

Example A 427×34

	400	20	7
30	12000	600	210
4	1600	80	28

$12000 + 600 + 210 + 1600 + 80 + 28$
  $= \mathbf{14518}$

Example B 427×34

$427 \times 34 = 427 \times (30 + 4)$

$$\begin{array}{cc} 427 & 427 \\ \times\, 30 & \times\, 4 \\ \hline 12810 & +\ 1708 \end{array}$$

so, **$427 \times 34 = 14518$**

Exercise 6

1 Work these out *without* using a calculator.

(a) 12×131 (b) 21×152 (c) 23×123

(d) 15×325 (e) 54×372 (f) 75×273

(g) 382×47 (h) 625×68 (i) 733×25

(j) 286×48 (k) 159×37 (l) 951×85

2 (a) Multiply 26 by 432.

(b) What is the result of multiplying 547 by 63?

(c) What is 69 times 153?

(d) What is the product of 85 and 611?

3 (a) During one month, a school canteen provided 387 meals for 24 days. Altogether, how many meals was this?

(b) In a supermarket a shelf holds 356 tins of fruit. If there are 15 shelves of fruit, how many tins is this?

(c) A girl's heart beats 75 times a minute. How many times does it beat in: (i) 1 hour? (ii) 1 day?

4 Copy this:

Now put the numbers 0, 1, 2, 3, 4, 5 and 6 in the boxes to make the multiplication correct.

5 Start with the number 19.

(a) Write down two or more numbers which add up to 19.

For example, $3 + 4 + 4 + 8 = 19$

(b) Now multiply these numbers together: $3 \times 4 \times 4 \times 8 = 384$

(c) What is the biggest number you can make this way?

(d) Try the same puzzle starting with different numbers.

(e) Describe any patterns or anything else you notice.

Russian multiplication

For several generations, Russian peasants used this special method for multiplying large numbers together.

Example 19 × 35

	Left	Right	
① Divide the left-hand number by 2 – but ignore the remainders. Carry on until you reach 1	19	35	② Multiply the right-hand number by 2. Carry on until there are enough to pair with the left-hand column.
	9	70	
③ Cross out any pair where there is an even number on the left.	4̶	1̶4̶0̶	④ The answer is found by adding up the numbers remaining on the right.
	2̶	2̶8̶0̶	
	1	560	

35 + 70 + 560 = **665** so 19 × 35 = **665**

Exercise 7

1 Use the Russian multiplication method to work these out.

(a) 24 × 15   (b) 25 × 22

(c) 18 × 17   (d) 34 × 32

(e) 44 × 45   (f) 67 × 52

(g) 25^2 (h) 33^2

25^2 means
'25 squared'.
$25^2 = 25 \times 25$

Assignment 2   Russian multiplication

In Exercise 7, you have multiplied 2-digit numbers.

* Try the Russian multiplication method on numbers larger than 100. Does it still work? Show your results.

* Try to explain why the Russian method of multiplication works.

Assignment 3   Play your cards right

- Arrange these five cards as a multiplication as shown.

- What is the largest possible answer?

- What is the smallest possible answer?

- Try different numbers on the five cards.

- Try using more than five cards.

- Write down any patterns that you notice.

Approximating

Key fact

An approximate value is one which is close to the real value.

It often makes sense to give an approximate value rather than the actual value.

It is reasonable to say this stereo system costs about £130.

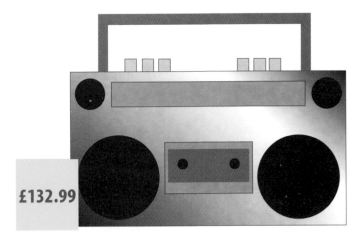

£132.99

The attendance at a football match is 23 943, but it may be reported as 24 000 on the news.

In Maths, an approximate value of a number is found using a process called **rounding**.

Key fact

The symbol ≈ means 'is about'.

21 ≈ 20

88 ≈ 90 (88 is nearer to 90 than 80)

182 ≈ 200 (182 is nearer to 200 than 100)

4235 ≈ 4000 (4235 is nearer to 4000 than 5000)

Each number has been 'rounded' to one digit followed by enough zeros to make it approximately the same size.

386 ≈ 400   386 has 3 digits.

one digit + 2 zeroes   400 also has 3 digits.

Exercise 8

Use one digit and enough zeros to keep it the correct size.

1 Use the rounding method to give approximate values for each of these numbers.

(a) 31   (b) 63   (c) 49   (d) 44

(e) 78   (f) 86   (g) 103   (h) 198

(i) 477   (j) 615   (k) 333   (l) 25

2 Use the same rounding method for these numbers.

(a) 210   (b) 690   (c) 899   (d) 912

(e) 3004   (f) 4210   (g) 5950   (h) 3694

(i) 978   (j) 1499   (k) 1501   (l) 1500

3 Rewrite these sentences using approximate values.

(a) A tennis court is 78 feet long.

(b) The island of Malta has an area of 316 square kilometres.

(c) The radius of the Earth is 6378 kilometres.

(d) Mount Everest is 8848 metres high.

(e) Angel Falls in Venezuela drops 979 metres and is the highest waterfall in the world.

Estimating

Estimating is an important skill. You can use your knowledge of approximating to estimate the answers to calculations.

Example

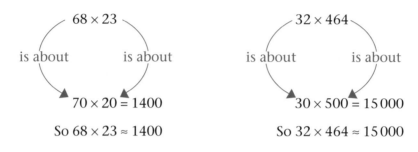

68×23
is about   is about
$70 \times 20 = 1400$
So $68 \times 23 \approx 1400$

32×464
is about   is about
$30 \times 500 = 15\,000$
So $32 \times 464 \approx 15\,000$

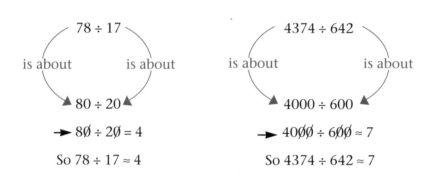

$78 \div 17$
is about   is about
$80 \div 20$
$8\cancel{0} \div 2\cancel{0} = 4$
So $78 \div 17 \approx 4$

$4374 \div 642$
is about   is about
$4000 \div 600$
$40\cancel{0}\cancel{0} \div 6\cancel{0}\cancel{0} \approx 7$
So $4374 \div 642 \approx 7$

Test your ability to make estimates in the next exercise.

Exercise 9

1 (a) 32×21 (b) 49×32 (c) 23×78 (d) 44×93

   (e) 68×72 (f) 48^2 (g) 7×97 (h) 283×3

2 (a) 21×310 (b) 43×195 (c) 48×632 (d) 378×68

   (e) 881×53 (f) 97×108 (g) 302×697 (h) 755×945

Check your estimates using a calculator.

3 (a) $62 \div 23$ (b) $87 \div 13$ (c) $198 \div 38$ (d) $476 \div 53$

   (e) $821 \div 184$ (f) $2320 \div 77$ (g) $4850 \div 725$ (h) $6745 \div 91$

Using estimations

You can use your knowledge of number patterns together with your estimating skills to check answers to problems.

Example

Is the multiplication $87 \times 32 = 284$ true or false?

First, check the last digit of the answer.
$7 \times 2 = 14$ so the last digit of the answer will be 4.
The last digit of 284 is 4, so it could be true.

$$8\ 7\ \times\ 3\ 2$$
$$1\ 4$$

Next, estimate the size of the answer.

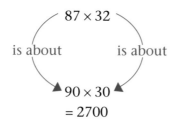

$$87 \times 32$$
is about — is about
$$90 \times 30$$
$$= 2700$$

Because 2700 is much larger than 284
$$87 \times 32 \neq 284$$
and the multiplication $87 \times 32 = 284$ is false. (The correct answer is 2784).

$\neq$ means 'is not equal to'.

Exercise 10

1 For each of these, estimate the answer. Say whether the equation is true or false.

(a) $9 \times 49 = 871$

(b) $62 \times 11 = 682$

(c) $7 \times 327 = 2184$

(d) $32 \times 47 = 1504$

(e) $48 \times 52 = 2510$

(f) $23 \times 37 = 8501$

(g) $62 \times 97 = 5952$

(h) $16 \times 122 = 1952$

(i) $72 \times 319 = 22\ 968$

(j) $222 \times 888 = 18\ 946$

Show your working.

2 For each of these, decide which is the correct answer, (i), (ii) or (iii).

(a) $82^2 =$ (i) 6724   (ii) 674   (iii) 6516

(b) $523^2 =$ (i) 1046   (ii) 273526   (iii) 273529

(c) $627 \div 19 =$ (i) 3   (ii) 33   (iii) 333

(d) $9312 \div 32 =$ (i) 31   (ii) 292   (iii) 291

(e) $5005 \div 715 =$ (i) 5   (ii) 7   (iii) 71

Review Exercise

1 Calculate these as easily as possible, without using a calculator.

(a) $42 + 54 + 8$

(b) $27 + 46 + 13$

(c) $88 + 35 + 12 + 50 + 5$

(d) $5 \times 42 \times 2$

(e) $4 \times 185 \times 25$

(f) $20 \times 92 \times 4 \times 5 \times 25$

2 Calculate these without using a calculator.

(a) 8×40

(b) 9×35

(c) 52×34

(d) 69×85

(e) 13×151

(f) 45×237

(g) 235×65

(h) 947×57

3 Write down approximate values for these numbers.

(a) 51

(b) 88

(c) 102

(d) 528

(e) 876

(f) 2957

(g) 7321

(h) 962

4 Make estimates for these calculations. Check your answers using a calculator.

(a) 41×19

(b) 57×51

(c) 231×72

(d) 525×372

(e) $83 \div 18$

(f) $3872 \div 28$

5 Rewrite this sentence using approximate values.
Ms Jones is 43 years old and she earns £23 412 per year.

6 A pair of compasses costs 76 pence. A Maths department buys sets for a class of 28 pupils. Approximately how much does this cost?

7 For each of these, decide which is the correct answer, (i), (ii) or (iii).

(a) $92 \times 53 =$

(i) 476

(ii) 4785

(iii) 4876

(b) $72 \times 389 =$

(i) 2888

(ii) 28 008

(iii) 28 431

(c) $58^2 =$

(i) 116

(ii) 3236

(iii) 3364

(d) $814 \div 22 =$

(i) 37

(ii) 47

(iii) 372

Assignment 4   Products in a number square

You need to pick out any 2×2 square on a blank 100-number grid.

The example shown here is the '14, 15, 24, 25' square.

1	2	3	4	5	6	7	8	9	10
11	12	13	14	15	16	17	18	19	20
21	22	23	24	25	26	27	28	29	30
31	32	33	34	35	36	37	38	39	40
41	42	43	44	45	46	47	48	49	50
51	52	53	54	55	56	57	58	59	60
61	62	63	64	65	66	67	68	69	70
71	72	73	74	75	76	77	78	79	80
81	82	83	84	85	86	87	88	89	90
91	92	93	94	95	96	97	98	99	100

14	15
24	25

- Calculate the product of the numbers on each diagonal.
  In this example: 14×25 and 15×24.

- What do you notice?
  Does this always happen?
  Why?

- Try to find other patterns by investigating further.

> The product is the answer found by multiplying two numbers.

Using angles

→ how to work out the angles in and around polygons
→ how to make some more 3D shapes
→ how to work out the angles formed by a line crossing parallel lines
→ how to locate a point using angles

Starting points

Before starting this chapter you will need to know:

• the words used to describe angles

• the sum of the angles in a triangle

• how to construct an angle with ruler and compasses

• how to measure and draw angles using a protractor.

Measuring the angles in a triangle

The three angles of a triangle can fit together to make a straight line.

What does this tell you about the total number of degrees in the three angles in a triangle?

If you are measuring an angle and its line is not long enough to cross the scale on the protractor, use a piece of paper to extend it, like this.

 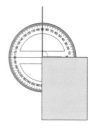

Exercise 1

1 Write down the total number of degrees in the three angles in a triangle.

2 (a) Copy this table.

Triangle	Angle a	Angle b	Angle c	Sum of angles
A				
B				
C				
D				
E				
F				

(b) Carefully measure all the angles in each of these triangles. Write your answers in your copy of the table.

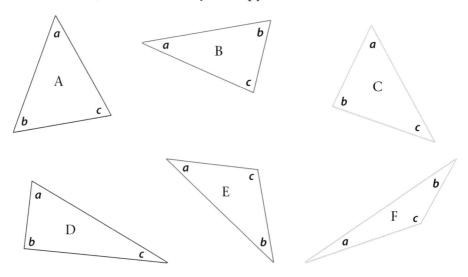

(c) Write down the sum of the three angles in the last column.

(d) Measure the angles again if this answer does not seem correct.

3 (a) Look back at Question 2 and write down at least two angles that are acute.

(b) Now write down at least two angles from Question 2 that are obtuse.

Constructing angles

Exercise 2

1 On a sheet of plain paper, mark a dot and label it A. Draw one line, length 5 cm, which starts at A.
Draw another line to make an angle of 40° at A.

2 Use a sheet of plain paper for your answers to this question.

(a) Mark a dot and label it A. Draw an angle of 65° at A.

(b) Mark a dot and label it C. Draw an angle of 156° at C.

(c) Mark a dot and label it D. Draw an angle of 215° at D.

> **Check your angles carefully with a protractor.**

3 Using only a ruler and compasses, construct these angles on a sheet of plain paper.

(a) 90° (b) 60° (c) 45° (d) 30° (e) 120° (f) 135°

4 (a) Construct angles of 15° and $22\frac{1}{2}°$, showing clearly how you carried out the construction.

(b) Write down any other angles you think you can construct with a ruler and compasses.

(c) Explain how you would construct them.

The sum of the angles around a point

This arrow points straight up the page.

Now it has turned 60° clockwise around point A.   **A**

If it continues to turn clockwise until it is facing straight up the page again it will have turned through another 300°.

The angles about a point add up to 360°.

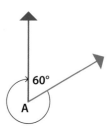

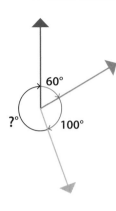

Exercise 3

1 At first, this arrow points straight up the page.
Then it turns through 60° clockwise and turns again, through 100° clockwise.

If the arrow continues to turn clockwise until it is facing straight up the page again, through how many more degrees will it turn? Explain how you worked out your answer.

2 Calculate the size of the angles marked a, b and c in these diagrams.

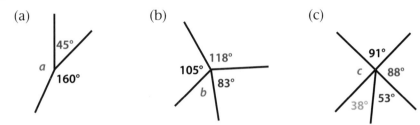

(a)   (b)   (c)

3 (a) Imagine you are standing facing the front of your classroom.

(b) Now you turn round until you are facing the front of the room again.

(c) Write down at least three different ways to tell a friend to make the same movement.

Key fact

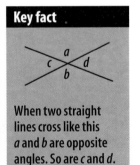

When two straight lines cross like this a and b are opposite angles. So are c and d.

4 (a) Draw two straight lines which cross each other.
Measure and write down the size of each of the four angles formed.

(b) Repeat activity (a) two more times.
Use what you know about angles around a point to check that your measurements are correct.

(c) What can you say about the **opposite angles** formed when two straight lines cross?

5 Write down the size of the angles marked a to g in these diagrams.

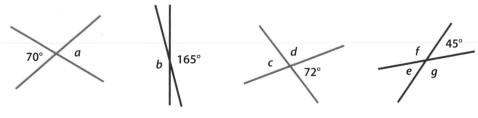

Angle properties of polygons

- Draw an arrow 5cm long on a piece of tracing paper

- Draw a triangle on a piece of plain paper with one end of each side extended.

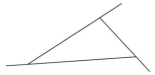

- Place the arrow along one side of the triangle with the blunt end at a vertex, and slide it until this end reaches the next vertex.

> Vertex is the name for a corner.

 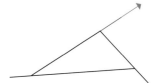

- Now, turn the arrow to point along the next side, repeating these steps until the arrow has returned to its original position.

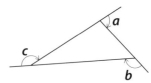

- How many degrees have you turned the arrow through? Your arrow turned through angle *a*, then *b*, then *c*.

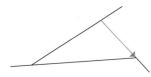

angle *a* + angle *b* + angle *c* = _____ °

- Repeat this activity first with a hexagon and then with an octagon.

Assignment 2   Computer drawn triangles

- Use LOGO on a computer to draw a triangle.

  Make sure you finish exactly at the same place as you start.

  Keep a record of the commands you use.

- What is the total of the turn commands for your triangle?

- Draw two more triangles. What is the total of the turn command for each triangle?

Assignment 3   Angles and polygons

- Draw a pentagon.

  Choose one vertex of the pentagon and join it to all the others.

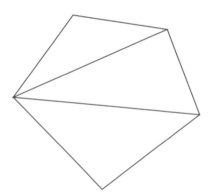

> The angles in the pentagon are made up of the angles of the three triangles.

- What is the total of all the angles in the pentagon?
  Write down how you worked out your answer.

- Use the same method to find the total of all the angles in a hexagon.

  Draw a diagram to help you to explain your answer.

- Now use the same method to find the total of all the angles in an octagon.

- Find a rule connecting the number of sides of the polygon and the total of all the angles.

  Write down your rule as clearly as you can.

Exercise 4

1 The interior angles of a regular polygon are all the same.

Calculate the size of *each* angle in:

(a) A regular triangle

(b) A regular quadrilateral

(c) A regular pentagon

(d) A regular hexagon

(e) A regular octagon.

> A regular triangle is called an **equilateral triangle.**
>
> A regular quadrilateral is called a **square.**

Write down how you found your answers.

2 Using a protractor and a ruler, draw each of these shapes accurately on plain paper:

(a) A regular hexagon with each side 5 cm long

(b) A regular octagon with each side 4 cm long

(c) A regular pentagon with each side 6 cm long

3 On plain paper, using only a ruler, compasses and pencil, construct these shapes:

(a) A regular hexagon with each side 6 cm long

(b) A regular octagon with each side 5 cm long

Assignment 4   Computer drawn polygons

• Use LOGO on a computer to draw a polygon.

• Make sure you finish exactly at the same place as you start.

• Keep a record of the commands you use.

• What is the total of the turn commands for your polygon?

• Draw two more polygons.

What is the total of the turn commands for each polygon?

Constructing 3D shapes

Exercise 5

Add glue tabs to help stick the shape together.

1 (a) Draw this net carefully on stiff paper or thin card.

All the shapes are equilateral triangles. Make each side 5 cm long.

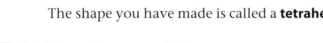

(b) Cut out, fold and glue your shape.

The shape you have made is called a **tetrahedron.**

2 (a) Draw this net carefully on stiff paper or thin card.

All the shapes are equilateral triangles. Make each side 5 cm long.

(b) Cut out, fold and glue your shape.

The shape you have made is called an **octahedron.**

3 (a) Draw this net carefully on stiff paper or thin card.

All the shapes are regular pentagons. Make each side 2.5 cm long.

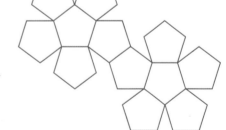

(b) Cut out, fold and glue your shape.

The shape you have made is called a **dodecahedron.**

4 (a) Draw this net carefully on stiff paper or thin card. The shapes are equilateral triangles and regular hexagons. Each side should be 3 cm long.

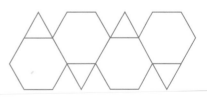

(b) Cut out, fold and glue your shape.

The shape you have made is called a **truncated tetrahedron.**

5 (a) Construct a dodecahedron as in Question 3.

(b) Construct 12 shapes using this net.

Each section is an isosceles triangle. The two larger angles are 72°.

Add a glue tab on all the 2.5 cm sides and on one of the 4 cm sides.

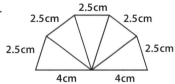

> An isosceles triangle has two sides of equal length and two equal angles.

(c) Cut out and fold each of your shapes. Join the 4 cm sides to form pyramids. Stick a pyramid to each face of the dodecahedron. The shape you have made is called a **small stellated dodecahedron.**

6 (a) Construct the solid from this net.

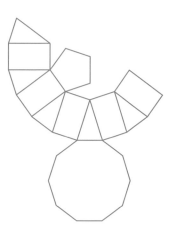

Each triangle looks like this: Each rectangle looks like this:

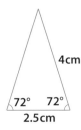   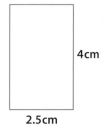

(b) Try joining 12 of these solids by sticking the rectangular faces together with the edges of the pentagons touching.

Assignment 5   Making another solid shape

• Find another interesting 3D shape from a book. Draw its net and construct it.

Angle properties of parallel lines

Exercise 6

Key fact

Two straight lines are parallel if they are the same distance apart everywhere. (Parallel lines never cross.)

1 Which of these diagrams show parallel lines?

(a)
(b)
(c)

(d)
(e)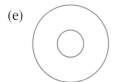

Key fact

Straight lines which cross are called intersecting lines.

2 If you think that any of the diagrams in question 1 are not parallel, write down why.

Assignment 6   Constructing parallel lines

- Draw a straight line.

- Place the longest side of a set square carefully along the line.

- Place a ruler against one of the other sides of the set square.

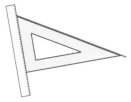 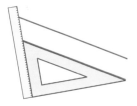

Parallel lines are shown by drawing arrows on them.

- Slide the set square along the ruler. Draw a line along the longest side of the set square.

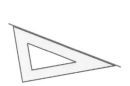

- The two lines you have drawn are parallel.

Assignment 7   **Alternate angles**

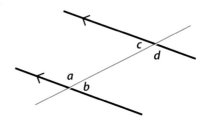
- Draw two parallel lines.

  Draw a straight line which crosses
  both of the parallel lines.

  Label the angles *a* to *d* like this.

  Measure the marked angles and record them in a table.

- Repeat this activity at least three more times.

- Write down everything you notice about the angles you have
  measured.

  In particular look for angles which are the same.

Assignment 8   **Lines crossing parallels**

- Draw two parallel lines.

- Draw a straight line which crosses
  both of the parallel lines.

  Label the angles *a* to *h* like this.

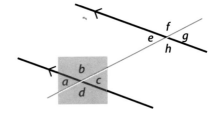

- Trace this part of your diagram.
  Fit your tracing carefully
  over the other angles.

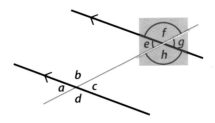

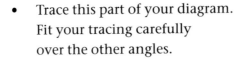

- Write down all the angles which are equal to angle *a*.

- Write down all the angles which are equal to angle *b*.

Exercise 7

1 Look at these diagrams. Use your knowledge of alternate angles and other angle facts to write down the size of the angles marked *a* to *m*.

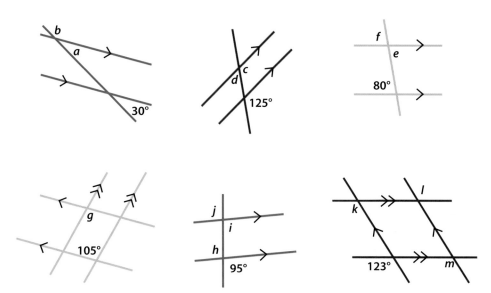

Locations

If you are standing at point O, you can describe the position of point A by the angle you turn clockwise from north (N) to face A and the number of rings from O to A.

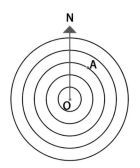

You will need to draw a line from O to A to help you to measure the angle.

In this example, the position of A from O is (30°, 3).

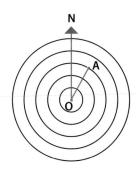

Assignment 9   **Measuring locations**

- First, you need to make a grid to measure locations.

  On tracing paper draw five circles, all with the same centre O and with radii 1 cm, 2 cm, 3 cm, 4 cm and 5 cm.

  Draw a straight line from the centre O to the outside circle. Label the line N for north.

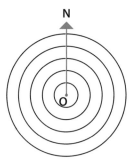

- Place your grid carefully on this map with the centre O on the point marked A and the line labelled N exactly over the line labelled N on the map.

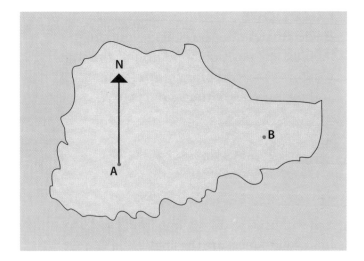

- Mark the position of B on your tracing paper.

- On your tracing paper draw a line from the centre O to point B.

- Measure the angle clockwise from the line N to the line to B.

- If the location of B from A is $(x°, y)$ what are the values of x and y?

Exercise 8

1 (a) By marking the points on your grid, find the location of:

   (i)   B from A   (ii) C from A   (iii) D from A

   (iv) A from E   (v)   D from E

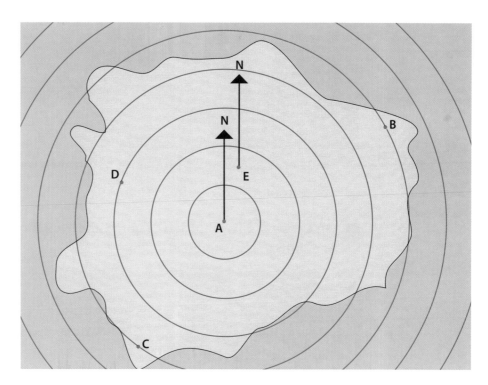

(b) If each ring represents 1 km, how far is:

   (i)   B from A   (ii) C from A   (iii) D from A

   (iv) A from E   (v)   D from E?

2 Draw a new grid on tracing paper.
Mark a point in the middle of a piece of
plain paper and label it P.
Draw a north line (N) with the base on P.

By measuring angles on your grid, mark
points at the following locations.

> You will need a
> north line (N) at
> each point.
> Make sure these
> lines are parallel.

   (a) A at (30°, 3)   (b) B at (90°, 5)   (c) C at (160°, 4)

   (d) D at (225°, 3.5)   (e) E at (292°, 2)   (f) F at (222°, 3.75)

3 On a copy of this map trace the north line and the points A, B and C.
(1 cm represents 1 km.)

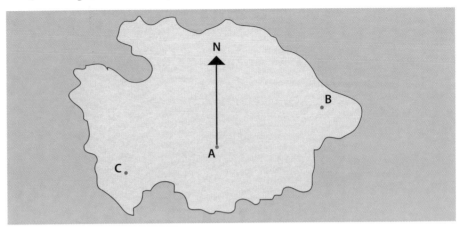

Using only a ruler and a protractor write down the location of:

(a) B from A   (b) C from A.

4 On a copy of this map, draw a north line from A parallel to the
one shown. 1 cm represents 1 km.

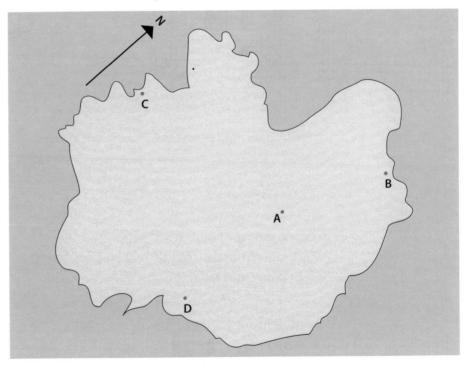

Write down the location of:

(a) B from A   (b) C from A   (c) D from A.

Bearings

A bearing is an angle measured clockwise from north. It tells you the direction to face.

Bearings are written using three digits, even for angles less than 100°. Originally, when bearings were given over the radio, three digits were used so that there would be no confusion.

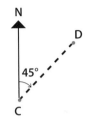

Example

045° means an angle of 45° clockwise from north.
You say 'the bearing of D from C is 045°'.

Exercise 9

1 What is the bearing of:

(a) B from A?

(b) D from C?

(c) F from E?

(d) H from G?

2 Which places are on these bearings from home?

(a) 090°

(b) 135°

(c) 290°

(d) 070°

(e) 200°

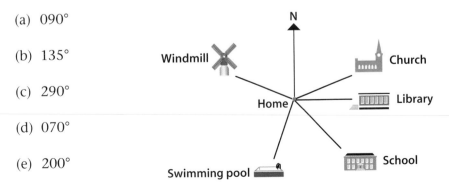

3 Which places are on these bearings from the lighthouse?

(a) 180°

(b) 097°

(c) 242°

(d) 033°

(e) 352°

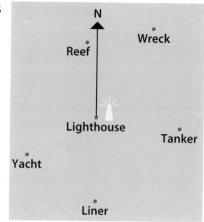

4 On this diagram 1 cm represents 1 km.

(a) How far is B from A?

(b) What is the bearing of B from A?

5 This map shows the route taken by a ship round an island. It starts and finishes at A.

(a) Use tracing paper to copy the points A, B and C and the north line. Draw a north line at each point.

(b) Write down the distance the ship sails and its bearing, for each stage of the journey round the island.

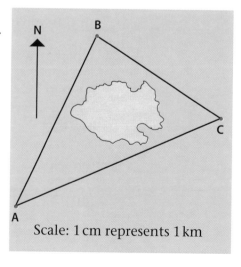

Scale: 1 cm represents 1 km

6 This map shows the places visited by a helicopter. It starts and finishes at A.

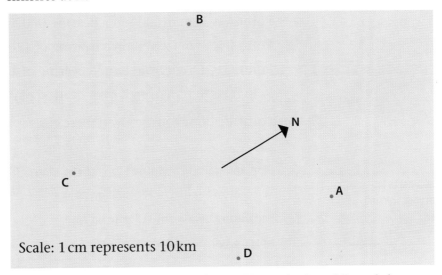

Scale: 1 cm represents 10 km

(a) Use tracing paper to copy the points A, B, C and D and the north line. Draw a north line at each point.

(b) Write down the bearing and distance the helicopter flies on each stage of the journey.

7 In an orienteering race, you have to visit all the points shown on this map.

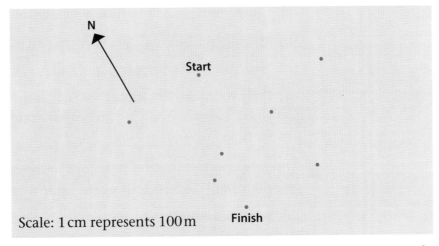

Scale: 1 cm represents 100 m   Finish

(a) Write down the order in which you would visit the points and the bearing of each point to the next.

(b) How far would you run?

(c) Discuss your answer with a partner.

8 Mark a point on a piece of plain paper and label it K.
Draw a north line from the point K and mark the following points.

Point A is 5 cm from K on a bearing of 070°.

Point B is 7 cm from K on a bearing of 120°.

Point C is 4.5 cm from K on a bearing of 180°.

Point D is 5.5 cm from K on a bearing of 200°.

9 On a treasure hunt you are given these clues.

> Draw a north line from your starting point.

> From the starting point, go 50 m on a bearing of 075°.
>
> Turn onto a bearing of 170° and go 70 m.
>
> Turn onto a bearing of 315° and go 30 m.
>
> Now go 100 m on a bearing of 225°.

(a) Start near the centre of a piece of plain paper.

(b) Using 1 cm to represent 1 m, draw the route you would follow.

(c) What is the bearing of the start from the point you have reached?

10 Set your own orienteering exercise.

(a) Draw a route which starts and finishes at the same point.

(b) Measure the bearing and distance from each point to the next.

(c) Write these on a piece of paper and pass it to a partner to draw.

(d) Does your partner's route look the same as yours? If not check who has gone wrong. If you cannot decide ask your teacher for help.

11 This diagram shows the bearings for a route followed by a helicopter. The pilot wants to return along the same route.

(a) What bearings should be used?

(b) Explain how you reached your answers.

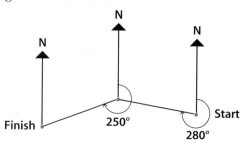

Review Exercise

1 (a) Write down the size of the angles marked *a*, *b*, *c* and *d*.

(b) Explain how you worked out your answers.

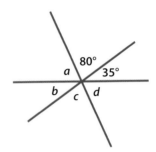

2 (a) Write down the size of the angles marked *a* to *f*.

(b) Explain how you worked out your answers.

> Remember: arrows show parallel lines.

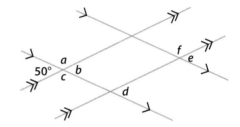

3 Give the bearing of each of the points of the compass shown.

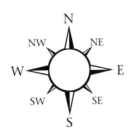

4 Using 1 cm to represent 1 km, draw this route:

6 km on a bearing of 035°, then

8 km on a bearing of 125°, then

10 km on a bearing of 268°.

5 (a) Explain how you can work out the angles inside a regular nine-sided polygon (a nonagon).

(b) Draw a regular nonagon with each side 3 cm long.

(c) Use LOGO to draw a regular nonagon.

(d) Write down the instructions you used.

Working with decimals

→ the importance of the position of a digit in whole numbers and decimal numbers
→ how to add and subtract decimal numbers without a calculator
→ how to multiply and divide whole numbers and decimal numbers by 10, 100 and 1000 without a calculator
→ how to use a calculator to solve a range of problems involving decimals, selecting an appropriate degree of accuracy

Starting points

Before starting this chapter you will need to know:

• about place value in whole numbers

• how to add and subtract whole numbers.

Exercise 1

1 Say these numbers to yourself and then write them down in words.
(a) 125   (b) 342   (c) 45   (d) 1351

2 In the 3-digit number 724:
the digit 7 stands for 7 **hundred**,
the digit 2 stands for 2 **tens** and
the digit 4 stands for 4 **units**.

Write down what the 3, the 5 and the 1 stand for in the number 351.

3 A pupil was asked to put the number 451 under these column headings:

thousands	hundreds	tens	units

This is what he did:

thousands	hundreds	tens	units
4	5	1	

Explain why he was wrong.

4 You are given these four number cards.

| **4** | **3** | **7** | **0** |

Do not use any number more than once.

(a) Write down as many 2-digit numbers as you can make.

(b) Write down as many 3-digit numbers as you can make.

(c) Write down as many 4-digit numbers as you can make.

(d) Arrange all the numbers you have made in parts (a), (b) and (c) in order of size, the smallest first.

5 Show how to add the numbers 437 and 39.

6 Show how to subtract 79 from 203.

> Check your answer with a calculator.

7 Find the difference between

(a) 436 and 674 (b) 326 and 519

(c) 436 and 374 (d) 519 and 674

> Subtract the smaller number from the larger number to find their difference.

8 Do these calculations.
Show your method clearly.

(a) 132 + 194 (b) 148 + 47

(c) 29 + 180 (d) 138 – 25

(e) 438 – 176 (f) 445 – 188

(g) 1000 – 632 (h) 303 – 171

9 These cards show the digits 0 to 9.

| **0** | **1** | **2** | **3** | **4** | **5** | **6** | **7** | **8** | **9** |

Select five different cards.
Use each card once only.
Find the two numbers which give the smallest difference.

Multiplication of whole numbers by 10, 100 and 1000

1 Use your knowledge of the 10 times table to calculate these.

(a) 2×10 　　 (b) 4×10 　　 (c) 10×10 　　 (d) 7×10

2 For a school concert chairs are put out in rows of 10. How many chairs will be needed for:

(a) 5 rows? 　 (b) 8 rows? 　 (c) 9 rows?

3 How many pence are there in:

(a) £1? 　　 (b) £3? 　　 (c) £5? 　　 (d) £7?

4 How many centimetres are there in:

(a) 1 m? 　　 (b) 6 m? 　　 (c) 3 m? 　　 (d) 8 m?

5 In a sports arena, the seats are arranged in rows of 100. How many seats will be needed for:

(a) 2 rows? 　 (b) 4 rows? 　 (c) 8 rows? 　 (d) 9 rows?

6 How many metres are there in:

(a) 1 km? 　 (b) 4 km? 　 (c) 8 km? 　 (d) 9 km?

7 How many grams are there in:

(a) 1 kg? 　 (b) 5 kg? 　 (c) 7 kg? 　 (d) 6 kg?

8 (a) What is special about the answer when you multiply a whole number by 10?

(b) What is special about the answer when you multiply a whole number by 100?

(c) What is special about the answer when you multiply a whole number by 1000?

Quick ways of multiplying

In Exercise 2 you discovered that there are quick ways of finding the answer when you multiply a single-digit number by 10, 100 and 1000. Now look at what happens when you start with larger numbers.

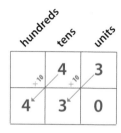

43 × 10 = 430

Key fact

The effect of multiplying by 10 moves all digits one place to the left.

Multiplying by 100 is the same as multiplying by 10, and then multiplying by 10 again.

43 × 100 = 4300

Key fact

The effect of multiplying by 100 moves all digits two places to the left.

Multiplying by 1000 is the same as multiplying by 10 – three times!

43 × 1000 = 43000

Key fact

The effect of multiplying by 1000 moves all digits three places to the left.

This number written in words is forty-three thousand.

Exercise 3

1 Copy and complete these diagrams.

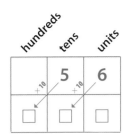

(a) **56 × 10** = _____

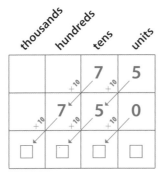

(b) **75 × 100** = _____

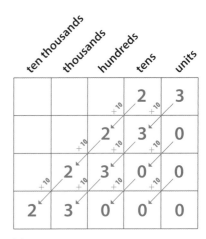

(c) **23 × 1000** = _____

2 Copy and complete these calculations.

(a) 61 × 10

(b) 121 × 10

(c) 10 × 565

(d) 2356 × 10

(e) 49 × 100

(f) 163 × 100

(g) 100 × 24

(h) 1257 × 100

(i) 54 × 1000

(j) 372 × 1000

(k) 1000 × 16

(l) 1000 × 6125

3 For these calculations write your answers in words.

(a) 10 × 35

(b) 42 × 100

(c) 16 × 10

(d) 12 × 1000

(e) 65 × 100

(f) 121 × 10

(g) 36 × 100

(h) 1000 × 43

Can you write any answers more than one way?

Dividing whole numbers by 10, 100 and 1000

Key fact

The effect of dividing by 100 moves the digits two places to the right.

The effect of dividing by 10 moves the digits one place to the right.

Dividing by 100 is the same as dividing by 10 – twice.

Dividing by 1000 is the same as dividing by 10 – three times.

Key fact

The effect of dividing by 1000 moves the digits three places to the right.

Exercise 4

1 Copy and complete these calculations.

(a) $40 \div 10$ (b) $60 \div 10$

(c) $50 \div 10$ (d) $400 \div 10$

(e) $800 \div 10$ (f) $5000 \div 10$

(g) $600 \div 100$ (h) $800 \div 100$

(i) $4000 \div 100$ (j) $9000 \div 1000$

(k) $24\,000 \div 1000$ (l) $58\,000 \div 1000$

2 How many pounds are the same as:

(a) 400 pence?   (b) 1200 pence?   (c) 2000 pence?

3 How many metres are the same as:

(a) 100 cm?   (b) 500 cm?   (c) 1800 cm?

4 How many kilograms are the same as:

(a) 1000 g?   (b) 8000 g?   (c) 80 000 g?

5 (a) What is special about the answer when you divide a whole number which ends in more than one zero, by 10?

(b) What is special about the answer when you divide a whole number which ends in more than two zeros, by 100?

(c) What is special about the answer when you divide a whole number which ends in more than three zeros, by 1000?

Assignment 1   **Pascal's triangle**

Describe how each row in this triangle is built up.

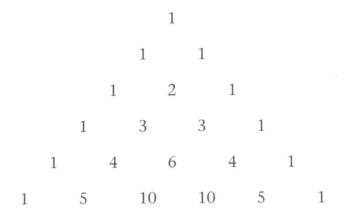

```
                    1
                1       1
            1       2       1
        1       3       3       1
    1       4       6       4       1
1       5       10      10      5       1
```

The seventh row of the triangle contains only one number which can be divided exactly by 10.

- Copy the triangle and add the next row.
  Which number in that row can be divided exactly by 10?
  Which row is the next to contain exactly one number that can be divided by 10?

When you multiply the numbers in the sixth row together the answer is 2500, which can be divided exactly by 100.

- Add some more rows to the triangle until you have 12 rows altogether. If you were to multiply the numbers in each row together, which is the first row to give an answer which can be divided exactly by 1000?

> You should not need to work out the answer for every row, to find out!

When the total of all the numbers in the ninth row, and all the numbers in the eleventh row are added together you should get 1280 which can be divided by 10.

- Find two other rows such that when you add the totals of the numbers in each row you obtain a number which can be divided by 10.

Using decimals in measurement

5.6 cm is the same as $5\frac{6}{10}$ cm.

The 6 represents 6 **tenths** of a centimetre.

1.05 m is the same as $1\frac{5}{100}$ m.

The 5 represents 5 **hundredths** of a metre.

The line AB shown here measures 4.3 cm.

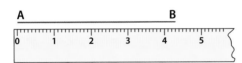

There are different ways of recording the measurement of the length of a line. For example: 4.3 cm is the same as 4 cm 3 mm and 43 mm.

Exercise 5

1 Copy and complete these statements.

(a) In the measurement 25.4 cm:

the 4 represents 4 _____ of a centimetre.

(b) In the measurement 6.13 m: the 6 represents 6 metres

the 1 represents 1 _____ of a metre

the 3 represents 3 _____ of a metre.

(c) In the measurement 1.52 m: the 1 represents 1 metre

the 5 represents 5 _____ of a metre

the 2 represents 2 _____ of a metre.

2 Measure this red line in centimetres and write down your answer.

Write your answer in as many ways as you can.

3 Write these measurements in centimetres.

(a) 3 m   (b) 1.04 m   (c) 1.52 m   (d) 5.4 m

Using place value

Numbers to two decimal places

From your work on measurement you have seen that the digits after the decimal point in a number represent a fraction of the number.

In 1.7, the 7 represents 7 **tenths**.

In 2.05, the 5 represents 5 **hundredths**.

This red line measures 5.2 cm to the nearest tenth of a centimetre.

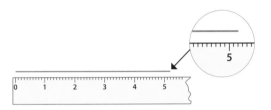

It is difficult to measure the line more accurately than this with an ordinary ruler.

The length of the line given as 5.2 cm is only accurate to one decimal place.

The height of this person is estimated to be 1.72 m.

Accuracy is important!

This estimate is in metres and is correct to two decimal places.

Problems involving money in pounds and pence are usually worked out correct to two decimal places.

224 pence = £2.24

Exercise 6

1 Measure these lines and write your answer in centimetres, correct to one decimal place.

(a) ⸻

(b) ⸻

(c) ⸻

(d) ⸻

2 Measure your handspan and give the answer in centimetres correct to one decimal place.

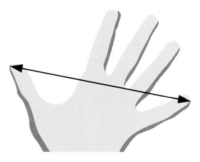

3 Estimate the height of your teacher:

(a) in centimetres to the nearest centimetre

(b) in metres to two decimal places.

4 Some pupils carry out some measuring in the school playground. They write down the results like this.

The distance from the main gate to the bicycle shed is 14 m.

The length of the wooden bench is 1.55 m.

The height of the netball post is 3.4 m.

The height of the fence is 2.25 m.

Copy down the sentences. Next to each one, write down whether you think the pupils had estimated to the nearest whole number of metres, to one decimal place, or to two decimal places.

5 The pupils tell their teacher that they estimate the height of the school building to be 15.01 m.

(a) Explain why it is not appropriate to estimate to this degree of accuracy in this case.

(b) Give a more sensible estimate for the height of the building.

6 (a) Estimate the length and height of some objects in your school playground, using an appropriate degree of accuracy.

(b) In each case, state whether your estimate is to the nearest whole number, to one decimal place or to two decimal places.

7 Look at the giraffe in this picture.

(a) Copy this sentence and complete it.

An estimate of the giraffe's height, to the nearest metre, is ___ metres .

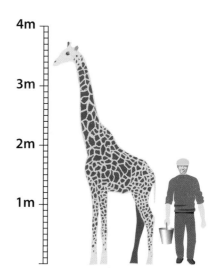

To the nearest tenth of a metre the giraffe is about 3.7 metres tall. This is correct to one decimal place.

(b) Copy this sentence and complete it.

An estimate of the giraffe's height in metres, correct to two decimal places, is ___ metres.

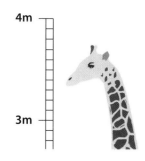

(c) Copy these sentences and complete them.

An estimate of the zoo keeper's height, to the nearest metre, is ___ metres.

An estimate of the zoo keeper's height, in metres to one decimal place, is about ___ metres.

An estimate of the zoo keeper's height, in metres correct to two decimal places, is about ___ metres.

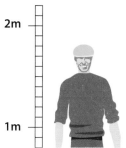

8 Write these amounts in pounds, using numbers with two decimal places.

(a) 500 pence   (b) 220 pence

(c) 452 pence   (d) 48 pence

(e) 908 pence   (f) 8 pence

(g) 350 pence   (h) 1245 pence

> Check that you have two decimal places in each of your answers.

Assignment 2   Choosing coins

You have these nine coins.

• Choosing only coins from this selection, how would you make £2.25, £2.05, £2.01, £2.07, £1.03 and £1.22?

• Write down all the sums of money it is possible to make with these coins between £1.00 and £1.50 inclusive.

Write each one as a decimal number using two places of decimals, e.g. £1.01, £1.02, etc.

Adding and subtracting decimal numbers

Exercise 7

1 Two children were saving to buy a new football.
One had saved £2 and the other had saved £1.20.

They added the amounts together and decided they had £1.22
towards the cost of the football.

(a) Explain why they were wrong.

It would have been better if the children
had written out the amounts and added
them like this:

	2	.	0	0
	1	.	2	0

> **Make sure you have a decimal point in your answer in the correct place.**

(b) Copy this sum and complete it.

> **Key fact**
> It is important to keep the decimal points underneath each other.

2 On a school trip, packed lunches are provided.

Each lunch consists of:
    a carton of juice costing 45p,
    a packet of sandwiches costing £1.24,
    a packet of crisps costing 25p and
    a cake costing 38p.

> **Check your answer with a calculator.**

Find the value of the packed lunch in *pounds*.

3 Here is a picture of a clown on stilts.

The clown is 1.72 m tall.

The stilts make the clown 0.85 m taller.

Write down an addition sum to show how tall
the clown becomes when he is on stilts.

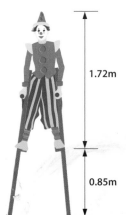

1.72m

0.85m

4 Copy the sum below and complete it to find the perimeter of this rectangle.

> The perimeter of a shape is the distance around its edge.

	units	tenths
	6 .	0
	4 .	3
	6 .	0
+	4 .	3

4.3m

6m

> 6 is written as 6.0 to keep digits with same value in line.

> Check your answer with a calculator.

5 Copy the addition below and complete it to find the perimeter of this rectangle.

8.1m

12.35m

	tens	units	tenths	100ths
	1	2 .	3	5
		8 .	1	0
	1	2 .	3	5
+		8 .	1	0

> Notice that 8.1 is written as 8.10. The addition is to two places of decimals.

6 Do these additions. Show your working.

(a) $2.3 + 8$

(b) $6.9 + 4$

(c) $12 + 3.65$

(d) $4.65 + 3.2$

(e) $3.62 + 1.8 + 0.6$

(f) $13.5 + 4.8 + 9$

> Check your answers with a calculator.

7 A child had saved £3.80 towards the cost of a new sweatshirt. The sweatshirt cost £17.50.

Copy this subtraction and complete it to show how much money the child still has to save.

	1	7 .	5	0
−		3 .	8	0

8 A box of chocolates cost £2.67.
Suppose you pay with a
£5 note.
Copy this subtraction and
complete it to show how
much change you would receive.

	5 .	0	0
−	2 .	6	7

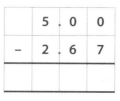

Write £5 as £5.00 in order to subtract using two places of decimals.

Write 2.3 as 2.30 in order to subtract using two places of decimals.

9 I want to make a shelf 1.75 m long.
I have a piece of wood 2.3 m long.

Copy this subtraction and complete it to work
out how much wood I will have to cut off
before making the shelf.

	units	tenths	100ths
	2 .	3	0
−	1 .	7	5

10 Show how you work out each of these subtractions.

Check your answers
with a calculator.

(a) 2.74 − 1.32 (b) 48.65 − 24.73 (c) 28.3 − 9.5

(d) 15 − 6.3 (e) 4.3 − 2.64 (f) 142.6 − 13.8

(g) 52.71 − 8.8 (h) 171.35 − 14.2 (i) 75.6 − 32.95

11 (a) Using three of these cards, make the largest possible decimal
number less than 10.

(b) Using four of these cards, make the largest possible decimal
number less than 100.

(c) Find the difference between your answers to (a) and (b).

Assignment 3   **Record breakers!**

- Use the *Guiness Book of Records* to find out the name and height
  (in metres) of the tallest person ever and the shortest person ever.

- Find the difference between their heights and yours (or a friend's).

- Find out more information involving measurements.

  Carry out some subtractions to make comparisons.

- Make a poster to show your findings!

Multiplying decimal numbers by 10, 100 and 1000

Look at your ruler to check that 8.6 cm is the same as 86 mm.

8.6 cm equals 86 mm because there are 10 millimetres in every centimetre. So

$8.6 \times 10 = 86$

Look at a metre ruler to check 0.86 m equals 86 cm. 0.86 m equals 86 cm because there are 100 centimetres in every metre. So

$0.86 \times 100 = 86$

You have seen that the effect of multiplying whole numbers by 10, 100 and 1000 results in digits moving to the left. This is also true when decimal numbers are multiplied by 10, 100 and 1000.

By writing appropriate column headings, you can see clearly what happens:

8.6 = 8 **units** and 6 **tenths**.

When you multiply by 10:

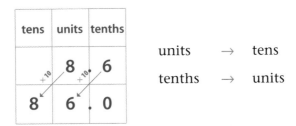

So $8.6 \times 10 = 86.0 = 86$

What happens if you multiply by 100?

To multiply by 100, you multiply by 10 and then by 10 again.

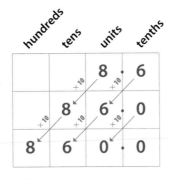

860.0 is written more simply as 860.

So $8.6 \times 100 = 860.0 = 860$

Exercise 8

1 Copy and complete these.

(a)

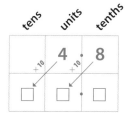

4.8 × 10 = _____

(b)

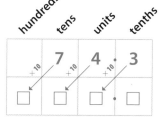

74.3 × 10 = _____

(c)

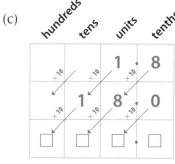

1.8 × 10 = _____

1.8 × 100 = _____

(d)

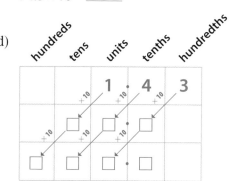

1.43 × 10 = _____

1.43 × 100 = _____

2 Copy and complete the diagrams to find the values of 2.3 × 1000 and 1.42 × 1000.

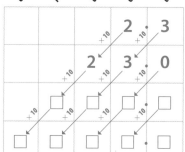

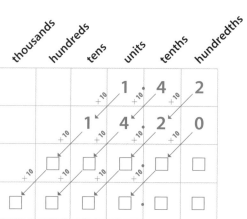

2.3 × 10 = _____

2.3 × 100 = _____

2.3 × 1000 = _____

1.42 × 10 = _____

1.42 × 100 = _____

1.42 × 1000 = _____

3 Now copy and complete these multiplications without drawing columns.

(a) 1.8×10

(b) 19.6×10

(c) 0.6×10

(d) 0.05×10

(e) 2.51×100

(f) 7.9×100

(g) 18.2×100

(h) 81.08×100

(i) 9.8×1000

(j) 0.3×1000

(k) 12.6×1000

(l) 6.85×1000

(m) 12.91×1000

4 Copy these and complete them.

(a) $7.2 \, \text{cm}$ is the same as ____ mm. $7.2 \times 10 =$ ____

(b) $35.4 \, \text{cm}$ is the same as ____ mm. $35.4 \times 10 =$ ____

(c) $0.54 \, \text{m}$ is the same as ____ cm. $0.54 \times 100 =$ ____

(d) $1.65 \, \text{m}$ is the same as ____ cm. $1.65 \times 100 =$ ____

(e) $1.5 \, \text{km}$ is the same as ____ m. $1.5 \times 1000 =$ ____

5 Multiply by 10, 100 or 1000, to change

(a) $4.2 \, \text{cm}$ to mm   (b) $8.9 \, \text{m}$ to cm   (c) $0.8 \, \text{m}$ to cm

(d) $4.1 \, \text{km}$ to m   (e) $0.5 \, \text{cm}$ to mm   (f) $12.25 \, \text{m}$ to cm

6 Copy and complete this diagram to join the metric measurements which are equivalent. Two have been done already.

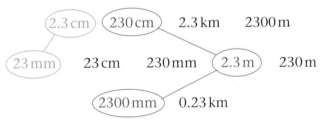

7 (a) Choose any number between 4 and 5. Multiply it by 10.

(b) Choose any number between 7 and 8. Multiply it by 10.

(c) Add your answers to (a) and (b).

(d) Repeat (a), (b) and (c) a few more times.

All possible answers lie between two certain whole numbers. What are they?

Dividing decimal numbers by 10, 100 and 1000

10 mm = 1 cm

To change millimetres into centimetres, you must divide by 10.

$$8\,\text{mm} = 8 \div 10\,\text{cm} = \frac{8}{10}\,\text{cm} = 0.8\,\text{cm}$$

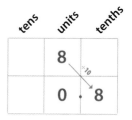

100 cm = 1 m

To change centimetres into metres, you must divide by 100.

$$8\,\text{cm} = 8 \div 100\,\text{m}$$

$$= \frac{8}{100}\,\text{m}$$

$$= 0.08\,\text{m}$$

1000 m = 1 km

To change metres into kilometres, you must divide by 1000.

$$8\,\text{m} = 8 \div 1000\,\text{km}$$

$$= \frac{8}{1000}\,\text{km}$$

$$= 0.008\,\text{km}$$

Dividing a whole number by 10, 100 or 1000 can lead to a decimal answer. Digits moving to the right sometimes fall under the headings tenths, etc.

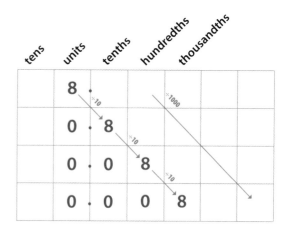

Decimal numbers are divided by 10, 100 and 1000 in the same way:

$$32.3 \div 10 = 3.23 \qquad\qquad 21.3 \div 100 = 0.213$$

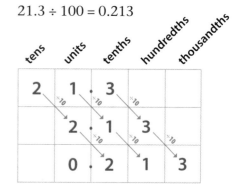

Exercise 9

1 Copy and complete these.

(a)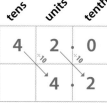

42 ÷ 10 =

(b)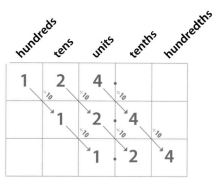

124 ÷ 10 = _____
124 ÷ 100 = _____

(c)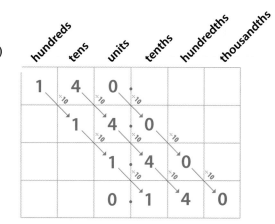

140 ÷ 10 = _____
140 ÷ 100 = _____
140 ÷ 1000 = _____

2 Copy and complete these calculations without drawing columns.

(a) 4.2 ÷ 10   (b) 21.3 ÷ 10   (c) 43 ÷ 10

(d) 0.5 ÷ 10   (e) 0.08 ÷ 10   (f) 16.9 ÷ 100

(g) 8.4 ÷ 100   (h) 6 ÷ 100   (i) 843.1 ÷ 100

(j) 215 ÷ 1000   (k) 82 ÷ 1000   (l) 9 ÷ 1000

3 Convert these.

(a) 59 mm to cm   (b) 17 cm to m   (c) 6 cm to m

(d) 12 cm to m   (e) 4 m to km   (f) 85 m to km

(g) 144 g to kg   (h) 2 g to kg   (i) 525 ml to litres

Assignment 4　**Dice game**

You need an ordinary six-sided dice and a blank dice.

- Label the sides of the blank dice:

    ×10　÷10　×100　÷100　×1000　÷1000

- Throw the two dice together.
  Reading the top faces, write down a multiplication or division and
  its answer, e.g. 6 ÷ 10 = 0.6. Repeat this 20 times.

- Which division leads to the smallest possible answer?

- Which multiplication leads to the largest possible answer?

- How many different possible answers are there?

Solving problems involving decimals

For each problem in the next exercise decide which operation you need
to carry out to solve it: addition, subtraction, multiplication or division?

Find the answer to each problem, without using a calculator, and show
your working.

Exercise 10

1 A bar of chocolate costs 27 pence. How much will 10 bars cost?

2 450 kg of potatoes are to be put into 10 kg bags. How many bags are
needed?

3 Cars are parked in rows of 10. If there are 80 cars, how many rows
will there be?

4 900 trees are planted in rows of 100. How many rows of trees will
there be?

5 A woman buys her lunch which costs £1.72 and pays with a £5 note.
How much change should she receive?

6 A man buys 1.2 kg of apples, 0.5 kg of bananas and 0.8 kg of pears.
What is the total weight of fruit?

7 Make up some more problems of your own that can be solved without
a calculator. Write each one down and show how to find the answer.

Using a calculator to solve problems

Adding several numbers

Sometimes it is quicker to use a calculator.

Example

I buy a packet of sandwiches for £1.49, a cake at 85p, a packet of crisps at 35p, a drink for 45p and a carrier bag for 6p.

To find the total amount spent, these amounts must be added.

£		p	
1	.	4	9
0	.	8	5
0	.	3	5
0	.	4	5
0	.	0	6
3	.	2	0

> **Check this answer using a calculator.**

The answer on the calculator is 3.2.

This should be written as £3.20.

Key fact

The area of a rectangle is found by multiplying the length by the width.

Finding areas of rectangles

This rectangle is made up of six rows of $2\frac{1}{2}$ centimetre squares.

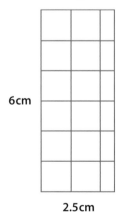

6cm

2.5cm

Its area $= 6\,\text{cm} \times 2\frac{1}{2}\,\text{cm}$

$= 6\,\text{cm} \times 2.5\,\text{cm}$

$= 15$ square centimetres

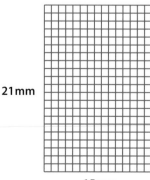

21mm

15mm

In this rectangle there are 21 rows of 15 millimetre squares.

The area of the rectangle is
$21\,\text{mm} \times 15\,\text{mm} = 315$ square millimetres.

Problems involving money

Example

I buy 3.2 m of fabric at £5.95 per metre.

I estimate the cost of fabric in this way:

> **Using a calculator**
> 3.2 × £5.95 =
> £19.04

3.2 m is a bit more than 3 m
£5.95 is just less than £6
3 m at £6 per metre is £18.

Rounding the decimal numbers helped me to see that a multiplication was needed and to work out an estimate of the answer.

Four of us are going to share the cost of the fabric.

£19.04 is just less than £20.

I can estimate roughly how much we will each have to pay.

> **Using a calculator**
> £19.04 ÷ 4
> = £4.76

My estimate is: £20 ÷ 4 = £5.

In the next exercise, show clearly whether you have used addition, subtraction, multiplication or division.

Exercise 11

> Use a calculator to help you with these questions.

1 (a) Calculate the areas of these rectangles in square millimetres.

(b) Write down the length and width of each rectangle in centimetres and calculate the area of each one in square centimetres.

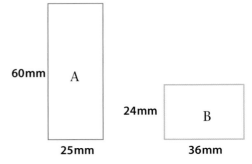

2 A piece of wood 14.8 m long is to be cut into five equal pieces.

(a) By rounding, estimate roughly how long each piece of wood will be.

(b) Find the exact length of each piece of wood.

In Questions 3 and 4, first estimate by rounding.

3 A shopkeeper sells chairs at £45.25 each. In one day he sells 29 chairs. Calculate how much money he takes that day.

4 A rectangular room measures 4.2 m by 5.4 m.

  (a) What is the perimeter of the room in metres?

  (b) What is the area of the room in square metres?

  (c) Carpet costs £12 per square metre.
        Calculate the cost of carpet for the room.

5 One kilogram in weight is approximately the same as 2.2 pounds.

  (a) What will an 11-pound bag of potatoes weigh, in kilograms?

  (b) What is the weight of a 25-kg sack of potatoes, in pounds?

6 Books weighing 1.24 kg each are packed into crates which weigh 0.5 kg. Each crate can hold 25 books.

  (a) Calculate the total weight of one full crate.

  (b) Calculate the weight of 50 full crates.

Assignment 5 — Area of 40

- Find at least eight rectangles with an area of 40 square centimetres.

- Calculate the perimeter of each of your rectangles.

Selecting an appropriate degree of accuracy

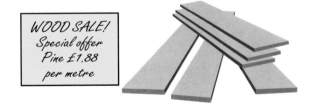

WOOD SALE!
Special offer
Pine £1.88
per metre

The total cost of 1.6 m of this wood is £1.88 × 1.6 = £3.008

This is the same as 300.8 pence.

.8 pence is more than $\frac{1}{2}$p

We have no coin for .8 pence so it is sensible to round 300.8p to 301p, and to charge 301p or £3.01 for 1.6 m of wood.

Exercise 12

1 Round these amounts to the nearest penny.

(a) 4.3p   (b) 25.8p   (c) 1.356p   (d) 2.921p

2 Find the cost of 1.2 kg of apples at £1.78 per kg.

3 2.8 m of fabric is needed to make a dress. The fabric costs £4.99 per metre. How much will the fabric cost?

4 Seven friends share the cost of a take-away pizza, costing £8.95. Each person decided to pay £1.28.

(a) Explain why this is fair.

(b) Does the shop selling the pizza gain by this arrangement?

5 A car travels 330 miles on 25 litres of petrol.

(a) How far does the car travel on 1 litre of petrol?

(b) If petrol costs 53.4p per litre, how much does petrol cost for the whole journey?

> Give the answers to the nearest penny.

Review Exercise

1 Measure these lines and write your answers in centimetres, correct to one decimal place.

(a) ——————————————   (b) —————————

2 Estimate the height of your desk, in metres, correct to two decimal places.

> Check by measuring.

3 Show how to work out each of the following additions and subtractions.

(a) $3.7 + 9$

(b) $12.5 - 4.6$

(c) $345.8 - 135$

(d) $13 + 8.6$

(e) $123.78 + 13.625$

(f) $200.4 - 34.55$

> Check your answers with a calculator.

4 Find the perimeter and area of a rectangular pond measuring 2.5 m by 0.75 m.

5 Copy and complete these calculations.

(a) 7×10

(b) 45×100

(c) $230 \div 10$

(d) 65×1000

(e) $7800 \div 100$

(f) $46 \div 10$

(g) $1300 \div 100$

(h) $690 \div 10$

(i) 3×1000

6 Copy and complete these calculations.

(a) 5.6×10

(b) $12.3 \div 10$

(c) $35.65 \div 10$

(d) 0.54×10

(e) 3.6×100

(f) $4.5 \div 10$

(g) 12.5×1000

(h) $78.1 \div 100$

(i) $0.6 \div 100$

7 A recipe for cheese scones requires 75 g of cheese.

(a) Write 75 g in kilograms.

(b) If cheese costs £3.80 per kg, find the cost of the cheese needed to make the scones. Round your answer to the nearest penny.

8 A family of four share the cost of a take-away meal that cost £17.84.

(a) By rounding, estimate the cost per person.

(b) Use a calculator to find the exact cost per person.

9 If petrol costs 55.3p per litre, find the cost, in pounds, of 36.5 litres of petrol. Round your answer to two decimal places.

10 Two pupils are helping to run a school shop.
They can buy rulers for 14p each, pens for £1.34 per box of 20 and rubbers for £4.99 per box of 100.

(a) How much will it cost them to buy 50 rulers, two boxes of pens and one box of rubbers?

(b) They do not set out to make any profit, but must charge enough to cover their costs. What would be a fair price to charge for:

(i) the pens?   (ii) the rubbers?

(c) A pupil has £1.50 to spend in the shop. He buys a ruler and a rubber and as many pens as possible with the money he has left.

(i) How many pens can he buy?
(ii) How much money does he have left?

Assignment 6   Feeding an elephant!

Here is a typical daily menu for an elephant in a zoo.

Morning

2.00 kg stud pellets
1.50 kg dry biscuits
6.20 kg apples
3.00 kg carrots
2.15 kg bananas
0.20 kg dates
1.70 kg potatoes
0.20 kg oranges
5.00 kg hay

11.00 am

4.00 kg hay

12.00 noon

1.50 kg apples
2.60 kg carrots
0.50 kg oranges
0.20 kg dates
0.90 kg potatoes
0.25 kg bananas
1.50 kg dry biscuits
6.00 kg hay

Evening

1.50 kg dry biscuits
2.00 kg stud cubes
2.15 kg apples
4.00 kg carrots
1.00 kg potatoes
0.25 kg cabbage
0.20 kg dates
8.00 kg hay
0.80 kg brown bread
0.10 kg oranges

- Find the total weight of each fruit eaten in a day on this diet.

- Find out the cost per kilogram of each fruit and estimate the amount it costs to feed the elephant this quantity of fruit for a week. How much would it cost to feed the elephant for a year?

```
        B.X.T
  73-78 ARTHUR AVENUE
    WESTBURY PARK

22-12-95          #1

DAIRY           0.99
DAIRY           0.99
OFF LC          2.99
OFF LC          2.99
MEAT            1.99
GROCERY         0.99
MEAT            4.99
MEAT            2.85
F & VEG         1.25
F & VEG         1.25
F & VEG         1.25
GROCERY         0.75
DAIRY           0.79
F & VEG         0.71
GROCERY         1.49
GROCERY         1.57
GROCERY         1.99
TOTAL          29.83

ITEM  17
CLERK 4 7339 09:42TM
```

Assignment 7   Shopping!

- Collect some supermarket receipts which show individual food items and their cost. Use receipts which show a large number of items.

- Split the items on each receipt into different food categories, e.g. fruit and vegetables, dairy products, meat, etc.
  Find the amount spent on food in each category.

- If possible, visit the local supermarket and look for special offers where if you buy several of one product it is cheaper than buying one of them.
  List the products and the price per item, with and without the offer. How much is saved per item?

Sequences and graphs

In this chapter you will learn:

→ **how to relate position to terms in sequences**
→ **how to find the *n*th term of a sequence**
→ **how to produce mappings**
→ **how to plot linear graphs**

Starting points

Before starting this chapter you will need to know how to:

* continue patterns

* continue simple number sequences

* generate sequences

* express simple sequences in words.

Exercise 1

1 Copy and continue these sequences.

(a) 2, 4, 6, 8, __ , __ , __

(b) 5, 10, 15, 20, __ , __ , __

(c) 1, 5, 9, 13, __ , __ , __

(d) 1, 2, 4, 8, __ , __ , __

(e) 1, 3, 6, 10, __ , __ , __

(f) 15, 13, 11, 9, __ , __ , __,

(g) 1, 1, 2, 3, __ , __ , __

Describe, in your own words, how you worked out the next three terms.

2 In each of these sequences, the first three terms have been given.
Copy each sequence and continue it for three more terms.

(a)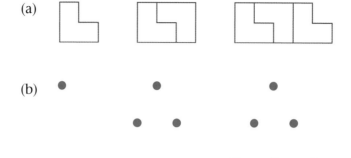

(b)

(c)

(d)

(e)

3 Write down the first five terms in each of the sequences described
in these statements.

(a) Start with 3 and add on 2 each time.

(b) Start with 1 and add on 3 each time.

(c) Start with 20 and subtract 2 each time.

(d) Start with 1 and double the result each time.

(e) Start with 2 and add on 3 each time.

(f) Start with 10 and subtract 1 each time.

(g) Start with 48 and halve the number each time.

Searching for a pattern

A line of cards with numbers written on them are laid face down.

When the first 4 cards are turned over, a pattern connecting the numbers can be seen. This pattern will allow you to predict the next numbers.

> The pattern connecting the terms is called the difference.

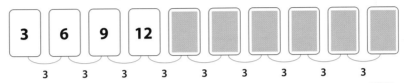

| 3 | 6 | 9 | 12 |
3   3   3   3   3   3   3   3   3

> Cards in a sequence are called terms.

The terms in the sequence are shown in this table. Notice that the difference is the same every time.

> *n* stands for any term

Term	1	2	3	4	5	6	7	n
Sequence	3	6	9	12	15	18	21	$3n$

3   3   3   3   3   3

> The difference between each pair of consecutive terms is 3

> This value is found by multiplying the term by the difference

To calculate any term in this example the rule is:

$3 \times$ the term

Each term is 3 times the term number.
This is usually written as

$n \rightarrow 3n$

or $s = 3n$

> *s* is shorthand for sequence.

So the 9th term is $3 \times 9 = 27$.

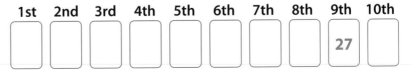

1st   2nd   3rd   4th   5th   6th   7th   8th   9th   10th

| | | | | | | | | 27 | |

Using this method you can find the 1000th term

$3 \times 1000 = 3000$

Exercise 2

1 Copy and complete the following tables.

For each one write a general rule in the form $s = $.

(a)

Term (n)	1	2	3	4	5	6	7	8	n
Sequence (s)	2	4	6	8					

(b)

Term (n)	1	2	3	4	5	6	7	8	n
Sequence (s)	6	12	18	24					

(c)

Term (n)	1	2	3	4	5	6	7	8	n
Sequence (s)	4	8			20				

(d)

Term (n)	1	2	3	4	5	6	7	8	n
Sequence (s)	10	20				60			

(e)

Term (n)	1	2	3	4	5	6	7	8	n
Sequence (s)		5		10		15		20	

More complex patterns

The pattern of some sequences often involves more than one operation.

Example

Term (n)	1	2	3	4	n
Sequence (s)	3	5	7	9	

$$\qquad 2 \qquad 2 \qquad 2$$

Here the difference is 2. Is the rule $s = 2n$?

The rule $s = 2n$ would give this pattern.

Term (n)	1	2	3	4	n
Sequence (s)	2	4	6	8	$2n$

The rule is close, but not quite there.

To obtain the original sequence it is necessary to add 1 to each term.

Term (n)	1	2	3	4	n
$\times 2$	2	4	6	8	$2n$
$+1$	$+1$	$+1$	$+1$	$+1$	$+1$
Sequence (s)	3	5	7	9	$2n+1$

Then the rule is

$$s = 2n + 1$$

This means for the 1000th term, with $n = 1000$,

$$s = (2 \times 1000) + 1 = 2001$$

Example

In this sequence, the difference is 4.

Term (n)	1	2	3	4	5	n
Sequence (s)	1	5	9	13	17	?

4   4   4   4

First, try the rule $s = 4n$.

	1	2	3	4	5	n
$\times 4$	4	8	12	16	20	$4n$
-3	-3	-3	-3	-3	-3	-3
	1	5	9	13	17	$4n-3$

4   4   4   4

The rule is close, but 3 must be subtracted from every term.

So the rule is $s = 4n - 3$.

Exercise 3

1 Copy and complete the following tables. For each one, write a general rule in the form $s = $.

(a)

Position of term (n)	1	2	3	4	5	6	n
Sequence (s)	2	5	8	11			

(b)

Position of term (n)	1	2	3	4	5	6	n
Sequence (s)	1	4	7	10			

(c)

Position of term (n)	1	2	3	4	5	6	n
Sequence (s)	2	6	10	14			

(d)

Position of term (n)	1	2	3	4	5	6	n
Sequence (s)	0	2	4	6			

(e)

Position of term (n)	1	2	3	4	5	6	n
Sequence (s)	5	9	13	17			

(f)

Position of term (n)	1	2	3	4	5	6	n
Sequence (s)	0	3	6	9			

(g)

Position of term (n)	1	2	3	4	5	6	n
Sequence (s)	−1	1	3	5			

(h)

Position of term (n)	1	2	3	4	5	6	n
Sequence (s)	9	8	7	6			

Exercise 4

1 These tiles have been drawn using only lines and dots.

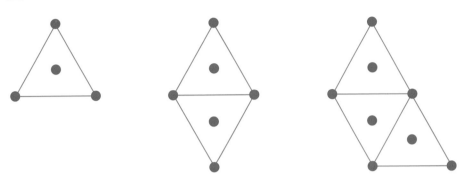

(a) Copy this table.

Number of tiles (*n*)	Number of dots (*d*)	Number of lines (*l*)
1	4	3
2	6	5
3	8	7
4		
5		
n		
1000		
10 000		

(b) Fill in the values as the number of tiles grows.

(c) The number of dots forms a sequence: 4, 6, 8, …

The number of lines also forms a sequence: 3, 5, 7, …

Write down, in your own words, how you found the values of the terms in each sequence.

(d) Write the general rule for each sequence in the form:
$d =$
$l =$

2 In these diagrams, hexagons have been connected.
Each hexagon is made of lines and dots.

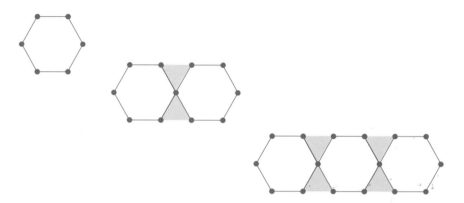

(a) Copy this table and complete it.

Number of hexagons (n)	Number of triangles (t)	Number of dots (d)	Number of lines (l)
1	0	6	6
2	2	11	14
3	4		
4			
5			
6			
n			
20			
100			

(b) Explain, in your own words, the relationship between:

    (i)   the number of hexagons and the number of triangles

    (ii) the number of hexagons and the number of dots

    (iii) the number of hexagons and the numbers of lines.

(c) Write down each of these mappings in its general form:

$t =$

$d =$

$l =$

3 These shapes have been made using straws.

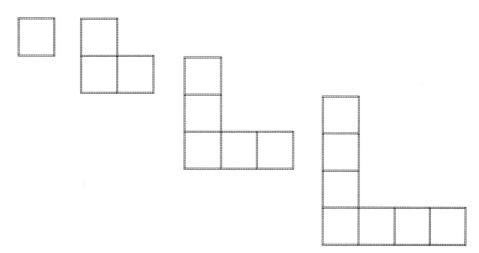

There are three different sequences to look for: the number of squares (*s*), the number of straws in the perimeter (*f*) and the total number of straws (*m*).

(a) Copy this table of values and complete it.

Length of side (*n*)	Number of squares (*s*)	Perimeter in straws (*p*)	Number of straws (*m*)
1	1	4	4
2	3	8	10
3			
4			
5			
6			
n			

(b) Write, in your own words, how you found the values of the terms in each sequence.

(c) Write the general rule for the sequences in the form

$s =$

$p =$

$m =$

Graphing linear relationships

All the sequences looked at so far, if graphed, result in a straight line. They are described as **linear** sequences.

This table shows the sequence $s = 2n + 1$.

Number of term (n)	1	2	3	4	n
Value of term (s)	3	5	7	9	$2n + 1$

Another way to write this is as a **mapping** between the term number and the values of the terms in the sequence.

Input (n)	$n \longrightarrow s$	Output (s)
1	$\longrightarrow$	3
2	$\longrightarrow$	5
3	$\longrightarrow$	7
4	$\longrightarrow$	9
n	$\longrightarrow$	$2n + 1$

This mapping or relationship can also be shown as a graph.

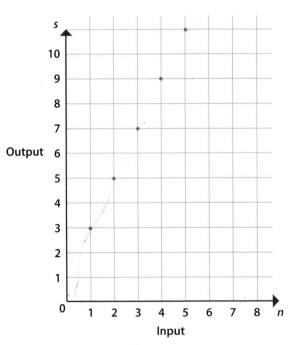

Input values *(n)* are placed on the horizontal axis (across the page).

Output values *(s)* are placed on the vertical axis (up the page).

Linear relationships produce straight line graphs.

Exercise 5

1 With axes for $n = 1$ to $n = 8$, and $s = 1$ to $s = 12$ draw a graph for each of these mappings.

(a)

In		Out
0	→	0
1	→	3
2	→	6
3	→	9
n	→	$3n$

(b)

In		Out
1	→	1
2	→	4
3	→	7
4	→	10
n	→	$3n - 2$

(c)

In		Out
0	→	2
1	→	4
2	→	6
3	→	8
n	→	$2n + 2$

(d)

In		Out
1	→	$\frac{1}{2}$
2	→	1
3	→	$1\frac{1}{2}$
4	→	2
n	→	$\frac{1}{2}n$

(e)

In		Out
0	→	12
1	→	11
2	→	10
3	→	9
n	→	$12 - n$

(f)

In		Out
1	→	8
2	→	6
3	→	4
4	→	2
n	→	$10 - 2n$

2 (a) Make up a table of values for each of these general rules by inputting the values {1, 2, 3, 4, 5}.

    (i) $n \rightarrow n + 2$ (ii) $n \rightarrow 2n + 5$

    (iii) $n \rightarrow 3n - 2$ (iv) $n \rightarrow \frac{1}{2}n + 1$

    (v) $n \rightarrow 4n + 2$ (vi) $n \rightarrow 2n - 3$

    (vii) $n \rightarrow 8 - n$ (viii) $n \rightarrow 15 - 2n$

  (b) Draw a graph for each of the mappings in part (a).

Working backwards

Look carefully at this graph.

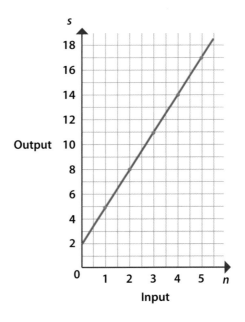

The values of points on the line can be read from the Input and Output axes and they can be placed in a mapping diagram like this.

Input (n)		Output (s)
0	$\longrightarrow$	2
1	$\longrightarrow$	5
2	$\longrightarrow$	8
3	$\longrightarrow$	11
4	$\longrightarrow$	14
5	$\longrightarrow$	17

The difference between each pair of terms is 3, and you can see from the values in the table that the relationship is:

multiply by 3 and add 2

You write this as:

$$n \rightarrow 3n + 2$$

or $\quad s = 3n + 2$

Exercise 6

1 Study these graphs. Then, for each of them, complete a mapping diagram from the information displayed in the graph.

(a)
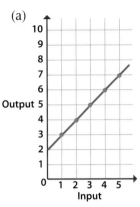

(b)
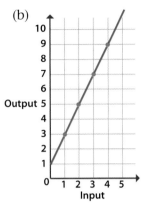

(c)
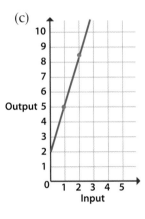

(d)
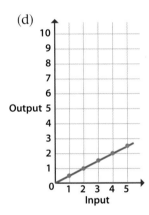

(e)
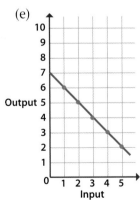

(f)
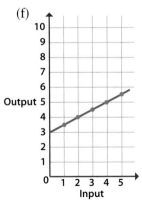

2 (a) For each graph in Question 1, write down the general rule for each line, in your own words.

    (b) Now rewrite these in the form $n \rightarrow$.

Assignment 1 | **What's a number for?**

This graph shows the rule $s = 3n + 2$.

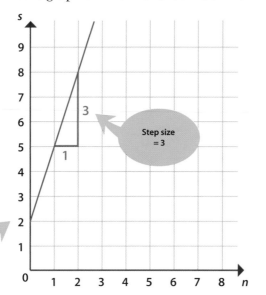

Step size is found by seeing how high up the graph goes for one square across.

The **cutting point** is the place where the graph line cuts the vertical axis.

Cutting point is 2

Step size = 3

From the graph, it is possible to make this table.

General rule	Step size	Cutting point
$s = 3n + 2$	3	2

- Copy this table and complete the information in the three columns for all the graphs in Exercise 6.

- Write down what you notice about the information in the first column and the numbers in the other two columns.

Linear equations

The input and output values used to plot graphs are called the **coordinates**.

The 'input' value is called the x-coordinate.

The 'output' value is called the y-coordinate.

Example

The mapping $n \rightarrow 2n + 1$ or the rule $s = 2n + 1$ becomes the equation $y = 2x + 1$.

The axes on the graph are labelled x and y, and the line is labelled with the 'equation of the line'.

x	$\rightarrow$	$y = 2x + 1$
0	$\rightarrow$	1
1	$\rightarrow$	3
2	$\rightarrow$	5
3	$\rightarrow$	7
4	$\rightarrow$	9

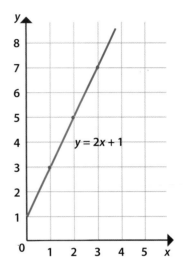

The rule is that the y-coordinate is twice the x-coordinate plus 1.

Write this as $y = 2x + 1$

This is the **equation** of the line drawn in the graph.

Example

To draw the graph of the equation $y = x + 4$ for values of x from 0 to 5, first produce the mapping diagram. This is produced by substituting the values of x into the equation to find the corresponding y-values.

If $x = 1$ then $y = 1 + 4 = 5$.

These points (0,4) (1,5) and so on are then plotted and joined to make a straight line.

x	$y = x + 4$
0	4
1	5
2	6
3	7
4	8
5	9

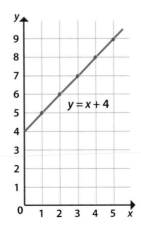

Exercise 7

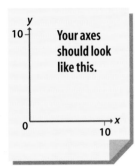

y
10
Your axes should look like this.

0   x
         10

1 (a) Produce mapping diagrams for each of these linear equations. Use values of x from 0 to 5.

(i) $y = x + 3$ (ii) $y = x - 1$ (iii) $y = x - 3$

(iv) $y = x$ (v) $y = 6 - x$ (vi) $y = 3 - x$

(b) Using axes with x and y going from 0 to 10, draw the graphs for the equations in part (a).

2 Write down what you notice about the lines you have drawn for question 1.

3 (a) Produce mapping diagrams for each of these linear equations. Use values of x from 0 to 5.

(i) $y = 2x$ (ii) $y = 3x$ (iii) $y = 6x$

(iv) $y = 5x$ (v) $y = 4x$ (vi) $y = \frac{1}{2}x$

(b) Using one pair of axes, draw the graphs of all these equations. (Your y-axis will need to be longer than 10 this time.)

4 Write down what you notice about each of the lines drawn for question 3.

5 (a) Draw mapping diagrams for each of these linear equations. Use values of x from 0 to 5.

(i) $y = x + 1$ (ii) $y = 2x - 1$ (ii) $y = 3x + 1$

(iv) $y = 4x + 2$ (v) $y = \frac{1}{2}x - 2$ (vi) $y = 4x - 1$

(vii) $y = \frac{1}{2}x + 3$ (viii) $y = 5 - x$ (ix) $y = 7 - x$

(b) Using only one pair of axes, draw the graphs of all of these equations.

Make sure your y-axis is long enough before you start.

6 Write down what you notice about each of the lines drawn for question 5.

Assignment 2   **Drawing graphs on a computer**

- Using a graph drawing package, investigate the effect of changing the step size and the cutting point in this linear equation.

$y = \text{step size} \times x + \text{cutting point}$

In shorthand this is written as $y = mx + c$.

> m means step size
> c means cutting point

- Use positive numbers, negative numbers and fractions for m and c.

Nonlinear sequences

Not all sequences are linear. Here is the sequence of square numbers.

1, 4, 9, 16, 25, ...

What are the differences between pairs of terms in this sequence?

Term	1	2	3	4	5	n
Sequence	1	4	9	16	25	n^2

       3   5   7   9

The difference between the terms is not the same every time. If you were to plot this relationship you would not get a straight line graph.

The graph and its sequence are no longer described as being linear. Instead they are called nonlinear.

What are the 'second differences' – the differences between the values of the first differences?

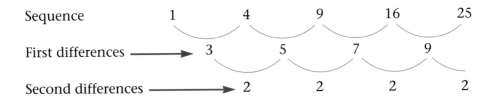

If the second differences are all the same, this shows that the relationship involves $n \times n$.

Exercise 8

1 This is the mapping diagram for the sequence of square numbers.

Term (n)	1	2	3	4	5	6
Sequence (s)	1	4	9	16	25	36

(a) Plot the points of the mapping diagram as pairs of coordinates. (Do not use a ruler to join the points.)

(b) Write down what you notice about the points you have plotted.

2 Here are the first three in a sequence of patterns of nails on a pin board.

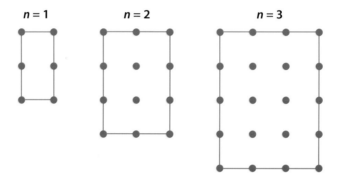

(a) Copy and complete this table to produce a mapping diagram.

Width of rectangle (n)	1	2	3	4	5	6	10	n
Number of pins	6	12	20					

(b) Plot the points of your mapping diagram as pairs of coordinates.

(c) If you join the points what shape will you draw? (Do not use a ruler to join the points. Try to draw a smooth curve.)

Curves should never be drawn with a ruler. Always draw them free hand or use curve-drawing equipment.

Assignment 3   Handshakes

As people arrive at a meeting, they shake hands with everyone already there.

- Copy and complete this table to show the number of handshakes.

People	1	2	3	4	5	6	10	n
Handshakes								

- Draw a graph of the sequence generated.

- Find the relationship between the number of people and the number of handshakes.

Review Exercise

1 These patterns of connected squares have dots at their corners.

$n = 1$ $n = 2$ $n = 3$ $n = 4$

   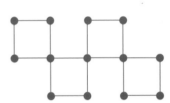

  (a) Copy this table of values and complete it.

Number of squares (n)	1	2	3	4	5	10	100
Number of dots (d)	4	7					
Number of sides (s)	4	8					

  (b) Draw a mapping diagram to show the relationship between the number of squares (n) and the number of dots (d).

  (c) Draw a straight-line graph to illustrate this relationship.

  (d) Draw a straight-line graph to show the relationship between the number of squares (n) and the number of sides (s).

2 (a) On one pair of axes draw the graphs of all these linear equations.

(i) $y = x$ (ii) $y = 2x$ (iii) $y = -x$

(iv) $y = 4x$ (v) $y = 3x + 2$ (vi) $y = 3x - 1$

(b) Describe the effect that the value of the number multiplying x has on the graph.

(c) Describe the effect that the value added to or subtracted from the x-term has on the graph.

3 Four different relationships generate sequences in these patterns: the width, the number of squares, the number of dots and the number of crossing points.

 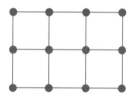 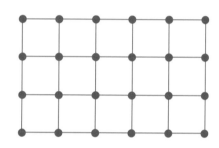

(a) Copy and complete this mapping diagram.

Height (h)	Width (w)	Number of squares (s)□	Number of dots (d)●	Number of crosses (c)+
1	1	1	4	0
2	3	6	12	2
3	5	15		
4				
5				
6				
7				

(b) Draw a separate graph of each mapping.

(c) Describe each of the relationships in your own words, and in the form $w = \ldots$, $s = \ldots$, $d = \ldots$ and $c = \ldots$.

Working with 2D shapes

→ **how to move a shape without turning**
→ **how to reflect a shape in a mirror line**
→ **how to rotate a shape around a point**
→ **how to use these movements to form tessellations**

Starting points

Before starting this chapter you will need to know how to:

• measure and draw angles

• draw shapes using coordinates

• work out angles round a point

• work out angles of polygons

• work out angles on parallel lines.

Exercise 1

1 (a) Measure each of the angles *a* to *g*.

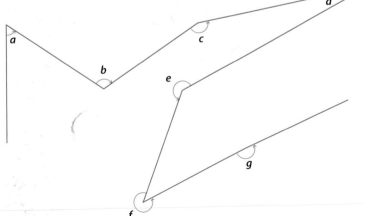

   (b) Angle *a* is an acute angle. Write down the word used to describe the type of angle of angles *b* to *g*.

2 Draw these angles.

(a) 55°   (b) 155°   (c) 255°   (d) 355°

3 Write down the coordinates of the points A to L.

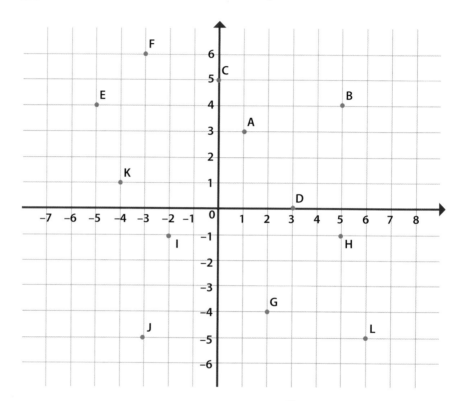

4 (a) Draw a set of axes like those in question 3.

(b) Mark each of these points and join them up in order.

(−7, 3), (− 4, 6), (−1, 6), (1, 4), (8, 4), (8, 2), (7, 1), (6, 2),

(5, 1), (4, 2), (3, 1), (2, 2), (1, 0), (2, −2), (3, −1), (4, −2),

(5, −1), (6, −2), (7, −1), (8, −2), (8, −3), (−7, −3)

5 (a) Draw a shape on a set of axes.

(b) Record the coordinates of every corner on a piece of paper.

(c) Pass the paper to a partner to draw the shape.

(d) Compare your shapes and discuss any differences.

6 (a) Work out the size of each of the angles *a* to *h*.

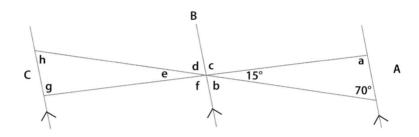

> Remember ⟶ shows parallel lines.

(b) Explain clearly how you found each answer.

7 Shapes A and B are regular.
The sides of shape C are all equal.

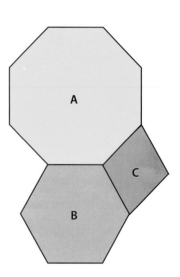

(a) Write down the size of the angles in shape C. Explain carefully how you arrived at your answer.

(b) What are the names of shapes A, B and C?

Reflection

Assignment 1   Ink devils

You will need a piece of plain paper and some paint or ink.

• Fold the paper in half, then unfold it.

• Place a blob of paint or ink on one half of the paper.

• Fold the paper again and press firmly, then open it.

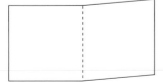 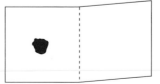 

• Make other patterns. Try using several smaller blobs, or more than one colour.

Exercise 2

A line of symmetry is a mirror line.

1 On a copy of these shapes draw on each one a line of symmetry.

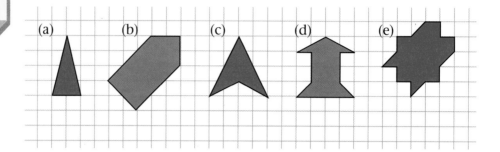

(a) (b) (c) (d) (e)

2 On a copy of these shapes add what is needed to make the blue line a line of symmetry.

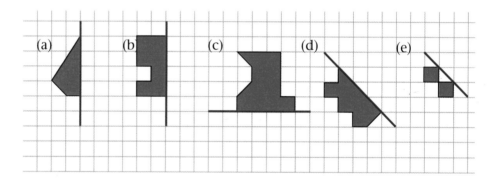

(a) (b) (c) (d) (e)

Check your answers using a mirror.

3 On a copy of these shapes add as many lines of symmetry as possible.

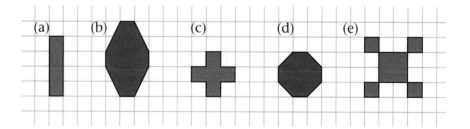

(a) (b) (c) (d) (e)

4 (a) Draw five different regular polygons accurately.

(b) Write down the name of each polygon.

(c) Draw all the lines of symmetry on each of your shapes.

Check your answers using a mirror.

5 Copy each of these shapes, and show what you would see if a mirror were placed along the blue line.

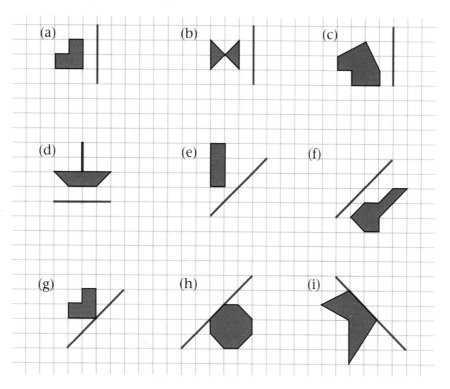

(a)

(b)

(c)

(d)

(e)

(f)

(g)

(h)

(i)

6 On a copy of these shapes, show what you would see if a mirror were placed along the blue line.
You may find tracing paper helpful.

(a)

(b)

(c)

(d)

(e)

7 • Draw an interesting shape of your own.

• Draw a mirror line.

• Reflect your shape in the mirror line.

| Assignment 2 | **Reflection patterns** |

Have you seen this effect in two mirrors?

You can achieve this yourself in the following way.

- Copy this diagram and draw the reflection of the shape in the blue mirror line.

- Now reflect the whole diagram in the red mirror line.

- This time reflect the whole diagram in the blue mirror line.

- Continue to reflect in the blue mirror line and then the red mirror line until your page is full.

- Draw your own diagram with two mirror lines. Repeat the steps you carried out before.

| Assignment 3 | **Reflecting on a computer** |

There are many different ways of reflecting shapes using a computer.

- Using a drawing package try drawing a shape and reflecting it. Can you reflect the shape in a diagonal mirror line?

- Use another package to reflect shapes.
  You could try a geometry package like **Cabri Geometre** or **Geometer's Sketchpad** if you have one. You could use **LOGO**.

- Make a display showing the results that you have achieved.

- Write a short account of your work. Which package did you find easiest to use to reflect shapes?

Exercise 3

1 (a) Copy this diagram, and show the result of reflecting the flag in the mirror line which joins the points (4, 0) and (4, 6).

(b) On the same diagram draw another mirror line between the points (0, 3) and (8, 3). Reflect both of your flags in this new mirror line.

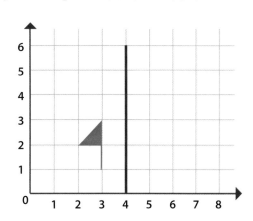

2 (a) Draw a set of axes and plot these points to make five shapes.

Shape A: (0,1), (0, 3), (0, 2), (1, 2), (1, 3), (1, 1)

Shape B: (3, 1), (2, 1), (2, 2), (3, 2), (2, 2), (2, 3), (3, 3)

Shape C: (4, 3), (4, 1), (5, 1)

Shape D: (6, 3), (6, 1), (7, 1)

Shape E: (8, 1), (8, 3), (9, 3), (9, 1), (8, 1)

(b) Join each set of points. (You should get a message!)

(c) Draw a line from (0, 0) to (10, 0). Use this as a mirror line to reflect all of the message.

(d) Copy out the coordinates you used above. Under each one write the coordinate of the same point on the reflection. Write down anything you notice which connects the two lists.

(e) Draw a line from (0, −6) to (0, 6). Use this as a mirror line to reflect both messages again.

(f) Record the coordinates as you did before. Write down anything you notice.

(g) Write your own name on a set of axes and reflect it. Check your patterns and look for others.

Your grid should look like this.

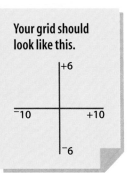

Rotation

Assignment 4 | **Rotating a triangle**

*   Construct this triangle on plain paper using only a pencil, ruler and compasses.

    Make a copy of the triangle on tracing paper.

*   Place the tracing over the triangle and put a pin in at point A.

    Turn the tracing until the 5 cm side lies on top of the long side of the triangle.

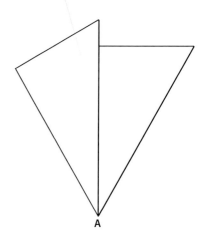

5 cm

30°

A

Draw a second triangle in this new position.

*   Repeat this until you return to the starting triangle.

A

Exercise 4

1 (a) Trace this shape.

(b) Rotate the tracing, using the black dot as the centre of rotation, until it lies exactly on top of the original shape.

(c) Repeat this until the tracing paper has returned to its original position.

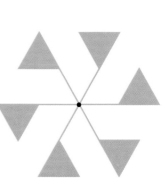

(d) Write down the number of times you rotated the tracing paper.

(e) What is the order of rotational symmetry of the shape?

2 (a) Write down the order of rotational symmetry for each of these shapes.

(i)

(ii)

(iii)

(iv)

(v)

(b) On a copy of each shape, mark the position of the centre of rotation.

3 Draw shapes with these orders of rotational symmetry.

(a) 2   (b) 4   (c) 6   (d) 3   (e) 5   (f) 7   (g) 1

4 (a) Copy this diagram.
Draw a line from A at an angle of 45° clockwise from the line AB.

(b) Trace the red flag.

(c) Using the tracing, rotate the flag around point A until the pole is on top of the new line.

(d) Draw the flag in this position.

B

A

5 (a) Copy this diagram.

Use tracing paper to rotate the shape through 60° clockwise around point A.

(b) Draw the shape in the new position.

A

6 Copy these diagrams, and rotate each shape through the angle given around the point marked.

(a) 90° anticlockwise   (b) 120° anticlockwise   (c) 180° clockwise

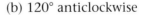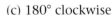

Draw each shape in the new position.

7 (a) Copy this diagram. Draw a line joining point A to point B.

Use this to help you to rotate the shape 135° clockwise around A.

(b) Copy this diagram again and draw a line joining point A to point C.

Use this to help you to rotate the shape 135° clockwise around A.

Compare your answers to parts (a) and (b). If they are not exactly the same check your work very carefully.

8 Copy each of these diagrams and rotate the shape through the angle given around the point marked.

(a) 180° clockwise

(b) 50° anticlockwise

(c) 100° clockwise

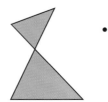

(d) 90° anticlockwise

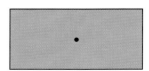

9 (a) Copy this diagram and rotate the shape through 90° clockwise around point A.

(b) Now rotate the new shape through 90° clockwise around point A.

(c) Continue to rotate your latest shape through 90° clockwise around A until it lies exactly on top of the original shape.

(d) Write down the order of rotational symmetry of the complete shape you have created.

10 Draw a new set of axes for each part of this question.

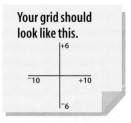

Your grid should look like this.

(a) Plot these points: (2, 1), (2, 4), (1, 3), (2, 1). Rotate 90° anticlockwise using (4, 3) as the centre of rotation.

(b) Plot these points: (1, 6), (3, 6), (3, 4), (2, 4), (2, 5), (1, 5), (1, 6). Rotate 180° using (5, 5) as the centre of rotation.

(c) Plot these points: (6, 2), (6, 3), (7, 3), (8, 4), (8, 2), (6, 2). Rotate 90° clockwise using (1, 2) as the centre of rotation.

(d) Plot these points: (4, 2), (3, 3), (3, 5), (4, 6), (5, 5), (5, 3), (4, 2). Rotate 90° anticlockwise using (4, 4) as the centre of rotation.

11 (a) Copy this diagram. Write down the coordinates of the corners of shape A.

(b) Rotate shape A 90° anticlockwise using (0, 0) as the centre of rotation. Label the new shape B.

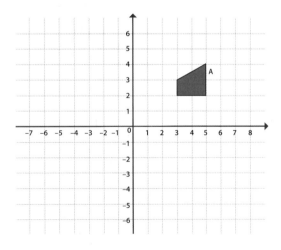

(c) Rotate shape B 90° anticlockwise using (0, 0) as the centre of rotation. Label the shape C.

(d) Rotate shape C 90° anticlockwise using (0, 0) as the centre of rotation.

(e) Write down the order of rotational symmetry of the complete pattern of shapes you have created.

(f) For each of the shapes in the pattern, list the coordinates in the same order as you listed them for the original shape. Write down any connections or patterns you notice.

12 Copy these four diagrams.

For each shape repeat the rotation around the point marked until the rotated shape lies exactly on top of the original shape.

(a) 120° anticlockwise   (b) 45° anticlockwise

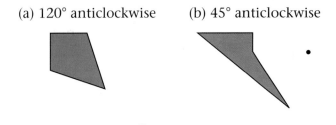

(c) 180° clockwise   (d) 80° clockwise

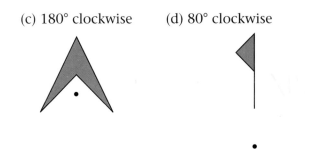

Write down the order of rotational symmetry of each complete shape you have created.

13 Copy these five diagrams using tracing paper. Use the tracing paper to help you to mark the centre of rotation for each pair of shapes.

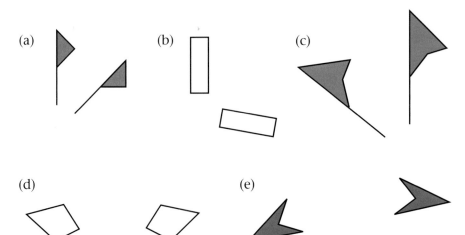

(a)   (b)   (c)

(d)   (e)

Assignment 5   **Rotating on a computer**

There are many different ways of rotating shapes using a computer.

- If you have a drawing package at school or at home, try drawing a shape and rotating it.

  Can you rotate the shape through angles other than 90° and 180°?

  Can you use a centre of rotation which is not on the shape?

- Use another package to rotate shapes.

- Make a display showing the results you have achieved.

- Write a short account of your work.

  Describe which drawing package you found the easiest to use to rotate shapes.

Assignment 6   **Following rules**

- Try to draw shapes A, B and C which fit these rules.

  Shape A must have one line of symmetry and rotational symmetry of order 1.

  Shape B must have one line of symmetry and rotational symmetry of order 2.

  Shape C must have two lines of symmetry and rotational symmetry of order 2.

- Consider various combinations of lines of symmetry and order of rotational symmetry.

  Which of the combinations that you have chosen are possible?

  Which ones are not possible?

  You could start by thinking about shapes where the number of lines of symmetry is the same as the order of rotational symmetry.

Translation

Look at these two shapes.

Shape B is a translation of shape A. The translation is the movement 6 to the right and 2 up.

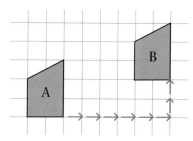

There is a shorter way of writing the movement of a shape. Write the numbers in brackets with the movement across above the movement up.

This is called vector notation.

For example, this movement is written as $\binom{6}{2}$.

Exercise 5

1 On squared paper, copy this diagram, and draw the same shape six squares to the right of the original.

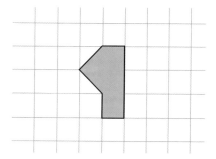

2 On squared paper, copy this diagram, and draw the same shape four squares up the page from the original.

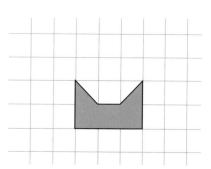

3 On squared paper, copy this diagram, and draw the same shape six squares to the right and four squares up the page from the original.

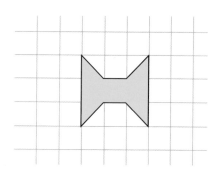

4 Describe how the blue shape must move to reach the position of the red shape in each of the following.

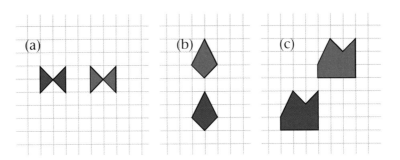

(a)   (b)   (c)

5 Use vector notation to write down the movements of each blue shape to each red.

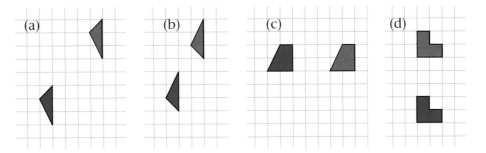

(a)   (b)   (c)   (d)

6 Copy this shape onto squared paper.

Draw the result when the shape is moved by these vectors.

(a) $\begin{pmatrix} 3 \\ 4 \end{pmatrix}$ (b) $\begin{pmatrix} 1 \\ 5 \end{pmatrix}$ (c) $\begin{pmatrix} 2 \\ 2 \end{pmatrix}$ (d) $\begin{pmatrix} 4 \\ 0 \end{pmatrix}$ (e) $\begin{pmatrix} 0 \\ 3 \end{pmatrix}$

Vector diagrams

The arrow shows how the point (2, 3) moves if it is translated with the vector $\begin{pmatrix} 5 \\ 4 \end{pmatrix}$.

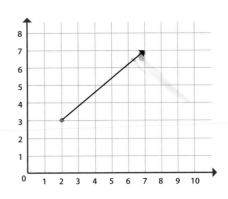

Exercise 6

1 These arrows show translations.
For each arrow write down:

(i) the coordinates of the point that has been translated

(ii) the vector for the translation.

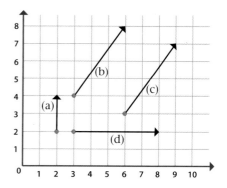

2 Draw arrows to show these translations.

(a) the point (1, 1) translated with the vector $\begin{pmatrix} 2 \\ 4 \end{pmatrix}$

(b) the point (5, 3) translated with the vector $\begin{pmatrix} 3 \\ 1 \end{pmatrix}$

(c) the point (0, 0) translated with the vector $\begin{pmatrix} 3 \\ 3 \end{pmatrix}$

(d) the point (2, 2) translated with the vector $\begin{pmatrix} 3 \\ 0 \end{pmatrix}$

(e) the point (1, 4) translated with the vector $\begin{pmatrix} 0 \\ 4 \end{pmatrix}$

3 (a) Draw arrows to show the translation of five different points with the vector $\begin{pmatrix} 3 \\ 4 \end{pmatrix}$.

(b) Describe the five lines you have drawn.

(c) Write down the coordinates of the beginning and end of each arrow.

(d) Write down a rule for working out the coordinate of the end of the arrow if you know the beginning and the vector.

(e) Test that your rule works for other vectors.

Congruence

Exercise 7

1 List any sets of these shapes that are congruent.

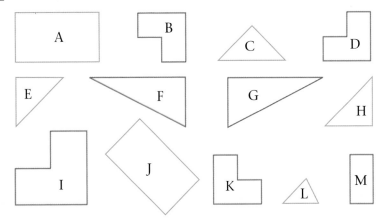

2 Draw this triangle accurately.

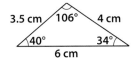

Write down whether each of the following triangles is congruent to the one you have drawn. If it is not congruent draw an accurate diagram that shows why.

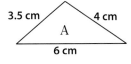
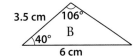
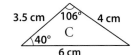

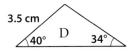
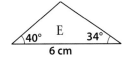
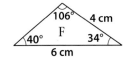

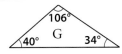
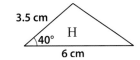
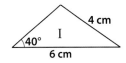

Tessellations

Tessellations are patterns created by translating a shape. The shapes must fit together without any gaps.

Tessellating with a rectangle produces a brick wall effect. Tessellating with a hexagon produces a honeycomb pattern.

To produce more interesting tessellations a simple shape may be reflected or rotated to make a new shape. The new shape is then translated to make the tesselation.

Exercise 8

1 This tessellation can be produced by translations of the shape outlined in red.

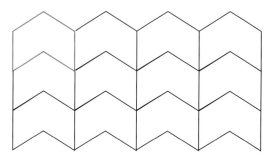

(a) Produce a tessellation of your own which only involves translating a shape.

(b) Describe any symmetry you can see in this tessellation.

2 (a) Construct a tessellation using only rotation of this shape and the shapes produced.

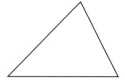

(b) Try to produce a different tessellation starting with the same shape and still only using rotations.

3 You will need a copy of this tessellation.

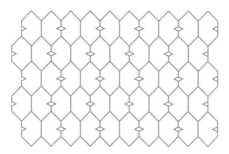

Try to find:

(a) a reflection in a horizontal mirror line

(b) a reflection in a vertical mirror line

(c) a reflection in a mirror line at 45° to the horizontal.

If you find the movement, outline the shapes and draw the mirror line.

Now try to find:

(d) rotations through as many different angles as possible.

Outline the shapes on a copy of the tessellation and mark the centre of rotation.

Describe any symmetry in this tessellation.

4 (a) Describe how the shape outlined in red can be moved onto the shape outlined in blue.

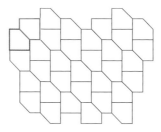

(b) What other types of movement can you find in this tessellation? Describe them clearly using a copy of the tessellation to help you.

(c) Describe any symmetry you can see in this tessellation.

5 (a) Identify as many
different rotations as
possible in this
tessellation.

(b) Describe any symmetry
you can see in this
tessellation.

6 (a) Use reflection, rotation and translation to form a tessellation
of your own.

(b) Describe the symmetry in your tessellation.

7 (a) Use a computer package to form a tessellation.

(b) Describe how you used reflection, rotation and translation.

Review Exercise

1 (a) Copy this diagram.
Move the shape using the
vector $\begin{pmatrix} 3 \\ 5 \end{pmatrix}$.
Label the new shape B.

(b) Move shape B using the
vector $\begin{pmatrix} 2 \\ 4 \end{pmatrix}$.
Label the new shape C.

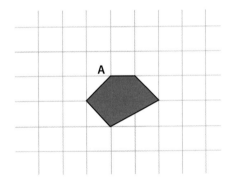

(c) Write down a vector which will move shape A straight to
position C.

2 Copy this diagram, and rotate
the shape 60° anticlockwise around
the point marked A.

3 (a) On a copy of this diagram, mark the centre of rotation of shape A onto shape B with a dot.

(b) Write down the angle of rotation.

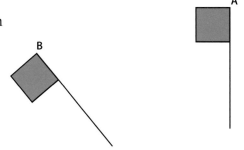

4 (a) Copy this diagram. Draw the reflection of shape A in a mirror line along the line joining (6, 0) and (6, 8).

(b) On the same diagram, draw the reflection of shape B in a mirror line along the line joining (0, 4) and (9, 4).

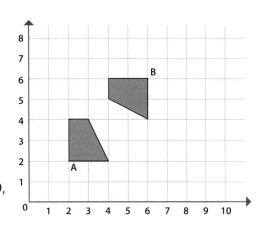

(c) Write down the coordinates of two points on the line which shows the position of the mirror to reflect shape A onto shape B.

5 (a) Draw a pair of parallel lines.

Draw a second pair of parallel lines which cross the first pair.

What quadrilateral have you drawn?

(b) Draw a diagonal of the quadrilateral.

Draw a line parallel to the diagonal through each of the other vertices.

Describe the transformations needed to start from one of the triangles and move onto each of the others.

6 On a copy of this diagram, draw all the lines of symmetry on each shape and write down the order of rotational symmetry of each shape.

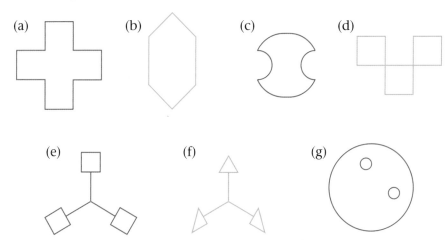

(a) (b) (c) (d)

(e) (f) (g)

7 (a) Draw a shape with exactly one line of symmetry.

(b) Draw a shape with exactly two lines of symmetry.

(c) Draw a shape with exactly three lines of symmetry.

(d) Draw a shape with rotational symmetry of order 5.

(e) Draw a shape with rotational symmetry of order 7.

8 (a) Draw a shape with three lines of symmetry which does not have rotational symmetry of order 3.

(b) Draw at least three more shapes where the number of lines of symmetry is different from the order of rotational symmetry.

Parts and percentages

In this chapter you will learn:

→ more about the links between fractions, decimals and percentages
→ how to multiply fractions
→ how to add simple fractions
→ how to find fractions of amounts
→ how to find percentages of amounts

Starting points

Before starting this chapter you will need to be able to:

- recognise the importance of the position of a digit in a number

- recognise equivalent fractions

- change fractions into decimals

- recognise percentages

- change decimals into percentages.

Exercise 1

1 What fraction of each of the following diagrams has been shaded?

(a)   (b)   (c)   (d)

                  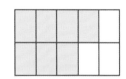

2 Copy and complete these equivalent fractions.

(a) $\frac{1}{2} = \frac{\square}{8}$ (b) $\frac{\square}{10} = \frac{70}{100}$ (c) $\frac{4}{5} = \frac{\square}{20}$

(d) $\frac{3}{8} = \frac{6}{\square}$ (e) $\frac{18}{24} = \frac{3}{\square}$ (f) $\frac{25}{100} = \frac{\square}{20} = \frac{1}{\square}$

3 Write down the value of the 4 in each of these numbers.

(a) 24.6 (b) 12.4 (c) 428 (d) 9.24 (e) 48.2 (f) 1.04

4 Write these sets of numbers in order of size, starting with the smallest.

(a) 100.97   19.07   9.170   70.91

(b) 3.8   3.038   3.83   3.803

(c) 0.25   0.205   0.52   0.502

5 Write these fractions as percentages.

(a) $\frac{82}{100}$ (b) $\frac{170}{200}$ (c) $\frac{36}{50}$

(d) $\frac{7}{10}$ (e) $\frac{15}{20}$ (f) $\frac{20}{25}$

6 Write these fractions as decimals.

(a) $\frac{1}{4}$ (b) $\frac{7}{10}$ (c) $\frac{3}{4}$

(d) $\frac{4}{5}$ (e) $\frac{5}{8}$ (f) $\frac{7}{8}$

7 Write these decimals as percentages.

(a) 0.23   (b) 0.58   (c) 0.25

(d) 0.07   (e) 0.4   (f) 0.13

Assignment 1   Exploring fractions

- Write down any five numbers.

- Make as many fractions as possible with your numbers.
  For example, using the five numbers 1, 2, 3, 4, 5 some possible fractions are:

  $\frac{1}{3}$ $\frac{3}{1}$ $\frac{3}{3}$ $\frac{2}{5}$

- Divide your fractions into three groups:

  less than 1   *equal to one*   *bigger than 1*

- Within each of these groups arrange the fractions in order of size.

How big is a fraction?

Here are three possible ways to help you to decide on the size of a fraction.

Recognising the fraction and its size

Example

The shaded areas on these area diagrams represent $\frac{3}{4}$ and $\frac{1}{2}$.

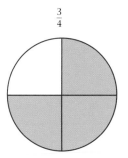
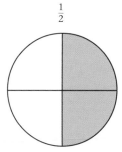

The left circle has more shading so $\frac{3}{4}$ is bigger than $\frac{1}{2}$.

Drawing a graph to show the fraction sizes

Example

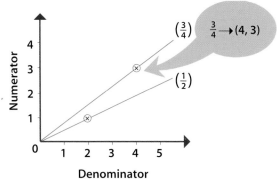

The line representing $\frac{3}{4}$ lies above the one representing $\frac{1}{2}$ so $\frac{3}{4}$ is the bigger fraction.

Changing the fractions into decimals

Example

Key fact
> means
'is bigger than'.

$\frac{3}{4} = 0.75$ $\frac{1}{2} = 0.5$

As 0.75 is bigger than 0.5 then $\frac{3}{4} > \frac{1}{2}$.

Exercise 2

1 By recognising the size of fractions, find which is the bigger in each of these pairs of fractions.

(a) $\frac{1}{2}, \frac{1}{3}$ (b) $\frac{7}{10}, \frac{4}{5}$ (c) $\frac{3}{4}, \frac{7}{8}$

2 By graphing these fractions, place them in size order.

$\frac{3}{4}$ $\frac{7}{10}$ $\frac{4}{5}$ $\frac{2}{3}$ $\frac{8}{10}$ $\frac{5}{8}$

> $\frac{3}{4}$ means
> 3 divided by 4
> or 3 ÷ 4

3 By changing these fractions into decimals, place this list in order, smallest first.

$\frac{3}{5}$ $\frac{4}{7}$ $\frac{2}{3}$ $\frac{5}{6}$ $\frac{3}{8}$ $\frac{5}{12}$

Key fact

The numerator is the top number of a fraction.

The denominator is the bottom number.

Fractions bigger than 1

Fractions bigger than 1 are called top heavy, because the numerator is larger than the denominator.

They are also called improper fractions.

Here are some top heavy – or improper – fractions.

$\frac{11}{5}$ $\frac{21}{7}$ $\frac{19}{4}$ $\frac{3}{2}$

It is sometimes helpful to rewrite a top heavy fraction as a mixed number.

> A mixed number has both whole numbers and fractions e.g. $3\frac{1}{2}$

Examples

$\frac{11}{5}$ means $11 \div 5$

$$\begin{array}{r} 2^{\,r\,1} \\ 5\overline{)11} \end{array}$$

$11 \div 5 = 2\frac{1}{5}$

> Check that $\frac{19}{4} = 4\frac{3}{4}$
>
> and that $\frac{3}{2} = 1\frac{1}{2}$

$\frac{21}{7}$ means $21 \div 7$

$21 \div 7 = 3$

Exercise 3

Write these improper fractions as mixed numbers.

1 $\frac{3}{2}$ **2** $\frac{5}{2}$ **3** $\frac{8}{3}$ **4** $\frac{11}{3}$ **5** $\frac{9}{5}$

6 $\frac{11}{7}$ **7** $\frac{13}{6}$ **8** $\frac{5}{3}$ **9** $\frac{24}{6}$ **10** $\frac{300}{100}$

11 $\frac{17}{10}$ **12** $\frac{11}{5}$ **13** $\frac{14}{3}$ **14** $\frac{20}{9}$ **15** $\frac{26}{5}$

Mixed numbers to fractions

Sometimes we need to change mixed numbers to improper fractions.

$$2\frac{2}{3} = \frac{6}{3} + \frac{2}{3} = \frac{8}{3}$$

Exercise 4

Write these mixed numbers as improper fractions.

1 $2\frac{1}{2}$ **2** $1\frac{1}{3}$ **3** $1\frac{1}{4}$ **4** $1\frac{3}{4}$ **5** $2\frac{2}{3}$

6 $1\frac{1}{5}$ **7** $3\frac{1}{4}$ **8** $1\frac{1}{7}$ **9** $1\frac{3}{5}$ **10** $5\frac{5}{6}$

11 $2\frac{4}{5}$ **12** $2\frac{3}{8}$ **13** $11\frac{2}{3}$ **14** $8\frac{3}{7}$ **15** $6\frac{2}{5}$

Assignment 2   Exact or recurring?

Some fractions give exact decimals, e.g. $\frac{1}{5} = 0.2$ $\frac{3}{8} = 0.375$

Other fractions give recurring decimals, e.g. $\frac{1}{3} = 0.333\,333\,...$

Key fact

$0.\dot{3}$ means $0.333...$
$0.\dot{5}\dot{4}$ means $0.5454...$
$0.\dot{1}23\dot{4}$ means
$0.123\,412\,341\,23...$

- Choose some fractions and change them into decimals.
- Put them into three groups:

  exact   *recurring*   *not sure*

- Explore more fully some of the fractions you could not decide on. (You may need to abandon your calculator.)

Assignment 3 | Refreshing decimals

On a copy of this diagram, complete the missing sections.

Adding

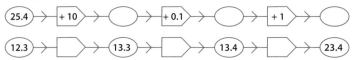

Subtracting

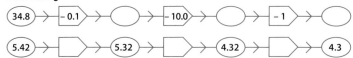

Multiplying and dividing

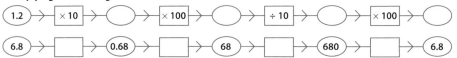

- Now invent your own decimal chains to change a number into a different number. You can use any sign but **only** the digits 0 and 1.

Assignment 4 | Healthy numbers

28 is a healthy number because the sum of its digits is exactly divisible by the number of digits

$(2 + 8) \div 2 = 5$

128 is not a healthy number because the sum of its digits is not exactly divisible by the number of digits

$(1 + 2 + 8) \div 3 = \frac{11}{3} = 3\frac{2}{3}$

- Explore other numbers to discover whether they are healthy.

- How many 2-digit numbers are healthy?

- Are there any patterns in the healthy values?

- What fraction of numbers less than 100 are healthy?

- What fraction of numbers less than 1000 are healthy?

- How far can you go … ?

Decimals to fractions

Exact decimals can be changed into fractions using place values, e.g.

0.23 means 2 tenths and 3 hundredths

$$0.23 = \frac{2}{10} + \frac{3}{100}$$

$\times 10$

$$= \frac{20}{100} + \frac{3}{100}$$

$$= \frac{23}{100}$$

Sometimes we can simplify the fraction.

$$0.45 = \frac{4}{10} + \frac{5}{100}$$

$$= \frac{40}{100} + \frac{5}{100}$$

$$= \frac{45}{100}$$

$\div 5$

$$= \frac{9}{20}$$

Exercise 5

Change these decimals into fractions.

1	0.1	**2**	0.2	**3**	0.8	**4**	0.01	**5**	0.05
6	0.3	**7**	0.7	**8**	0.9	**9**	0.4	**10**	0.25
11	0.37	**12**	0.04	**13**	0.375	**14**	0.425	**15**	0.103

Assignment 5   Every which way

- Write down any two numbers.

  Call one A and the other B.

- Find $A \div B$ and then $B \div A$.

- Multiply your two answers together.
  What do you notice?

- Try other values for A and B.

- Explain fully what you find, what you would expect and why.

Finding fractions of amounts

Sharing involves division, and calculating fractional values.

Example

Two people share £24.00
Find a half of £24.00.
£24.00 ÷ 2 = £12.00
They receive £12.00 each.

Example

A length of material is cut into three strips.
Find a third of 15 metres.
15 m ÷ 3 = 5 m
Each strip is 5 m long.

Here is another way of looking at this type of calculation.

Find a half of £24.00

$$\downarrow$$

$$\frac{1}{2} \quad \times \quad \frac{£24}{1} = \frac{£24}{2} = £12$$

'of' means ×

24 whole ones is the same as $\frac{24}{1}$.

Example

Find two-thirds of £24.00

$$\frac{2}{3} \times \frac{£24}{1} = \frac{£48}{3} = £16$$

Example

Find four-fifths of 22 metres.

$$\frac{4}{5} \times \frac{22m}{1} = \frac{88m}{5} = 17\frac{3}{5} \text{ metres}$$

Exercise 6

Calculate these fractional amounts.

1 A half of £16

2 A half of £48

3 A quarter of £12

4 A third of £12

5 A third of £30

6 A fifth of £100

7 $\frac{1}{2}$ of £32.00

8 $\frac{1}{4}$ of 90 km

9 $\frac{1}{8}$ of £68.00

10 $\frac{2}{5}$ of £10

11 $\frac{3}{4}$ of £72

12 $\frac{2}{3}$ of 90

13 $\frac{2}{5}$ of 200 m

14 $\frac{2}{9}$ of £900

15 $\frac{2}{3}$ of £3.60

16 $\frac{4}{5}$ of £10.00

17 $\frac{3}{5}$ of 56 km

18 $\frac{3}{20}$ of £24.00

19 $\frac{7}{10}$ of £700

20 $\frac{4}{7}$ of 210 kg

21 $\frac{5}{8}$ of 300 cm

22 $\frac{3}{10}$ of 50 kg

23 $\frac{2}{7}$ of 490 litres

24 $\frac{11}{100}$ of £3.00

25 $\frac{2}{3}$ of 250 m

26 $\frac{5}{6}$ of 39 litres

27 $\frac{3}{100}$ of £12

Fractions of fractions

For some calculations, the shading method on an area diagram is best.

Example

$\frac{1}{2}$ of $\frac{1}{4}$ is the same as $\frac{1}{8}$

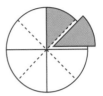

Alternatively, you can change 'of' to read 'multiply'.

Example

$\frac{2}{3}$ of $\frac{3}{4} = \frac{2}{3} \times \frac{3}{4} = \frac{6}{12} = \frac{1}{2}$

This can then be checked by looking at an area diagram.

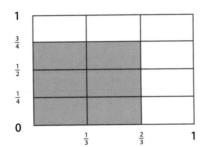

$\frac{2}{3} \times \frac{3}{4}$ represents the shaded area in the diagram.

Exercise 7

Calculate these, and check your answers with an area diagram.

1 $\frac{1}{2} \times \frac{1}{4}$ **2** $\frac{3}{4} \times \frac{1}{2}$ **3** $\frac{3}{5} \times \frac{1}{2}$

4 $\frac{2}{3} \times \frac{4}{5}$ **5** $\frac{3}{8} \times \frac{3}{4}$

Assignment 6   Multiplying mixed numbers

• Extend the method of using area diagrams to find a way of solving this problem.

$1\frac{1}{2} \times 2\frac{3}{5}$

• Check that your method works for other similar problems.

Assignment 7   The big one!

Find as many different ways as you can of multiplying three fractions together to give an answer of 1.

Here is one to start with: $\frac{3}{4} \times \frac{2}{9} \times \frac{6}{1}$

Simplifying

The arithmetic involved can be made easier if we simplify the fractions before multiplying.

Example

$$\frac{2}{5} \text{ of } \frac{15}{16} = \frac{2}{5} \times \frac{15}{16}$$

$$\div 2 \qquad = \frac{\overset{1}{\cancel{2}}}{\underset{1}{\cancel{5}}} \times \frac{3 \times \cancel{5}^{1}}{\underset{1}{\cancel{2} \times 8}} \qquad \div 5$$

$$= \frac{1}{1} \times \frac{3 \times 1}{1 \times 8}$$

$$= \frac{3}{8}$$

Exercise 8

Calculate these fractional amounts.

1 $\frac{2}{3}$ of $\frac{9}{10}$ **2** $\frac{4}{5}$ of $\frac{15}{16}$ **3** $\frac{3}{5}$ of $\frac{15}{16}$

4 $\frac{3}{4}$ of $\frac{5}{6}$ **5** $\frac{3}{4}$ of $\frac{5}{12}$ **6** $\frac{2}{3}$ of $\frac{3}{5}$

7 $\frac{3}{4}$ of $\frac{2}{3}$ **8** $\frac{3}{4}$ of $1\frac{1}{2}$ **9** $1\frac{1}{2}$ of $\frac{8}{9}$

10 $1\frac{1}{2}$ of $\frac{4}{9}$ **11** $1\frac{1}{4}$ of $\frac{5}{6}$ **12** $1\frac{3}{4}$ of $\frac{7}{8}$

Using a calculator

Most calculators have a fraction button.

Fractions can be entered as follows: $2\frac{1}{3} \rightarrow$

The display should look like this:

Calculators will give the simplest equivalent fraction.

Example

Enter $\frac{8}{10}$ using these keys:

and the display shows:

Adding fractions

Adding fractions without a calculator is easy if the fractions have the same denominator.

Example

$$\frac{3}{8} + \frac{1}{8} = \frac{4}{8} = \frac{1}{2}$$

The top number is called the numerator.

So, before adding, make sure the fractions have the same denominator. To do this, make an equivalent fraction.

Examples

$$\times 2 \left(\begin{array}{c} \frac{1}{2} + \frac{1}{4} \\ = \frac{2}{4} + \frac{1}{4} \end{array} \right.$$

$$= \frac{3}{4}$$

$$\times 5 \left(\begin{array}{c} \frac{2}{3} + \frac{1}{5} \\ = \frac{10}{15} + \frac{3}{15} \end{array} \right) \times 3$$

$$= \frac{13}{15}$$

Exercise 9

Calculate these.

1 $\frac{1}{2} + \frac{3}{8}$

2 $\frac{1}{3} + \frac{1}{6}$

3 $\frac{2}{5} + \frac{7}{10}$

4 $\frac{3}{4} + \frac{7}{8}$

5 $\frac{4}{5} + \frac{2}{3}$

6 $\frac{3}{7} + \frac{3}{5}$

Check your results with a calculator.

7 An Arabian Prince left his famous collection of horses to his sons. The eldest received half of the collection, the next received a quarter, the third received one fifth and the fourth received 48 horses. How many horses made up the complete collection?

8 A large medal collection was stolen. The thief buried half of them and threw half of the remainder into a lake. Only 500 remained in the thief's possession. How many medals were stolen in total?

Assignment 8   Fraction sum squares

Here is the working for a particular sum.

	2	3
3	+	9
5	10	15

$\rightarrow \frac{19}{15} = 1\frac{4}{5}$

- What is the sum being worked above?

  Explain the working fully.

- Will this method always work?
  Try examples of your own to find out.

- Would you recommend the method?

  Explain fully the reasons for your answer.

Key fact

The reciprocal of a number is 1 divided by that number.
So the reciprocal of 3 is $\frac{1}{3}$.

Assignment 9   Number patterns

- Write down a number pattern of your choice, e.g.
  1, 3, 5, ... or 1, 3, 6, 10, ...

- Now rewrite it as a pattern of reciprocals and sum them, e.g.

  $\frac{1}{1} + \frac{1}{3} + \frac{1}{5} + ...$ or $\frac{1}{1} + \frac{1}{3} + \frac{1}{6} + \frac{1}{10} + ...$

- What do you find? Try other patterns.

Exercise 10

1 Give a simple equivalent fraction for each of these.

    (a) $\frac{15}{20}$ (b) $\frac{12}{36}$ (c) $\frac{120}{150}$ (d) $\frac{24}{120}$ (e) $\frac{9}{1332}$

    (f) $\frac{91}{273}$ (g) $\frac{143}{1001}$ (h) $\frac{21}{847}$ (i) $\frac{35}{225}$ (j) $\frac{33}{1542}$

2 Calculate these:

    (a) $2\frac{2}{3} \times 1\frac{4}{5}$ (b) $3\frac{3}{4} \times 5\frac{3}{7}$ (c) $\frac{12}{13} \times 4\frac{3}{11}$

    (d) $1\frac{1}{2} + 3\frac{3}{7}$ (e) $6\frac{3}{4} + 2\frac{2}{3}$ (f) $\frac{4}{5} + \frac{2}{3} + 1\frac{1}{5}$

    (g) $1\frac{1}{2} - \frac{3}{4}$ (h) $3\frac{3}{4} - 1\frac{11}{12}$ (i) $3\frac{3}{4} \div 2\frac{1}{2}$

Assignment 10   Combining fractions

- If the only fractions available were $\frac{1}{2}$, $\frac{1}{4}$ and $\frac{1}{8}$, how many different fractions could be made by adding any combination of these three?

> Use each fraction only once.

- Another set of three fractions is now included with these three, namely 0.1, 0.2 and 0.4. Place the complete set of six in size order.

- How many different values are now possible by combining the complete set of six in the same way?

Percentages

Assignment 11   Advertisement study

- Make a collection of advertisements from newspapers and magazines that use percentages in any way.

- Which percentages are in most common use?

In your head

Many common percentages are easy to work out in your head.

Example

50% of £30.00

Half of £30 = £15

Example

75% of £80.00

Three quarters of £80 or half plus a quarter of £80

$$= £40 + £20$$

$$= £60.00$$

Exercise 11

Try to calculate these in your head and write down the answer.

1 50% of £100

2 50% of £50

3 50% of £48

4 25% of £16

5 75% of £36

6 50% of £19

7 50% of £13.50

8 75% of £10

9 25% of £50

10 12.5% of £200

Assignment 12   Swapping the order

*   Is 25% of £50 the same as 50% of £25?

    Guess first, then check your answer carefully.

*   Is 25% of £75 the same as 75% of £25?

    Explain your answer fully.

Percentages and fractions

Recognising the percentage as a fraction helps to make the calculations easier.

$$10\% \rightarrow \frac{10}{100} \rightarrow 0.10$$
$$\downarrow$$
$$\frac{1}{10}$$

$$30\% \rightarrow \frac{30}{100} \rightarrow 0.30$$
$$\downarrow$$
$$\frac{3}{10}$$

30 per cent means
30 hundredths

Also: $$81\% \rightarrow \frac{81}{100} \rightarrow 0.81$$
$$\downarrow$$
$$\frac{8}{10} + \frac{1}{100}$$

Exercise 12

Copy and complete this table by filling in the missing values.

	Percentage	Fraction	Decimal
1	10%		
2		$\frac{4}{5}$	
3	15%		
4		$\frac{7}{10}$	
5	95%		
6		$\frac{3}{8}$	
7	120%		
8			1.6
9		$\frac{1}{3}$	

Ten per cent

Ten per cent (10%) is a common percentage and easy to calculate.

$$10\% = \frac{10}{100} = \frac{1}{10}$$

To find 10%, simply multiply by $\frac{1}{10}$ or divide by 10.

This means you need only alter the place values of the digits in the amount.

Example

10% of £32.60 = £3.26

This also means that percentages such as 5% (half of 10%), 20% (double 10%) and combinations like 15% (10% + 5%) can be found very quickly.

Exercise 13

1 Calculate these amounts:

    (a) 10% of £34.50   (b) 10% of £3.20   (c) 10% of £124.00

    (d) 10% of £3400.00   (e) 10% of £0.60   (f) 20% of £46

    (g) 20% of £250   (h) 20% of £4.50   (i) 5% of £28.00

    (j) 5% of £2.50   (k) 5% of £480   (l) 15% of £24.80

    (m) 15% of £140   (n) 15% of £0.80   (o) 17.5% of £200

Answers to problems about money are given to the nearest penny.

17.5% = 10% + 5% + 2.5%

Assignment 13 — Working with VAT

A pocket computer costs £119.00 plus VAT.

A customer is entitled to 10% discount.

The shop assistant is not sure whether to calculate the discount first
and then add the VAT or to calculate it the other way round.

• Does it matter? Justify your answer fully.

Using a calculator

Most calculators have a percentage button. The way it works varies
from model to model. Check your own calculator's manual.
However, this method will always work.

Example

Find 32% of £128.00.

Enter by pressing these keys: **3** **2** **×** **1** **2** **8** **÷** **1** **0** **0** **=**

Your calculator should display: **40.96**

You should write your answer as £40.96

Remember to interpret the
display appropriately.

Exercise 14

Find these percentages using your calculator.

1 46% of £60.00	**2** 13% of £250	**3** 9% of £450
4 95% of £34.50	**5** 66% of £48.00	**6** 58% of £34.00
7 27% of £400	**8** 26% of £50	**9** 158% of £140
10 82% of £4.82	**11** 32% of £65.50	**12** 99% of £156.75

Assignment 14 — Price changes

A CD player made by Sonpo costs the same as a CD player made by
Hitchy. After one year Sonpo increases the cost by 5%, while Hitchy
increases the costs by 10%. The following year Sonpo increases the new
cost by 10% and Hitchy increases by 5%.

• Which is the cheaper player now? Explain your answer fully.

Percentage problems

- Read the problem through carefully at least twice.

- Plan your method carefully in small stages.

- Carry out your plan thoroughly.

- Check that your final answer is sensible.

- Include any units.

Key fact

Percentage profit is calculated by comparing the actual profit, with the original amount.

Exercise 15

1 A shopkeeper bought some hats for £4.90 each and sold them making 30% profit.
What was the selling price of each hat?

2 A water tank accidentally spilled 18 litres of water. It normally holds 240 litres.
What percentage loss is this?

3 An item costing £25 was recently sold making a loss of 8%.
What was the selling price?

4 All the items in a gift shop are to be sold for charity. It is agreed that 25% of each selling price will go to the charity.
How much money does an item costing £1.20 make for the charity?

5 A good wine is bought at £108 per dozen bottles. It is later sold at £32.40 per bottle.
What percentage profit does this wine make?

6 In a closing-down sale, goods are being sold off at a loss to clear the shop. One small item costing £1.44 makes a loss of 12.5%.
How much was it sold for?

7 A person on a diet manages to reduce weight from 200 lbs to 179 lbs.
What percentage of weight has been lost?

8 A person invests £1000 in a business. In the first year, the investment makes 5% profit and, subsequently, it makes 10% profit every year. If all the money is left in the business, how much is the investment at the end of 5 years?

Review Exercise

1 Write $\frac{3}{5}$ as a decimal and as a percentage.

2 Write 0.64 as a percentage and as a fraction.

3 Write 72% as a decimal and as a fraction.

4 Write 210% as a decimal and as a fraction.

5 A tank hold 42 litres when full. If it is two-thirds full, how many litres are there in the tank at the moment?

6 A recipe for 6 people needs 300 g of flour.

How much flour would be needed to make the recipe for

(a) 3 people?   (b) 2 people

7 Write these values in order of size with the smallest first.

$\frac{1}{3}$ 0.72   25%   0.3   79% $\frac{7}{10}$

8 Calculate these.

(a) $\frac{1}{3} + \frac{1}{3}$ (b) $\frac{1}{3} + \frac{1}{3}$ (c) $\frac{1}{3} \times \frac{1}{3}$

(d) $\frac{1}{3}$ of $\frac{1}{3}$ (e) half of 0.7

9 Find these percentages of £84.

(a) 25%   (b) 10%   (c) 15%   (d) 17.5%

10 Look at this advertisement for a camera.

If VAT is 17.5%, how much would you have to pay for this camera?

Only £160 +VAT

11 A pen is sold for £3.60. If the pen originally cost £1.60 what percentage profit has been made?

Assignment 15   The big one revisited!

How many ways can you find to make one by adding three different fractions together?

Here is one example: $\frac{1}{2} + \frac{1}{3} + \frac{1}{6}$

Conversions

In this chapter you will learn:

→ how to construct and use conversion graphs
→ how to use conversion tables
→ how to convert between units by calculation

....

Starting points

Before starting this chapter you will need to know how to:

- plot a straight-line graph

- read values from a graph

- read a variety of scales

- multiply decimal numbers.

Exercise 1

1 Draw a grid so that the axes are numbered from 0 to 10 and from 0 to 6 as shown.

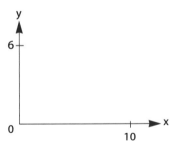

(a) Plot the points (2, 2), (6, 4), (8, 5) and (9, $5\frac{1}{2}$).

(b) Join the points with a straight line.

(c) Extend your line so that it crosses the y-axis. What are the coordinates at this point?

2 Look at this graph. Write down the coordinates of the points A, B, C, D and E.

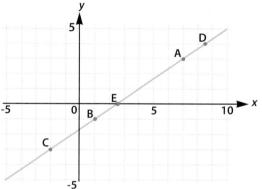

3 Measure these lines. Give your answers in the units shown.

(a) _____ (mm)

(b) _____ (cm)

(c) _____ (inches)

4 Read the measures shown on these scales.

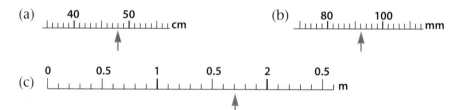

(a) 40   50 cm

(b) 80   100 mm

(c) 0   0.5   1   0.5   2   0.5 m

(d) Write your answers to (b) and (c) in centimetres.

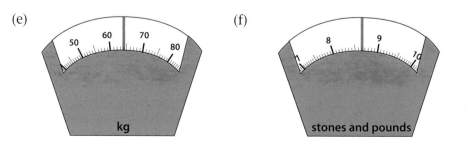

(e) 50 60 70 80 kg

(f) 7 8 9 10 stones and pounds

Conversion graphs

Conversion graphs are usually straight-line graphs which can be used to convert a quantity from one unit to another unit.

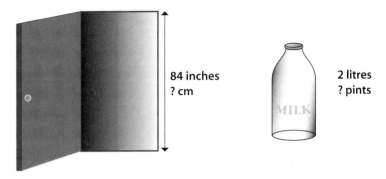

84 inches
? cm

2 litres
? pints

MILK

Assignment 1	Length: conversion of inches ↔ centimetres

You will need a ruler and a tape measure. Both must be marked in inches and centimetres.

- Copy this table.

Object	Measurement in inches	Measurement in centimetres
1 Height of table	30	76
2 Width of TV screen	13	33
3 Length of desk		
4 Width of door		
5 Height of pencil		
6 Length of textbook		
7 Height of window sill		
8 Perimeter of your head		
9		
10		

- Measure the items listed as 3 to 8.

  Items 1 and 2 have already been measured for you. Choose your own objects for items 9 and 10.

- Complete the table.

- Copy this pair of axes on to a sheet of graph paper. Use a scale of 1 cm for every 10 cm on the vertical (↑) axis, and 1 cm for every 5 inches on the horizontal (→) axis. Make sure you label the axes correctly.

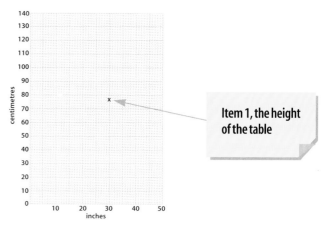

Item 1, the height of the table

Notice that item 1, the height of the table, has already been plotted:

  30 inches across

  76 centimetres up

- Using the data in your table, plot the rest of the objects on the same grid. There is no need to label each one.
  You should notice that the points are very nearly in a straight line.

Now draw a straight line through as many points as possible on your grid.

This line is called the **line of best fit**.

Your graph should look like this.

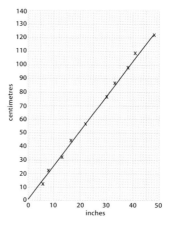

- Why does the line go through the origin (0, 0)?

Using conversion graphs

The graph you have drawn can be used to convert inches to centimetres. It can also be used to convert centimetres to inches.

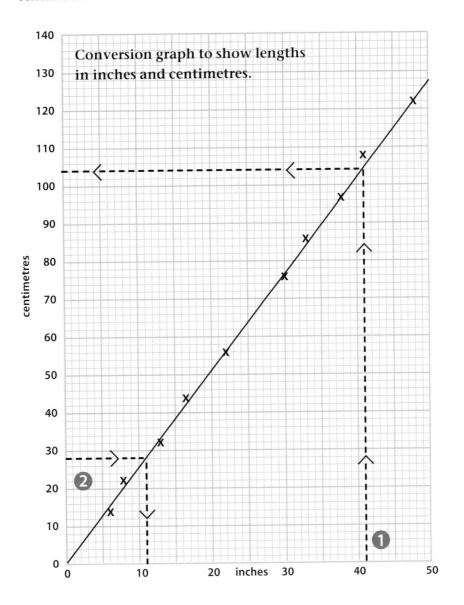

Conversion graph to show lengths in inches and centimetres.

The graph shows two examples: **1** and **2** .

Example **1** shows 41 ins = 104 cm (approximately).

Example **2** shows 28 cm = 11 in (approximately).

Exercise 2

Think! Use your common sense.

1 Use your graph to convert these lengths in inches to centimetres.

(a) 50 in   (b) 47 in   (c) 25 in   (d) 16 in   (e) 28 in

(f) 100 in   (g) 35 in   (h) 10 in   (i) 43 in   (j) 1 in

2 Use your graph to convert these lengths in centimetres to inches.

(a) 30 cm   (b) 54 cm   (c) 8 cm   (d) 66 cm   (e) 118 cm

(f) 100 cm   (g) 200 cm   (h) 500 cm   (i) 1000 cm   (j) 1 cm

3 A person wants to buy 1 yard of fabric but the shop uses metric measurements.

(a) How many inches are there in 1 yard?

(b) How many centimetres is this?

(c) How many metres should the person ask for?

> 12 inches = 1 foot
> 3 feet = 1 yard

Assignment 2   Weight: conversion of pounds ↔ kilograms

1 stone = 14 pounds

You will need bathroom weighing scales. They must be marked in stones/pounds and kilograms.

- Find your weight in kilograms (kg).
  Now find your weight in stones and pounds.
  Change this to pounds (lb).

- Now measure your 'strength' by squeezing the scales as hard as you can.
  You will need to maintain the reading for five seconds!
  Record your strength in both pounds and kilograms.

- Get strength readings from some other pupils. Record your results in a table.

- Draw a set of axes on graph paper.
  Use a scale of 1 cm to 10 lb along the horizontal axis (→) up to 150 lb.
  Use a scale of 1 cm to 5 kg along the vertical axis (↑) up to 75 kg.

Ask your teacher to check your graph before you try Exercise 3.

Plot your results and draw the line of best fit.

Give your conversion graph a title.

Exercise 3

1 Use your graph to convert these weights in pounds to kilograms.

(a) 30 lb   (b) 65 lb   (c) 122 lb

(d) 44 lb   (e) 100 lb   (f) 1 lb

2 Use your graph to convert these weights in kilograms to pounds.

(a) 52 kg   (b) 30 kg   (c) 63 kg

(d) 37 kg   (e) 10 kg   (f) 1 kg

3 A pet poodle weighs 15 kg.

(a) Use your graph to convert this to pounds.

(b) What is this weight in stones and pounds?

Assignment 3   Capacity: conversion of gallons ↔ litres

5 litres
1.1 gallons

Fuel tank capacity 13 gallons (59 litres)

Draw a set of axes on graph paper.
Use a scale of 1 cm to 1 gallon along the horizontal axis (→) up to 15 gallons.

Use a scale of 1 cm to 5 litres along the vertical axis (↑) up to 75 litres.

• Plot the capacities of the oil can and the car.

Draw a straight line through (0, 0) and as close as possible to the points plotted.

Ask your teacher to check your graph before you try Exercise 4.

• Give your conversion graph a title.

Exercise 4

1 Use your graph to convert these capacities in gallons to litres.

(a) 11 gallons   (b) 9 gallons

(c) 2.2 gallons   (d) 13.6 gallons

(e) 7.5 gallons   (f) 10 gallons

(g) 100 gallons   (h) 1 gallon

> Each centimetre across has five divisions so each division represents $1 \div 5 = 0.2$ gallons.

2 Use your graph to convert these capacities in litres to gallons.

(a) 55 litres   (b) 36 litres

(c) 23 litres   (d) 16 litres

(e) 30 litres   (f) 50 litres

(g) 100 litres   (h) 1 litre

3 A builder needs to install a water tank which must hold at least 15 gallons. In his store room, he has a water tank labelled 67.5 litres. Is it large enough?

Key fact

An exchange rate is the amount of a foreign currency that can be bought for £1.

Foreign currency conversions

This table shows the exchange rates for a day in 1969 – the year astronauts landed on the moon.

France	11.20 francs
Portugal	345 escudos
Germany	2.85 marks
Spain	211.50 pesetas
Greece	410 drachmae
Switzerland	3.95 francs
Italy	1920 lire
United States	2.12 dollars

Example

For France, the exchange rate was £1 = 11.20 francs.

So, £10 = 112 francs and £100 = 1120 francs.

This conversion graph has been drawn using these two points and (0, 0).

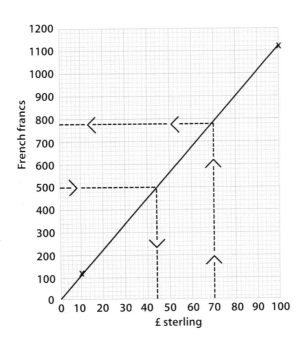

Sterling is the name given to British currency.

The graph can be used to convert amounts of money from pounds sterling (£) to francs and vice versa.

The examples on the graph show that £70 is approximately 780 francs and 500 francs is approximately £44.

Exercise 5

1 Use graph paper or squared paper to draw a conversion graph for pounds sterling (£) to US dollars ($). Use the exchange rate table on page 198.

Use your graph to convert these amounts.

(a) £70   (b) £28   (c) £98   (d) £55

(e) $140   (f) $128   (g) $110   (h) $36

Your axes should look like this

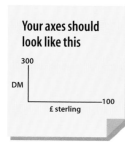

Your axes should look like this

2 Draw a conversion graph for pounds sterling (£) to German marks (DM).

Use the exchange rate table on page 198.

Use your graph to convert these amounts.

(a) £70   (b) £40   (c) £82

(d) £65   (e) DM150   (f) DM85

(g) DM155   (h) DM265

Temperature conversion

Sometimes the word 'centigrade' is used instead of 'Celsius'. They mean the same.

You can use conversion graphs to change temperatures in degrees Celsius (°C) to degrees Fahrenheit (°F). It can also be used to convert degrees Fahrenheit (°F) to degrees Celsius (°C).

Remember that the freezing point of water is 0°C or 32°F and the boiling point of water is 100°C or 212°F.

Exercise 6

1 Use graph paper or squared paper to draw a temperature conversion chart.

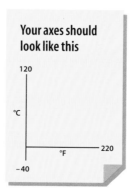

Your axes should look like this

Plot the points (32, 0) and (212, 100).

Join the points with a straight line and extend it both ways so that it meets the edges of the grid.

The line does not go through (0, 0).

Use your graph to convert these temperatures.

(a) 60°F   (b) 0°F   (c) 104°F

(d) 190°F   (e) 16°F   (f) 60°C

(g) 20°C   (h) 25°C   (i) −4°C

Conversion tables

Petrol used to be sold only in gallons. Now it is sold in litres.

During the 'change over' period, most filling stations displayed conversion tables to help motorists.

Here is an example of a typical conversion table.

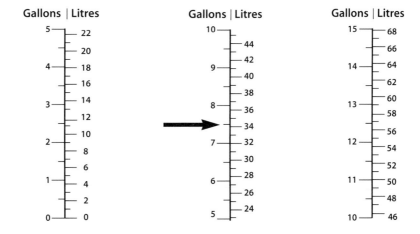

Example

A motorist usually fills her car with 7.5 gallons of petrol.

The table shows that this is about 34 litres.

Exercise 7

1 Use the motorists' conversion table to change these amounts into litres.

(a) 11 gallons   (b) 9.5 gallons   (c) 1.5 gallons

(d) 14.1 gallons   (e) 4.4 gallons   (f) 9.7 gallons

(g) 12 gallons   (h) 3 gallons

2 Use the motorists' conversion table to change these amounts into gallons.

(a) 32 litres   (b) 66 litres   (c) 25 litres

(d) 36.2 litres   (e) 18.1 litres   (f) 63.7 litres

(g) 60 litres   (h) 40 litres

Exercise 8

1

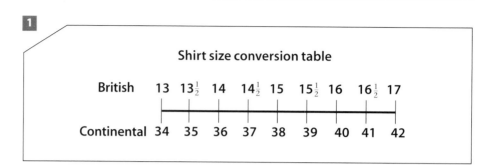

Shirt size conversion table

| British | 13 | $13\frac{1}{2}$ | 14 | $14\frac{1}{2}$ | 15 | $15\frac{1}{2}$ | 16 | $16\frac{1}{2}$ | 17 |

| Continental | 34 | 35 | 36 | 37 | 38 | 39 | 40 | 41 | 42 |

Use the table above to convert these British shirt sizes into continental shirt sizes.

(a) 15   (b) $16\frac{1}{2}$ (c) $13\frac{1}{2}$ (d) 18

Now convert these continental shirt sizes to British shirt sizes.

(e) 36   (f) 39   (g) 34   (h) 45

2

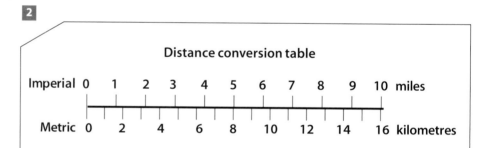

Distance conversion table

| Imperial | 0 | 1 | 2 | 3 | 4 | 5 | 6 | 7 | 8 | 9 | 10 | miles |

| Metric | 0 | 2 | 4 | 6 | 8 | 10 | 12 | 14 | 16 | kilometres |

Key fact

'Imperial' is the name given to British units.

Use the table above to convert these Imperial distances into metric distances.

(a) 5 miles   (b) 9 miles   (c) 2.5 miles

(d) 4.4 miles   (e) 7.8 miles   (f) 15 miles

Now convert these distances from kilometres to miles.

(g) 12 km   (h) 16.1 km   (i) 4.8 km

(j) 10.5 km   (k) 6 km   (l) 20 km

Converting between units by calculation

Look back at Exercise 3, Question 2(f).

You should have found that 1 kg is approximately 2.2 lb.

So 7 kg is approximately 15.4 lb.

$7 \times 2.2 = 15.4$

If you look at Exercise 2, Question 1(j) you should have found that 1 inch is approximately 2.54 cm.

So 15 inches is approximately 38.10 cm.

$15 \times 2.54 = 38.10$

Exercise 9

1 Convert these weights from kilograms into pounds.

(a) 2 kg   (b) 5 kg   (c) 9 kg

(d) 11 kg   (e) 10 kg   (f) 23 kg

(g) $\frac{1}{2}$ kg   (h) $6\frac{1}{2}$ kg   (i) 0.1 kg

(j) 0.6 kg   (k) 3.4 kg   (l) 14.7 kg

2 Convert these lengths from inches into centimetres.

(a) 2 inch   (b) 5 inches   (c) 9 inches

(d) 11 inches   (e) 10 inches   (f) 23 inches

(g) $\frac{1}{2}$ inch   (h) $6\frac{1}{2}$ inches   (i) 0.1 inch

(j) 0.6 inch   (k) 3.4 inches   (l) 14.7 inches

3 Convert these weights from kilograms into stones and pounds.

(a) 10 kg   (b) 35 kg

(c) 38 kg   (d) 64 kg

Write your answer to the nearest pound.

14 pounds = 1 stone

More converting between units by calculation

1 kg is approximately 2.2 lb so

$$1 \text{ lb is approximately } 1 \div 2.2 \approx 0.45 \text{ kg}$$

$$\therefore 3 \text{ lb is approximately } 3 \times 0.45 = 1.35 \text{ kg}$$

> $\approx$ means 'is about'
> $\therefore$ means 'therefore'

5 miles $\approx$ 8 kilometres so

$$1 \text{ mile} \approx 8 \div 5 = 1.6 \text{ km}$$

$$1 \text{ km} \approx 5 \div 8 = 0.625 \text{ miles}$$

Exercise 10

Key fact

1 kg $\approx$ 2.2 lb
1 lb $\approx$ 0.45 kg

1 Convert these weights into kilograms:

(a) 2 lb
(b) 5 lb
(c) 9 lb

(d) 11 lb
(e) 10 lb
(f) 32 lb

(g) 85 lb
(h) 100 lb
(i) 5 stone

(j) $6\frac{1}{2}$ stone
(k) $13\frac{1}{2}$ stone
(l) 2 stone 9 lb

Key fact

5 miles $\approx$ 8 km
1 mile $\approx$ 1.6 km

2 How far in kilometres is:

(a) 25 miles?
(b) 60 miles?
(c) 200 miles?

(d) 210 miles?
(e) 250 miles?
(f) 500 miles?

How far in miles is:

(g) 16 km?
(h) 84 km?
(i) 120 km?

(j) 160 km?
(k) 200 km?
(l) 800 km?

3 (a) Given that 1 inch $\approx$ 2.54 cm, calculate the equivalent of 1 cm in inches. Give your answer correct to 2 decimal places.

(b) Use your answer to (a) to express these lengths in inches.

(i) 2 cm
(ii) 5 cm
(iii) 9 cm

(iv) 11 cm
(v) 10 cm
(vi) 16 cm

(vii) 45 cm
(viii) 1 m
(ix) 3 m

Useful conversion tables

To convert from inches to centimetres, read from left to right ($\rightarrow$) so multiply by the factor 2.54.

To convert from centimetres to inches, read from right to left ($\leftarrow$) so multiply by the factor 0.394.

LENGTH	0.394 $\leftarrow$	inches : centimetres	$\rightarrow$	2.540
	0.039 $\leftarrow$	inches : millimetres	$\rightarrow$	25.40
	3.281 $\leftarrow$	feet : metres	$\rightarrow$	0.305
	1.094 $\leftarrow$	yards : metres	$\rightarrow$	0.914
	0.621 $\leftarrow$	miles : kilometres	$\rightarrow$	1.609
AREA	0.155 $\leftarrow$	square inches : square centimetres	$\rightarrow$	6.452
	10.76 $\leftarrow$	square feet : square metres	$\rightarrow$	0.093
	1.196 $\leftarrow$	square yards : square metres	$\rightarrow$	0.836
	2.471 $\leftarrow$	acres : hectares	$\rightarrow$	0.405
	0.386 $\leftarrow$	square miles : square kilometres	$\rightarrow$	2.590
VOLUME/	0.061 $\leftarrow$	cubic inches : cubic centimetres	$\rightarrow$	16.39
CAPACITY	35.31 $\leftarrow$	cubic feet : cubic metres	$\rightarrow$	0.028
	1.308 $\leftarrow$	cubic yards : cubic metres	$\rightarrow$	0.765
	1.760 $\leftarrow$	pints : litres	$\rightarrow$	0.568
	0.220 $\leftarrow$	gallons : litres	$\rightarrow$	4.546
WEIGHT/	0.035 $\leftarrow$	ounces : grams	$\rightarrow$	28.35
MASS	2.205 $\leftarrow$	pounds : kilograms	$\rightarrow$	0.454
	1.016 $\leftarrow$	tons : tonnes	$\rightarrow$	0.984

Example

To convert inches to millimitres, use 25.40

$$4 \text{ inches} = 4 \times 25.40 \text{ mm} = 101.6 \text{ mm}$$

To convert litres to pints, use 1.760

$$3 \text{ litres} = 3 \times 1.760 \text{ pints} = 5.28 \text{ pints}$$

To convert ounces to grams, use 28.35

$$4 \text{ ounces} = 4 \times 28.35 \text{ grams} = 113.4 \text{ g}$$

Exercise 11

1 Convert these amounts to the units shown:

(a) 3 metres to feet (b) 4 pints to litres

(c) 10 kilograms to pounds (d) 3 square yards to square metres

(e) 5 inches to millimetres (f) 7 pounds to kilograms

(g) 32 miles to kilometres (h) 6 cubic yards to cubic metres

Review Exercise

1 **Conversion graph for lengths in metres and feet**

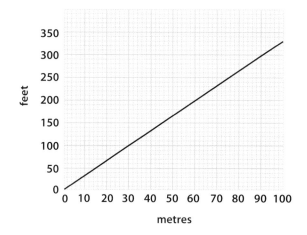

Use the graph to convert these lengths in metres to feet.

(a) 30m (b) 70m (c) 55m (d) 26m

Use the graph to convert these lengths in feet to metres.

(e) 250 feet (f) 130 feet (g) 310 feet (h) 75 feet

2 The exchange rate for Switzerland was £1 = 3.95 francs.
So £10 = 39.5 francs and £100 = 395 francs.

(a) Draw a set of axes on graph paper.
Use a scale of 1 cm to £10 along the horizontal axis (→) to £100.
Use a scale of 1 cm to 25 francs up the vertical axis (↑) to 400 francs.

(b) Use your graph to convert these amounts of money.

(i) £30 (ii) £85 (iii) 80f (iv) 185f

3

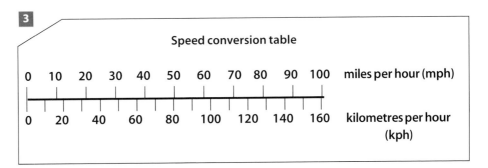

Speed conversion table

Use the table above to convert these speeds.

(a) 50 mph　　　　(b) 81 mph　　　　(c) 40 mph

(d) 40 kph　　　　(e) 144 kph　　　　(f) 90 kph

4

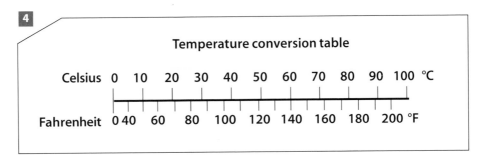

Temperature conversion table

Use the table to convert these temperatures.

(a) 60°C　　　　(b) 30°C　　　　(c) 21°C

(d) 35°C　　　　(e) 75°C　　　　(f) 100°C

(g) 50°F　　　　(h) 160°F　　　　(i) 104°F

(j) 185°F　　　　(k) 135°F　　　　(l) 32°F

5 Use the table on page 205 for these conversions.

(a) 5 inches into millimetres

(b) 8 metres into feet

(c) 6 kilometres into miles

(d) 15 square miles into square kilometres

(e) 24 square metres into square feet

(f) 5.7 ounces into grams

(g) 8.5 litres into pints

Directed numbers

In this chapter you will learn:

→ addition with numbers smaller than zero
→ subtraction with numbers smaller than zero
→ multiplication with numbers smaller than zero

Starting points

Before starting this chapter you will need to know how to:

* locate a point using coordinates

* to read scales.

Exercise 1

1 Write down the coordinates of the points marked A to J on these axes.

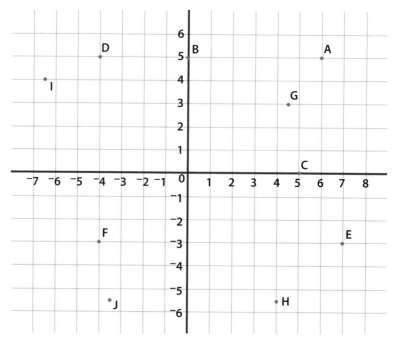

2 (a) Draw a set of axes like those in Question 1.
Plot these points on your axes and join them, in order.

(2, 3), (4, 5), (3, 2), (5, 1), (3, 0), (4, ⁻3), (2, ⁻1), (1, ⁻4), (0, ⁻1),
(⁻2, ⁻3), (⁻1, 0), (⁻3, 1), (⁻1, 2), (⁻2, 5), (0, 3), (1, 6), (2, 3)

(b) Write down the number of lines of symmetry the shape has.

(c) Write down the order of rotational symmetry of the shape.

3 (a) Draw a set of axes like those in Question 1.

(b) Draw a line through the two points (⁻6, 6) and (4, ⁻4).

(c) Plot these points and join them, in order to make a shape.

(⁻2, ⁻1), (⁻6, ⁻1), (⁻5, ⁻3), (⁻4, ⁻1)

(d) Reflect your shape in the line, and write down the coordinates
of the new shape.

4 (a) Write down the coordinates of the corners of the red and the
blue flags.

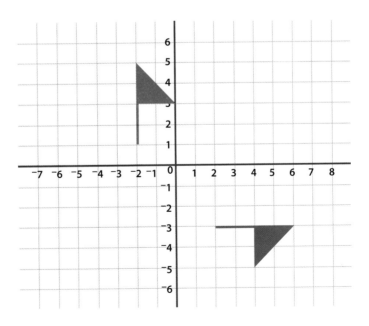

(b) The red flag has been rotated to the position of the blue flag.
Write down the coordinates of the centre of rotation.

(c) Write down the angle and direction of the rotation.

Extending the number line

Exercise 2

1 Look at each arrow and write down the number to which it points.

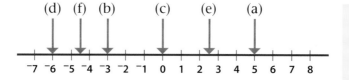

```
(d)  (f) (b)        (c)        (e)        (a)
 ↓    ↓   ↓          ↓          ↓          ↓
―――┼――┼――┼――┼――┼――┼――┼――┼――┼――┼――┼――┼――┼――┼――┼――
   ⁻7 ⁻6 ⁻5 ⁻4 ⁻3 ⁻2 ⁻1  0  1  2  3  4  5  6  7  8
```

> **Positive numbers are written without the sign '+'.**

2 This diagram shows the heights of various objects compared to sea level.

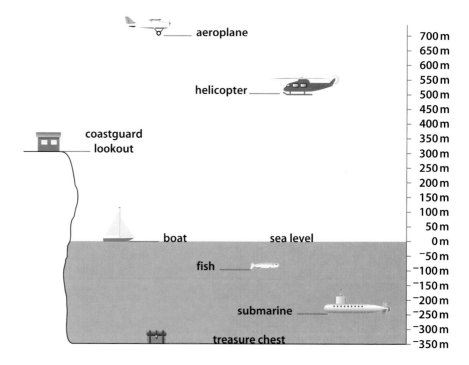

Write down the approximate height of these objects in the picture.

(a) aeroplane   (b) boat   (c) coastguard lookout

(d) fish   (e) helipcopter

(f) submarine   (g) treasure chest

3 Write down the temperatures shown on these thermometers.

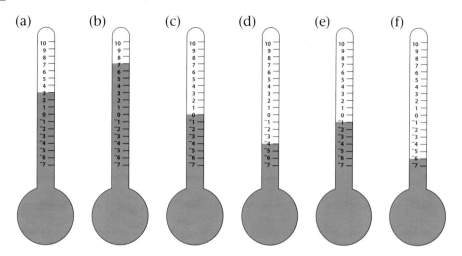

(a) (b) (c) (d) (e) (f)

Now write out the temperatures in order, from lowest to highest.

4 This diagram shows a mine cut into a mountain.

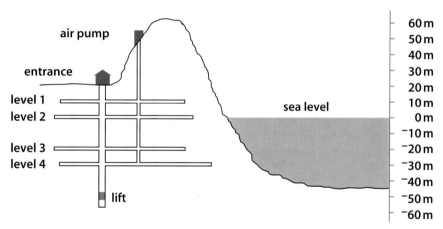

(a) Write down the approximate height of the entrance.

(b) Write down the approximate height of the lift.

(c) Write down the approximate height of each level of the mine.

(d) The lift rises from level 2 to level 1. How far does it travel?

(e) The lift rises from level 4 to level 2. How far does it travel?

(f) The lift goes down from level 1 to level 3. How far does it travel?

(g) The lift rises 30 m from level 3. Where does it stop?

(h) The lift goes down 40 m from the entrance. Where does it stop?

5 This map shows the temperatures at Edinburgh and Penzance in degrees Celsius (°C).

These thermometers show the same two temperatures as in the map.

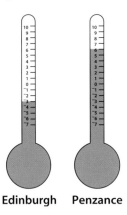

Edinburgh   Penzance

(a) Use the diagram to help you to work out how many degrees warmer Penzance is than Edinburgh.

(b) Write down the number of degrees that separate the temperatures in the places.

(i) Birmingham and London

(ii) Birmingham and Edinburgh

(iii) Newcastle and Swansea

(iv) London and Newcastle

(v) Penzance and Wick

(vi) Wick and Newcastle

(c) Draw a number line. Show where the temperature of each place on the map appears on the line.

(d) Write down which place is warmest and which is coldest.

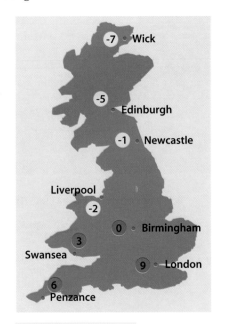

Draw thermometers if it helps you.

6 Look at this diagram again.

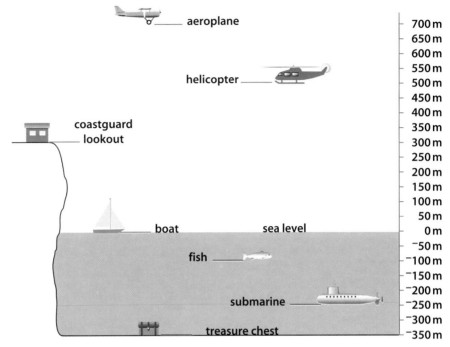

Write down the difference in height of these objects.

(a) the boat and the helicopter

(b) the coastguard lookout and the aeroplane

(c) the boat and the fish

(d) the treasure and the submarine

(e) the fish and the helicopter

(f) the submarine and the helicopter

(g) the submarine and the fish

(h) the boat and the submarine

Assignment 1   **Temperature differences**

Find out the lowest and highest temperatures that have been recorded near where you live in the last ten years.

• How many degrees separate these two temperatures?

• Try to find out which place in the British Isles has the largest difference between the lowest and highest recorded temperatures.

Adding negative numbers

Adding on the number line

On this number line, the points are 1 cm apart.

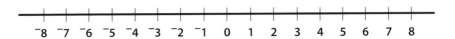

These two arrows can demonstrate adding 2 and 3.

One is 3 cm long, and the other is 2 cm long.

The arrows can be placed on the number line like this.

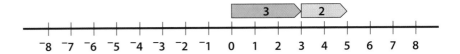

The first arrow must start at 0.
The second arrow starts at the end of the first and ends at 5.
5 is the answer to the sum 2 + 3.

Here is an arrow for ⁻2.

Notice that this arrow points the opposite way from the arrow for +2.

Placing the 3 arrow and the ⁻2 arrow on the number line like this demonstrates adding 3 and ⁻2.

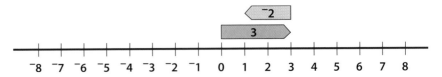

$3 + {}^-2 = 1$

Exercise 3

1 Use arrows on a number line for these additions.
Record your answers on a diagram and as a sum.

(a) $5 + {}^-2$

(b) $8 + {}^-1$

(c) $7 + {}^-4$

(d) $4 + {}^-4$

(e) $8 + {}^-8$

(f) ${}^-3 + 3$

(g) ${}^-2 + 8$

(h) $4 + {}^-6$

(i) $2 + {}^-5$

(j) $1 + {}^-8$

(k) ${}^-7 + 3$

(l) ${}^-5 + 2$

(m) ${}^-1 + {}^-2$

(n) ${}^-2 + {}^-4$

(o) ${}^-5 + {}^-3$

2 Write down as many ways as possible of using arrows on a number line to make the answer 4.

3 Write down as many ways as possible of using arrows on a number line to make the answer ${}^-4$.

4 Write down as many ways as possible of using arrows on a number line to make the answer 0.

Assignment 2   The 'end of the line' game

• For this game you will need a number line, a dice marked with the numbers
${}^-3,\quad {}^-2,\quad {}^-1,\quad 1,\quad 2,\quad 3$
and two markers.

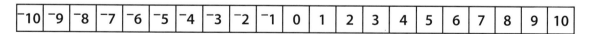

• Play this game with a partner.

Start with both your markers on 0.

• Take it in turns to throw the dice and move the number of places that it shows.

• The winner is the first person to move off either end of the line.

Subtracting negative numbers

Subtracting on the number line

Placing the 3 arrow and the 2 arrow on a number line like this,

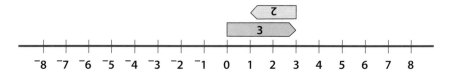

demonstrates taking 2 from 3.

The first arrow must start at 0.

The second arrow is turned upside-down and starts at the end of the first.

The end of the second arrow points at the answer.

$3 - 2 = 1$

This diagram demonstrates taking ⁻2 away from 3.

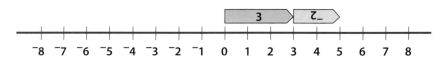

The second arrow has been turned upside-down as before.

$3 - {}^{-}2 = 5$

Exercise 4

1 Show how these subtractions can be demonstrated using arrows.

Show your answers on copies of the number line, using arrows.

(a) $4 - 1$ (b) $7 - 3$ (c) $5 - 5$

(d) $3 - 5$ (e) $5 - 7$ (f) $1 - 7$

(g) $4 - {}^{-}1$ (h) ${}^{-}3 - 1$ (i) ${}^{-}3 - {}^{-}1$

(j) $3 - {}^{-}3$ (k) $5 - {}^{-}1$ (l) $6 - {}^{-}3$

Exercise 5

1 Do these additions without using a calculator.

(a) $5 + {}^-3$

(b) $6 + {}^-2$

(c) $4 + {}^-4$

(d) ${}^-4 + 7$

(e) ${}^-7 + 10$

(f) ${}^-9 + 19$

(g) $4 + {}^-9$

(h) $3 + {}^-12$

(i) $0 + {}^-7$

(j) ${}^-8 + 7$

(k) ${}^-15 + 5$

(l) ${}^-12 + 0$

(m) ${}^-4 + {}^-5$

(n) ${}^-14 + {}^-6$

(o) ${}^-10 + {}^-10$

2 Do these subtractions without using a calculator.

(a) $5 - 7$

(b) $3 - 8$

(c) $0 - 7$

(d) ${}^-3 - 4$

(e) ${}^-6 - 5$

(f) ${}^-7 - 7$

(g) $8 - {}^-5$

(h) $1 - {}^-6$

(i) $0 - {}^-8$

(j) ${}^-4 - {}^-3$

(k) ${}^-6 - {}^-8$

(l) ${}^-4 - {}^-7$

(m) ${}^-5 - {}^-9$

(n) ${}^-10 - {}^-3$

(o) ${}^-11 - {}^-9$

3 Do these without using a calculator.

(a) $13 + {}^-7$

(b) $12 - 17$

(c) $10 - {}^-5$

(d) $13 + {}^-9$

(e) ${}^-10 - 6$

(f) ${}^-14 + 8$

(g) $15 - {}^-5$

(h) ${}^-8 + {}^-9$

(i) ${}^-9 - 9$

(j) ${}^-8 + 16$

(k) ${}^-13 - {}^-11$

(l) $13 - 25$

(m) ${}^-13 + 12$

(n) ${}^-13 + {}^-11$

(o) $0 - {}^-12$

4 Copy these problems and solve them by filling in the number missing from the square.

(a) $3 - \square = 1$

(b) $3 + \square = 1$

(c) $7 + \square = 3$

(d) ${}^-2 + \square = 6$

(e) ${}^-4 + \square = {}^-1$

(f) $5 - \square = 8$

(g) ${}^-6 - \square = {}^-10$

(h) ${}^-7 - \square = {}^-5$

(i) ${}^-8 - \square = 0$

(j) $\square + {}^-5 = 8$

(k) $\square - {}^-5 = 8$

(l) $\square + {}^-3 = {}^-6$

(m) $\square - {}^-3 = {}^-6$

(n) $\square - {}^-9 = 0$

(o) $\square + \square = 0$

Check all your answers with a calculator.

Multiplication with negative numbers

Multiplication on the number line

This arrow diagram shows $3 \times 2 = 6$.

As before the first arrow must start at 0. Three arrows, each 2 cm long are used.

This diagram shows the multiplication $2 \times 3 = 6$

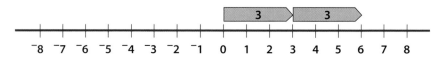

The first arrow starts at 0. Two arrows each 3 cm long are used.

This diagram shows $2 \times {}^-3 = {}^-6$.

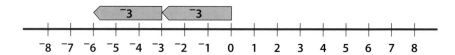

This diagram shows $3 \times {}^-2 = {}^-6$.

Notice that $3 \times {}^-2 = 2 \times {}^-3$.

> With multiplication the order of the numbers does not matter.
>
> $3 \times 2 = 2 \times 3$
>
> This rule works whether the numbers are positive or negative.

Exercise 6

1 Draw diagrams to show 2×3 and two other multiplications involving positive numbers.

2 Draw diagrams to show these multiplications.

(a) $2 \times {}^-3$ (b) $4 \times {}^-3$ (c) $3 \times {}^-4$

3 Copy and complete these multiplications.

(a) $3 \times {}^-5$ (b) $4 \times {}^-7$ (c) $6 \times {}^-4$

(d) ${}^-4 \times 6$ (e) ${}^-5 \times 7$ (f) ${}^-9 \times 8$

(g) $7 \times {}^-7$ (h) ${}^-9 \times 7$ (i) $9 \times {}^-8$

Problems involving negative numbers

For each question in this next exercise, write down the calculation you carry out to find the answer.

Exercise 7

1 One day in January, the temperature at 2 a.m. was ${}^-3°C$. By 8 a.m., it had risen to 2°C. By how many degrees had the temperature risen?

2 The next day the temperature at 2 a.m. was ${}^-5°C$. By 8 a.m., it had risen eight degrees Celsius. What was the temperature at 8 a.m?

3 The temperature falls from 10°C to ${}^-2°C$. How many degrees does it fall?

4 If the temperature drops by eight degrees Celsius from 2°C, what is the new temperature?

5 At 7 p.m. on a cold winter evening, the temperature was ${}^-5°C$. The temperature had dropped a further eight degrees Celsius by 11 p.m. What was the temperature at 11 p.m.?

6 A diver jumps into the sea from a helicopter hovering at 50 ft, and descends to 30 feet below sea level. How far is the diver below the helicopter?

7 An oil rig 47 m tall stands with its base on the sea bed. The depth of the sea is 28 m. What is the height of the rig above sea level?

8 The temperature at midnight was ${}^-12°C$. It then rose steadily by two degrees every hour. What was the temperature at 10 o'clock in the morning?

9 The temperature at 1600 hrs was 5°C. It then fell steadily at three degrees an hour. What was the temperature at 2300 hrs?

10 The temperature at 1730 hrs was ${}^-3°C$. By 2330 hrs, it had dropped to ${}^-9°C$. If the temperature dropped steadily, by how many degrees did it drop each hour?

Review Exercise

1 (a) Write down the names of the places on this map in order, from coldest to warmest.

(b) Which place is six degrees colder than Penzance?

(c) Which place is one degree warmer than Birmingham?

(d) How much colder is it in Edinburgh than in London?

(e) How much warmer is it in Penzance than in Swansea?

(f) What is the difference in temperature between Edinburgh and Liverpool?

2 For each of these questions, draw arrows on a copy of this number line to show the answers.

Label each line with the question and answer.

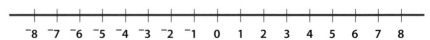

(a) $3 + {}^-2$

(b) ${}^-5 + 4$

(c) ${}^-4 + 1$

(d) $3 + {}^-6$

(e) ${}^-4 + {}^-2$

(f) $3 - 6$

(g) ${}^-2 - 3$

(h) $4 - {}^-5$

(i) ${}^-2 - {}^-4$

3 Work out these:

(a) $^-3 + 5$ (b) $^-6 + ^-9$ (c) $6 - 13$

(d) $^-5 - 8$ (e) $8 - ^-4$ (f) $^-7 - ^-5$

(g) $^-4 \times 7$ (h) $^-8 \times 3$ (i) $^-7 \times 6$

(j) $^-6 \times ^-8$ (k) $^-7 \times 9$ (l) $8 \times ^-9$

(m) $^-12 \div 3$ (n) $^-16 \div 4$ (o) $^-15 \div 3$

(p) $24 \div ^-6$ (q) $32 \div ^-8$ (r) $^-36 \div 4$

4 For each of these questions, write down the calculation you have to work out as well as the answer.

(a) The temperature at 9 a.m. was twelve degrees Celsius higher than it was at 1 a.m. If the temperature at 1 a.m. was $^-6°C$, what was the temperature at 9 a.m?

(b) Suppose that you are given £5 pocket money but you have to pay back £3.50 which you borrowed last week.
How much do you have left?

(c) If you borrow £27 and then pay back £12, how much do you still owe?

(d) The temperature at 11 p.m. was $^-3°C$. It fell steadily at three degrees per hour until 2 a.m.
What was the temperature at 2 a.m.?

Assignment 3   Negative numbers pictures

- Draw your own picture using negative numbers like those earlier in this chapter.

- Write some questions based on your own drawing.

Solving equations

In this chapter you will learn:

→ **how to solve simple equations**
→ **how to use formulae involving two operations**
→ **how to solve equations**

Starting points

Before starting this chapter you will need to know how to:

*   simplify algebraic expressions

*   use letters to represent numbers

*   substitute values into algebraic expressions

*   multiply out brackets.

Exercise 1

1 Simplify these expressions.

    (a) $2a + 3a + a$ (b) $5b - 3b$ (c) $2x + x + 2y$

    (d) $2a + 3a + 4b - 2b$ (e) $x + y + x + 2y - 2x$ (f) $3w + 3v - 4v$

    (g) $3x + x + 5$ (h) $9 - 2x - x$

2 If $a = 3$, $b = 5$ and $c = 7$, find the values of these expressions.

    (a) $2a + 3b + c$ (b) $5b - 3a$ (c) $2b + c - a$

    (d) $5a - 2b$ (e) $a + b + a + 2b - 2c$ (f) $3c + 3a - 4b$

> Each value inside the bracket is multiplied by the value in front of the bracket.

3 Multiply out these expressions.

    (a) $2(a + b)$ (b) $5(b - a)$ (c) $2(2b - a)$

    (d) $3(a - 2b)$ (e) $3(3b + 2a)$ (f) $3(2a - 4b)$

Assignment 1

- Use a copy of this diagram. Follow the direction of the arrows and fill in the values in the circles.

- You will need to substitute a value into each expression. The first one has been done for you: when $n = 5$, $n + 2 = 7$. For some circles, you need to work backwards.

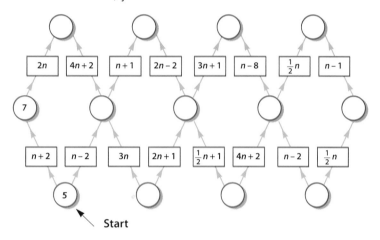

Sums with holes in them

Exercise 2

1 This is a section from a pupil's book.

```
1 (a)    + 4 + 11  ✓        (b) 6 +    = 15  ✓
  (c)  15 +    = 23  ✓        (d)    – 14 = 9  ✓
  (e)  24 +    = 60  ✓        (f)  54 –    = 28  ✓
  (g)    × 7 = 56  ✓          (h) 9 ×    = 45  ✓
  (i)    × 4 = 60  ✓          (j)    × 7 = 84  ✓
  (k)  36 ÷    = 4  ✓         (l)  64 ÷    = 8  ✓
  (m) 14 ÷    = 7  ✓          (n) 1   ÷ 9 = 12  ✓
```

Ink has been spilt on the page.

All the answers are correct.

Rewrite the exercise filling in the missing numbers.

2 In each of these equations, a number has been replaced by a coloured symbol.

Copy each equation and write down the number that the symbol represents.

(a) 8 + ■ = 16

  ■ =

(b) 3 + ● = 11

  ● =

(c) ▲ + 12 = 21

  ▲ =

(d) 17 + ● = 32

  ● =

(e) ▼ + 25 = 37

  ▼ =

(f) ■ + 24 = 41

  ■ =

(g) 36 + ◆ = 46

  ◆ =

(h) 52 + ● = 75

  ● =

(i) ▲ + 11 = 24

  ▲ =

(j) 19 + ■ = 34

  ■ =

(k) ◆ + 23 = 82

  ◆ =

(l) ▼ + 27 = 35

  ▼ =

Letters for numbers

In this equation, a number has been replaced by the letter f.

  $5 + f = 8$

You can illustrate this equation.

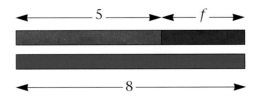

Then you can use your knowledge of numbers to work out the value of the letter.

You know that $5 + 3 = 8$.

Therefore $f = 3$.

Exercise 3

1 (i) Write down an equation to represent each of these diagrams.

(ii) Solve the equations to find the missing value in each one.

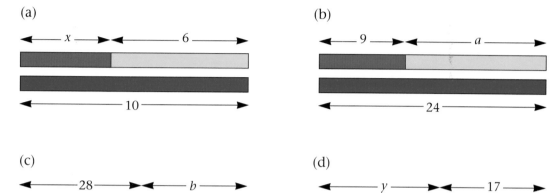

(a)

(b)

(c)

(d)

2 In each of these equations, the letter stands for a missing number. Write down the number represented in each case.

(a) $3 + a = 8$

$a =$

(b) $8 + k = 8$

$k =$

(c) $13 + g = 18$

$g =$

(d) $14 + c = 20$

$c =$

(e) $7 + s = 16$

$s =$

(f) $8 + y = 11$

$y =$

(g) $x + 3 = 8$

$x =$

(h) $9 + p = 15$

$p =$

(i) $15 + j = 32$

$j =$

(j) $x + 65 = 67$

$x =$

(k) $25 + r = 36$

$r =$

(l) $34 + m = 48$

$m =$

(m) $78 + n = 81$

$n =$

(n) $55 + f = 87$

$f =$

(o) $74 + h = 96$

$h =$

(p) $24 + g = 88$

$g =$

3 Look carefully at the questions and their answers.

(a) Write down a quick method for finding the solutions.

(b) Explain how your method works.

Taking away

This diagram illustrates the
equation $12 - x = 4$.

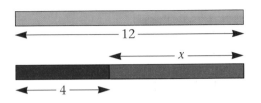

You can rewrite this as
$x = 12 - 4$
So, you can work out that $x = 8$.

Exercise 4

1 (i) Write down an equation to represent each of these diagrams.

   (ii) Solve the equations to find the missing value in each one.

(a)

(b)

(c)

(d)

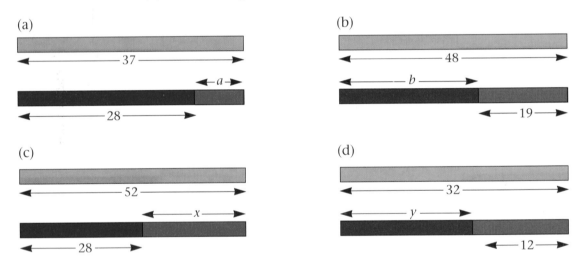

> **Remember to check
> your answers.**

2 Write down the value of the letters in each of these equations.

(a) $39 - a = 8$ (b) $8 - k = 8$ (c) $13 - g = 8$ (d) $44 - p = 20$

   $a =$ $k =$ $g =$ $p =$

(e) $37 - s = 16$ (f) $28 - y = 11$ (g) $14 - x = 8$ (h) $29 - r = 15$

   $s =$ $y =$ $x =$ $r =$

3 Look carefully at the expressions in Questions 1 and 2 and their
answers.

(a) Write down a quick method for finding the solutions.

(b) Explain how your method works.

Multiplying

If twice an unknown number is 38, you can illustrate it like this.

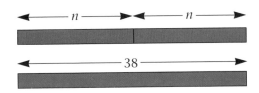

This can be written as $2n = 38$.

So, $n = 19$ because $2 \times 19 = 38$. ✓

Equations like this can also be solved without diagrams.

When multiplying using letters, leave out the multiplication sign.

Example

$4b = 20$ If four lots of something

$b = 5$ are worth 20 then one of
them must be worth 5.

Check:
$4 \times 5 = 20$

Exercise 5

1 (i) Write down an equation to represent each of these diagrams.

(ii) Solve the equations to find the missing value in each one.

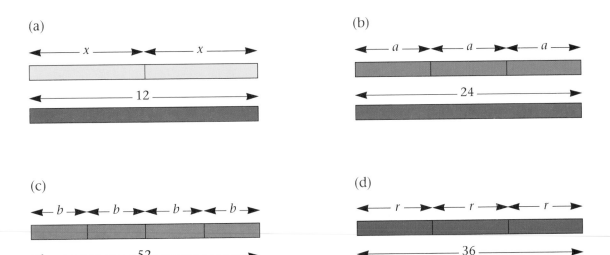

(a)

(b)

(c)

(d)

2 In each of the following, the letter stands for a number. Write down the number represented in each case.

(a) $3d = 9$

$d =$

(b) $8m = 8$

$m =$

(c) $2g = 8$

$g =$

(d) $5p = 20$

$p =$

(e) $3a = 3$

$a =$

(f) $4f = 32$

$f =$

(g) $9h = 36$

$h =$

(h) $4g = 28$

$g =$

(i) $2j = 20$

$j =$

(j) $3x = 48$

$x =$

(k) $3r = 6$

$r =$

(l) $2m = 18$

$m =$

(m) $3n = 21$

$n =$

(n) $9v = 27$

$v =$

(o) $2u = 46$

$u =$

(p) $3x = 18$

x

3 Look carefully at the equations in Questions 1 and 2 and their solutions.

(a) Write down a quick method for finding the solutions.

(b) Explain how your method works.

Dividing

When an unknown value is divided by a number you can still use your knowledge of numbers to work out the unknown value.

Example

A number divided by 2 is equal to 8.

You can write this as

$$\frac{a}{2} = 8$$

is the same as

$\frac{a}{2}$ $a \div 2$

The number must be 16 because

$$\frac{16}{2} = 8$$

Exercise 6

1 Complete each of the following.

(a) $\dfrac{b}{2} = 4$ (b) $\dfrac{m}{3} = 2$ (c) $\dfrac{e}{2} = 3$ (d) $\dfrac{a}{5} = 2$

$b =$ $m =$ $e =$ $a =$

(e) $\dfrac{a}{2} = 4$ (f) $\dfrac{b}{6} = 2$ (g) $\dfrac{f}{12} = 3$ (h) $\dfrac{t}{3} = 13$

$a =$ $b =$ $f =$ $t =$

(i) $\dfrac{b}{2} = 14$ (j) $\dfrac{m}{3} = 25$ (k) $\dfrac{e}{2} = 31$ (l) $\dfrac{a}{15} = 2$

$b =$ $m =$ $e =$ $a =$

2 Look carefully at the equations in Question 1 and their solutions.

(a) Write down a quick method for finding the solutions.

(b) Explain how your method works.

Two operators

The following problems involve using two of the processes you have worked on already.

To calculate the missing value this time you must carry out two operations.

d	d	3
	7	

Example

$2d + 3 = 7$ First, treat the $2d$ as one unknown number.
        This unknown number, added to 3, gives 7.
        The unknown number must be 4.

Check:
$2 \times 2 + 3 = 7$

$2d = 4$ Next, solve $2d = 4$
      Two times an unknown number is 4.

$d = 2$ The unknown number must be 2.

Exercise 7

1 (i) Write down an equation to represent each of these diagrams.

(ii) Solve the equations to find the missing value in each one.

(a)

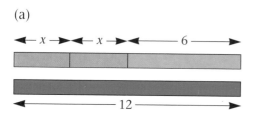

(b)

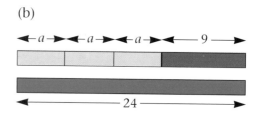

(c)

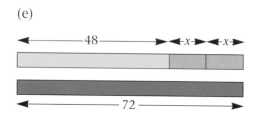

(d)

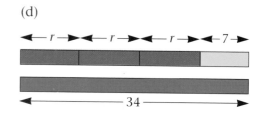

(e)

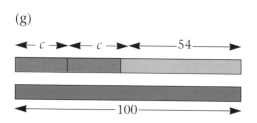

(f)

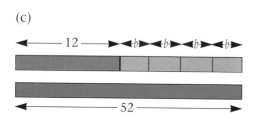

(g)

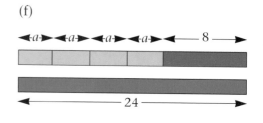

(h)

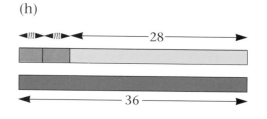

2 Complete each of the following.

(a) $2d + 5 = 9$

$2d =$

$d =$

(b) $8m + 3 = 19$

$8m =$

$m =$

(c) $2g + 5 = 15$

$2g =$

$g =$

(d) $5p + 3 = 18$

$5p =$

$p =$

(e) $3a - 1 = 2$

$3a =$

$a =$

(f) $4x - 2 = 30$

$4x =$

$x =$

(g) $9h - 3 = 33$

$9h =$

$h =$

(h) $4g + 2 = 30$

$4g =$

$g =$

(i) $3 + 2j = 23$

$2j =$

$j =$

(j) $3b - 4 = 44$

(k) $3r - 1 = 5$

(l) $2m - 5 = 13$

(m) $3p + 3 = 24$

(n) $1 + 9f = 28$

(o) $2x - 2 = 44$

Assignment 2   **Find four**

Look at the equations in this grid.

$\frac{1}{2}x - 1 = 1$	$3x + 1 = 7$	$2x + 1 = 13$	$5x + 3 = 13$	$5 - x = 2$
$x + 9 = 12$	$x + 7 = 11$	$4x - 1 = 7$	$x - 4 = 6$	$4 + 2x = 10$
$x - 3 = 2$	$\frac{1}{2}x + 1 = 2$	$2x - 1 = 7$	$2x + 1 = 7$	$5 - 3x = 2$
$3x - 2 = 4$	$3x - 1 = 14$	$4x + 1 = 9$	$3x = 12$	$x + 1 = 9$
$2x = 4$	$4x + 1 = 13$	$3x - 4 = 5$	$2x + 3 = 9$	$x + 1 = 4$

- Choose an equation and solve it

- Find four equations which have the same solution, that is, the same value of x which makes the equations true.

- If you are working in pairs you will each need to copy this grid. Take it in turns to solve an equation.

The winner is the first person to find four equations with the same solution.

Equations from words and diagrams

Problems are usually written as sentences or shown in diagrams.
Equations are then used to express the problem in letters and numbers.
Solving the equation solves the problem.

Example

When a number is multiplied by 2 and 1 is added, the result is equal to 7.

This can be written as: $2n + 1 = 7$

Solve this equation to show that the number is 3.

> Any letter can be used to represent the number you do not know.

Exercise 8

1 Write down and solve an equation for each of these statements.

  (a) I think of a number and then add 4. The answer is 6.

  (b) I think of a number. Then I take away 5. The answer is 12.

  (c) I think of a number, and then double it. The answer is 16.

  (d) I think of a number, and then divide it into two equal parts.
       The answer is 11.

  (e) I start with 6, and then add a number. The answer is 13.
       What number did I add?

2 Write down and solve an equation for each of these statements.

  (a) When a number is multiplied by 3, the result is equal to 9.

  (b) When 6 is added to a number, the answer is 13.

  (c) When 8 is subtracted from a number, 6 is left.

  (d) When a number is divided by 2, the answer is 5.

  (e) When four pupils are added to a group, there are 15 pupils.
       How many were there to start with?

  (f) If you have been on holiday for two weeks and it is four more
       weeks before you go back to school, how long was the holiday?

  (g) Three minibuses each carry the same number of pupils. If the
       total number of pupils is 48, how many were on each minibus?

3 Write down and solve an equation for each of these statements.

(a) When x is multiplied by 5 and then 3 is added, the result is 18.

(b) A number is doubled and then 5 is taken away. The result is 13.

(c) When t is multiplied by 3 and then 3 is added, the answer is 21.

(d) When x is multiplied by 2 and then 7 is added, the result is 23.

(e) A number is doubled and then 9 is taken away. The result is 21.

(f) You buy two identical posters and have £6 left.
If you started with £14, how much was each poster?

(g) You add 2 to a number and then multiply the result by 3.
The result is 21.
What was the original number?

4 Write a sentence to describe each of these equations.

(a) $2a = 6$ (b) $6 + b = 13$ (c) $12 - d = 8$

(d) $3s + 2 = 8$ (e) $2y - 3 = 15$ (f) $\frac{1}{2}x = 3$

5 Look at these diagrams.

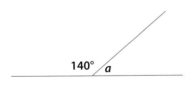

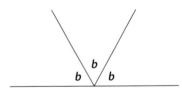

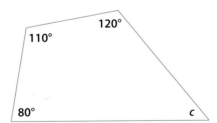

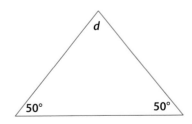

(a) Form an equation from each diagram.

(b) Solve your equations.

Expanding the brackets

This equation has brackets.

$$3(n + 2) = 21$$

One way to solve this type of equation is to multiply out the brackets.

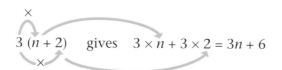

3 $(n + 2)$ gives $3 \times n + 3 \times 2 = 3n + 6$

> $\times$ and $\div$ before
> $+$ and $-$
> but brackets first

You can now solve $3n + 6 = 21$.

When you answer questions like these, your work should be set out in full like this.

$$5(a + 3) = 35$$
$$5a + 15 = 35$$
$$5a = 20$$
$$a = 4$$

> Make the
> $=$ signs line up.

Solve these equations by multiplying out the brackets.

1 $2(b + 3) = 16$ **2** $3(d + 4) = 18$ **3** $2(a + 2) = 28$

4 $3(x - 2) = 42$ **5** $5(n - 4) = 15$ **5** $4(k + 3) = 48$

7 $2(a + 3) = 20$ **8** $3(r - 3) = 63$ **9** $4(a + 7) = 36$

Dealing with negatives

All the equations you have solved up to this point in the chapter have had a positive solution. This is not always the case.

Example

> Check:
> $2 \times {}^-2 + 7 = 3$

$2a + 7 = 3$ The sum of $2a$ and 7 gives 3. So $2a = 3 - 7 = {}^-4$.
$2a = {}^-4$ Twice a equals ${}^-4$, so $a = {}^-2$.
$a = {}^-2$

Exercise 10

Copy and solve these equations.

1 $a + 7 = 3$ **2** $p - 6 = {}^-8$ **3** $2x = {}^-6$

4 $n \div 2 = {}^-6$ **5** $2x + 7 = 1$ **6** $3a + 8 = 2$

7 $2b - 3 = {}^-7$ **8** $5u + 13 = 8$ **9** $2k - 9 = {}^-7$

Assignment 3   Cross algebra

Copy this grid and complete it by filling in the solutions to the equations.

Down clues

2   $x + 17 = 43$
3   $2b = 20$
4   $\frac{1}{4}a = 4$
5   $x \div 11 = 12$
6   $a + 17 = 48$
7   $2r + 3 = 33$
9   $2a - 10 = 12$
12   $27 - x = 6$
13   $2x + 1 = 29$
15   $a + 10 = 31$
16   $26 - 2m = 6$
17   $80 - 2r = {}^-2$
19   $n \div 7 = 3$

Some clues have positive solutions and some have negative solutions.

Across clues

1   $2x = 24$
3   $2n - 1 = 37$
5   $2a + 1 = 21$
6   $3n - 2 = 106$
8   $d \times 2 = 26$
9   $3x - 8 = 25$
10   $a \div 5 = 10$
11   $n - 100 = 121$
14   $z + 11 = 33$
16   $q - 96 = 48$

18   $3p + 1 = 25$
19   $2d - 19 = 21$
20   $2m - 34 = {}^-4$
21   $2m + 6 = 2$
22   $8 + c = 6$
23   $d + 8 = 1$

Paired expressions

In Chapter 3 you found pairs of expressions that were equal.

For example $4x + 3 = 11$ and $2x + 7 = 11$.

Solution by trial and error

One way to solve this type of problem is to try substituting values into both sides of the equation until they are equal.

Using $x = 1$, $4x + 3 = 7$ and $2x + 7 = 9$. These are not equal so $x = 1$ is not a solution.

Using $x = 2$, $4x + 3 = 11$ and $2x + 7 = 11$, so $x = 2$ is a solution to $4x + 3 = 2x + 7$.

A systematic approach

Substituting values until you find one that works is not the best way to solve this type of problem.

Instead, try to think of these two expressions as being in balance.

Here is another example:

$$3a + 3 = a + 7$$

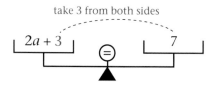

To solve this type of problem, aim to make both sides as simple as possible.

To keep the two sides balanced, you can add or subtract the same amount.

take a from both sides

$3a + 3$ = $a + 7$

Aim to have all the unknowns on one side only.

take 3 from both sides

$2a + 3$ = 7

Check your solution:
$3a + 3 = 6 + 3$
$\qquad = 9$
$a + 7 = 2 + 7$
$\qquad = 9$

You can multiply or divide both sides.

divide both sides by 2

$2a$ = 4

This means $a = 2$.

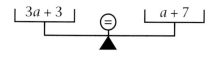

Assignment 4   Try it – change it

For each of these, there is only one number which will satisfy the equation.

- $3a + 4 = 2a + 11$

- $2x + 7 = 5x - 2$

- $3y - 40 = y - 4$

Substitute some values into each of the equations to see if you can find the solution that works.

If it does not work, use the more systematic approach instead.

Exercise 11

For each of these diagrams, find the value of the symbols which balance the two sides.

Keep the sides balanced at all times.

Try to make each side of the equation as simple as you can.

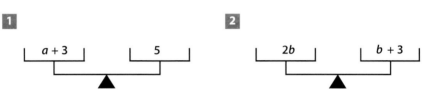

1 | $a + 3$ | 5 |

2 | $2b$ | $b + 3$ |

3 | $2c + 3$ | $3c$ |

4 | $5d + 4$ | $7d$ |

5 | $2e + 12$ | $e + 25$ |

6 | $3f + 8$ | $2f + 12$ |

Solving equations by balancing

Many equations can be solved this way. There is no need to draw the diagram, but you must remember to do the same thing to both sides of the equation, to keep it in balance.

Example

Solve the equation $3a + 3 = a + 7$

The process is written like this:

$$3a + 3 = a + 7$$

$$3a - a + 3 = a - a + 7 \quad \text{Take } a \text{ from both sides}$$

$$2a + 3 = 7$$

$$2a + 3 - 3 = 7 - 3 \quad \text{Take 3 from both sides}$$

$$2a = 4 \quad \text{Divide both sides by 2}$$

$$a = 2$$

> Check your solution by putting it back into the equation.
> $3(2) + 3 = 2 + 7$
> $9 = 9$ ✓

If the equation contains a bracket, you must multiply out the bracket first.

Example

Solve the equation $3(a + 1) = a + 5$.

The left-hand side has brackets so you must multiply out the brackets first.

The process is written like this:

$$3(a + 1) = a + 5$$

$$3a + 3 = a + 5$$

$$2a + 3 = 5$$

$$2a = 2$$

$$a = 1$$

> Check:
> $3(1 + 1) = 1 + 5$
> $6 = 6$ ✓

Exercise 12

1 Solve these equations.

The first question has been started for you.

(a) $7x + 5 = x + 23$

  $7x - x + 5 = x - x + 23$

  $6x + 5 = 23$

(b) $6b + 2 = 4b + 6$

(c) $8k + 3 = 3k + 18$

(d) $3s + 7 = 2s + 11$

(e) $6r + 6 = 34 + 2r$

(f) $5a + 9 = 9a + 1$

> Show all your working and check your answers.

2 Solve these equations.

(a) $4q + 5 = 3q + 8$ (b) $12w + 6 = 2w + 26$

(c) $13e + 6 = 6e + 13$ (d) $9r + 4 = r + 24$

(e) $4t - 5 = 3t + 1$ (f) $5y - 7 = 2y + 8$

(g) $12u - 5 = 8u + 3$ (h) $2p + 11 = 4p + 5$

(i) $2a + 20 = 5a + 2$ (j) $8s + 19 = 12s + 3$

(k) $6d + 1 = 3d + 10$ (l) $7f - 4 = 5f + 2$

(m) $7g + 3 = g + 21$ (n) $5h + 12 = h + 40$

(o) $2j + 26 = 4j + 10$ (p) $11k + 8 = 2k + 62$

3 Write down an equation for each of these sentences.
Then solve the equation.

(a) Multiplying a number by 3 and then taking away 5 gives the same result as multiplying the number by 2 and adding 2.

(b) Multiplying a number by 5 and then adding 4 gives the same result as multiplying the number by 3 and then adding 12.

Exercise 13

Solve these equations.

1 $2(x + 1) = x + 8$

2 $3(n - 2) = n + 2$

3 $3(a + 2) = a + 8$

4 $m + 10 = 4(m + 1)$

5 $2(x - 2) = x + 4$

6 $4(a - 2) = a + 1$

7 $2(2x + 2) = 3x + 7$

8 $3x + 6 = 2(x + 9)$

> Show all your working.

Review Exercise

1 Solve these equations. Show your working.

(a) $13 + a = 18$ (b) $5 + s = 7$ (c) $3 + d = 12$

(d) $5 + f = 8$ (e) $33 - y = 18$ (f) $25 - x = 7$

(g) $13 - t = 12$ (h) $15 - p = 8$ (i) $4s = 16$

(j) $3y = 12$ (k) $4x = 8$ (l) $3r = 15$

(m) $\frac{1}{2} a = 4$ (n) $\frac{1}{4} d = 2$ (o) $\frac{1}{3} t = 3$

2 Solve these equations. Show your working.

(a) $4f + 1 = 17$ (b) $3x + 2 = 14$ (c) $4a + 2 = 10$

(d) $3p + 2 = 17$ (e) $4 + 6t = 22$ (f) $1 + 9u = 73$

(g) $2b - 3 = 15$ (h) $3v - 1 = 20$

3 Solve these equations. Show your working.

(a) $2x + 13 = 5x + 1$ (b) $7a - 2 = 3a + 14$

(c) $9d + 6 = 6d + 12$ (d) $6r - 8 = 4r + 2$

(e) $23f - 12 = 13f + 28$ (f) $24x - 18 = 21x + 1$

4 Solve these equations. Show your working.

(a) $2m + 8 = 4(m + 2)$ (b) $2(6 + x) = 3x + 8$

(c) $3(x + 1) = x + 9$ (d) $4(2a - 3) = 2(3a - 9)$

Enlargements

→ to enlarge figures using a variety of methods
→ to identify and use the properties of enlargements
→ to enlarge more complex figures using scale drawings

....

Starting points

Before starting this chapter you will need to know how to:

- use coordinates to plot figures

- measure lengths accurately

- multiply measurements by simple numbers

- use a pair of compasses accurately.

Exercise 1

1 Draw a grid numbered from 0 to 5 along each axis, as shown.

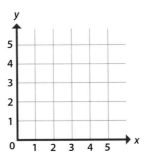

(a) Plot these points and join them up, in order.

(3, 1), (4, 4), (3, 5), (2, 4)

(b) Write down the name of this shape.

2 Draw a grid numbered as shown.

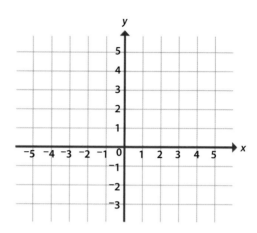

(a) Plot these points and join them up, in order.

($^-$4, $^-$3), (1, $^-$3), (0, $^-$2), ($^-$1, $^-$2)

(1, 3) (3, 3), (2, 1), (5, 1)

(4, 3) (4, 5), (3, 5), (3, 4)

(1, 4) ($^-$2, $^-$2), ($^-$3, $^-$2), ($^-$4, $^-$3)

(b) What picture do you get?

3 (a) Measure, to the nearest millimetre, the lengths a, b, c and d.

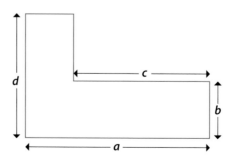

(b) Write these lengths in centimetres. (You will need to use decimals.)

4 Measure, to the nearest millimetre, these lengths.

(a) AB   (b) BC   (c) AC

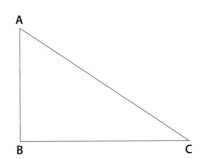

5 Suppose the length of each side of the triangle in Question 4 is doubled.

What would be the new lengths of these sides?

(a) AB   (b) BC   (c) AC

6 (a) Construct the triangle PQR with the base PQ = 12 cm.
Use a pair of compasses to construct sides PR and QR = 8.5 cm.

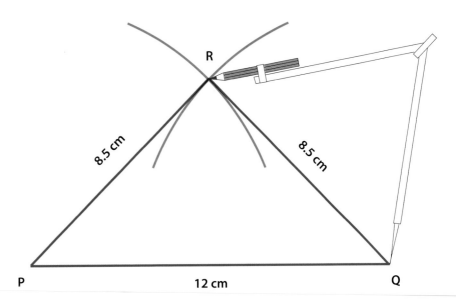

This diagram is not drawn to scale.
This means it is not drawn accurately.

(b) Measure, in degrees, the size of the angle at R.

Congruent and similar figures

Exercise 2

Look at these figures.

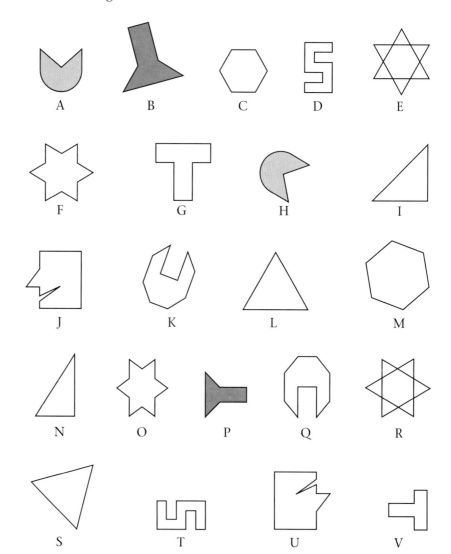

1 A and H are a pair of congruent figures. Write down as many pairs
of congruent figures as you can.

2 B and P are a pair of similar figures. Write down as many pairs of
similar figures as you can.

Enlargements

> 'Scaled up' means each measurement (or length) is multiplied by the same number.

When two figures are similar, one is an **enlargement** of the other.

To enlarge a shape, all measurements are scaled up by the same amount.

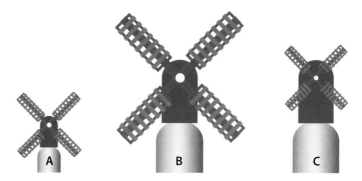

Figure B is an enlargement of Figure A. (It looks 'right'.)

Figure C looks 'different'. The sails have not been scaled up.

Exercise 3

1 Look at these diagrams. Decide which figure is not similar to the other two. Write down the letter of the 'odd one out' and explain how the figure is different.

(a)

(b)

(c)

(d)

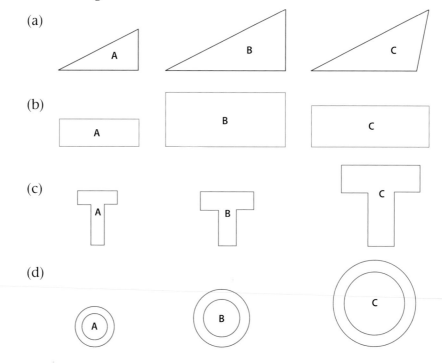

Drawing on grids

A drawing on a grid can be enlarged by copying it onto a larger grid.

You need to be very careful. Points on the small grid should be placed in the corresponding positions on the enlarged grid.

Original drawing

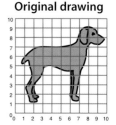

This enlarged drawing is two times as big as the original drawing.

It is called an **enlargement** of **scale factor 2** .

Enlarged drawing

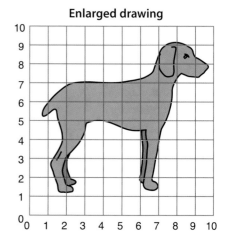

Assignment 1   Enlarging drawings using grids

- Choose at least two drawings and enlarge them onto a grid of 1-cm squares.

- Make your own drawing and copy it onto a larger grid.

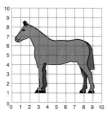

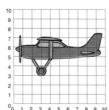

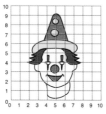

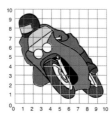

Warping ... an activity just for fun!

Usually you use a grid that is rectangular – all the 'squares' on the grid are squares.

With warped grids, this is not the case.

Here are some examples of grids that have been warped.

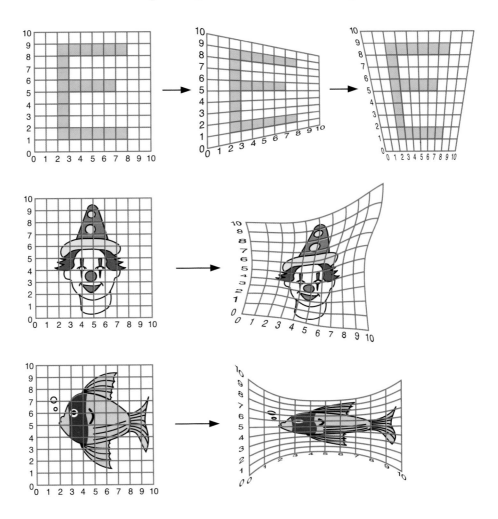

Assignment 2   **Warping**

You will need a sheet with warped grids.

- Design your own drawing and warp it using the grids.
- Design your own grids and warp your drawings in different ways.

Enlargements again

You have enlarged drawings using larger grids. A drawing can also be enlarged using the same grid.

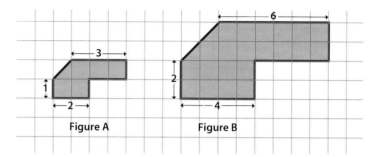

Figure A   Figure B

Each line in Figure B is twice as long as the corresponding line in Figure A. Some measurements have been put in to show you.

Exercise 4

You will need 5-mm squared paper for this exercise.

1 This diagram shows the start of an enlargement by scale factor 2. Copy the enlargement and complete it.

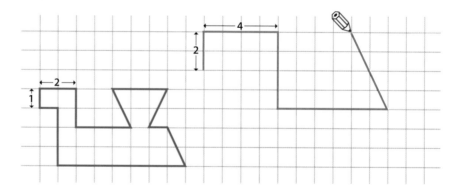

2 Copy this picture and then draw an enlargement of scale factor 3.

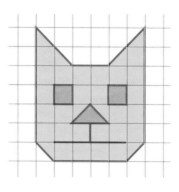

More scale factors

The lengths in
Figure B are all
three times the
corresponding
lengths in Figure A.

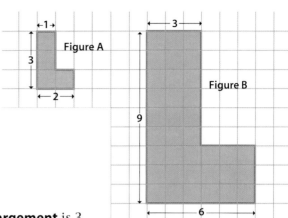

Figure A

Figure B

So the **scale factor of enlargement** is 3.

Exercise 5

1 Figure D is an enlargement of
Figure C.
What is the scale factor of
enlargement?

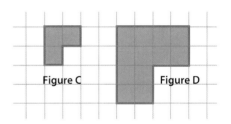

Figure C

Figure D

2 Figure F is an enlargement
of Figure E. What is the scale
factor of enlargement?

Figure F

Figure E

3 Triangles G, H, I and J are each enlargements of the shaded triangle.
What are their scale factors of enlargement?

The scale factor
may not be a
whole number.

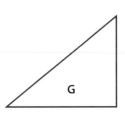

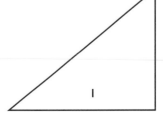

G

H

I

J

Growing from a point

Look carefully at these shape patterns.

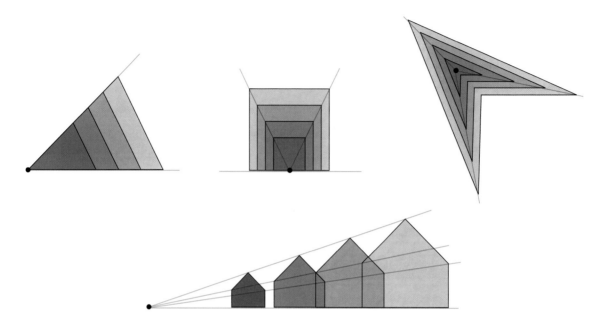

They all grow (enlarge) from a single point.

This point is called the **centre of enlargement**.
The lines from this point are called **projection lines**.

Projection lines pass through the corresponding corners of the shapes.

To find the centre of enlargement of similar shapes:

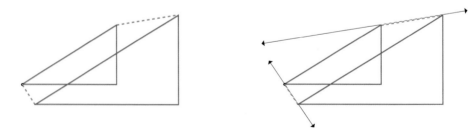

1   Draw a line joining corresponding corners.

2   Extend the line to make a projection line.

3   Repeat steps 1 and 2 for other corners to find their projection lines.

The centre of enlargement is where the projection lines cross.

Exercise 6

Use a copy of the following and find the centre of enlargement for each shape.

Use the method given above.

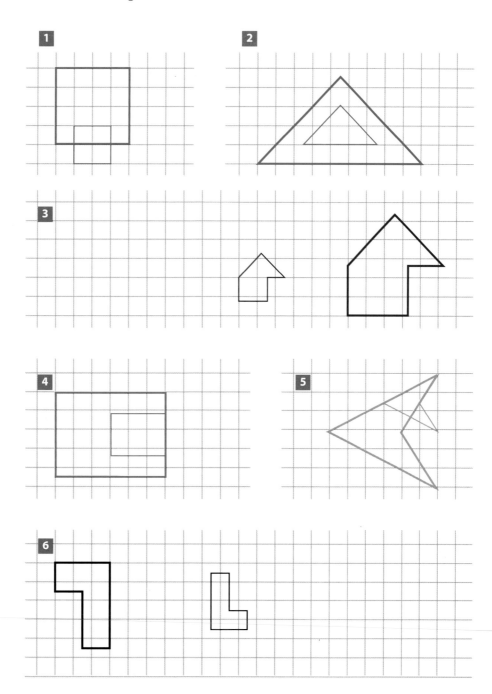

Enlargements by measuring

Exercise 7

1 Work through these steps to enlarge the quadrilateral ABCD by scale factor 2 using point O as the centre of enlargement.

(a) On a copy of the diagram, draw projection lines from O through each corner.

> Try to draw the projection lines as lightly as possible.

(b) Measure the distance from O to corner A (22 mm). Multiply this distance by 2 (44 mm). Mark the corresponding corner A′ at a distance of 44 mm from O.

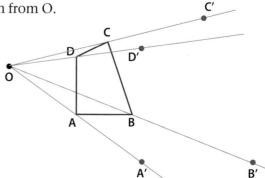

(c) Repeat for corners B, C and D.

(d) To draw the enlargement, join up the points A′, B′, C′ and D′.

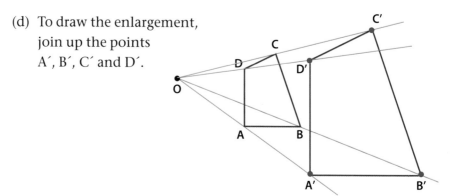

2 On a copy of these shapes, enlarge each by scale factor 2.

3 On a copy of this arrow, enlarge it by scale factor 3.

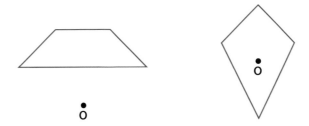

4 (a) Copy this right-angled triangle, and the points P, Q and R on to a sheet of paper.

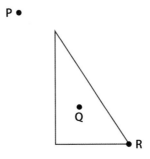

Enlarge it by scale factor 2 using the point P as centre of enlargement.

(b) On the same diagram, enlarge the original triangle by scale factor 2, using point Q as the centre of enlargement.

(c) Then enlarge the triangle by scale factor 2 from point R.

5 Describe the position of the enlarged star after each enlargement, using the points A, B, C, D and E as centres of enlargements.

Do not draw any enlargements for Question 5. Use what you have noticed so far to answer it.

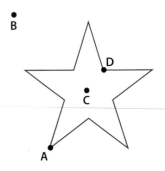

Enlargements using construction methods

Exercise 8

1 Work through these steps to enlarge the triangle ABC by scale factor 2, using O as the centre of enlargement.

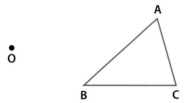

(a) Copy the diagram above. Draw a projection line from O through corner A.

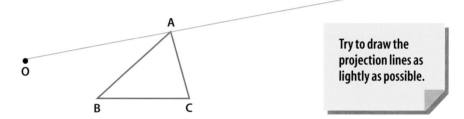

> Try to draw the projection lines as lightly as possible.

(b) Set your compasses to the distance OA.
Use your compasses to step off this distance from A.
Mark this point A′. Distance OA′ = 2 × OA.

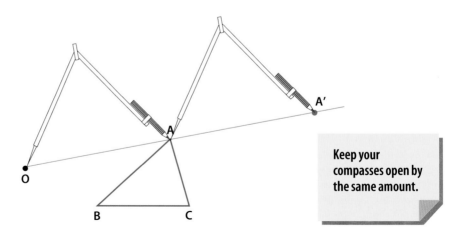

> Keep your compasses open by the same amount.

(c) Draw a projection line from O through corner B.

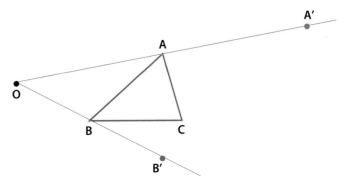

Open your compasses to the distance OB.
Use your compasses to step off this distance from B.
Mark this point B'. Distance OB'= 2 × OB.

(d) Draw a projection line from O through corner C.

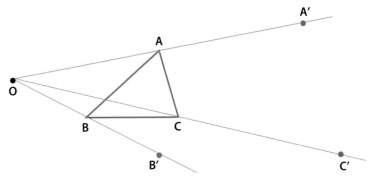

Open your compasses to the distance OC.
Use your compasses to step off this distance from C.
Mark this point C'. Distance OC' = 2 × OC.

(e) Join the points A', B' and C' to form a triangle.

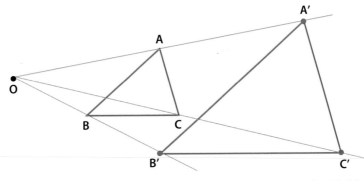

Triangle A'B'C' is an enlargement of triangle ABC by scale
factor 2 from point O.

2 On copies of these shapes, use the construction method to enlarge:

(a) by scale factor 2 from point P

(b) by scale factor 2 from point Q

(c) by scale factor 3 from point R.

(a)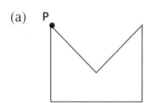

(b)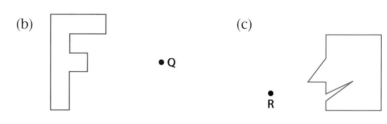

(c)

3 (a) Draw your own shape and enlarge it by a suitable scale factor from a point.

(b) Try different scale factors and other centres of enlargement.

Enlargements and coordinates

Assignment 3	An investigation using coordinates

Using 5-mm squared paper, draw a grid with axes numbered from 0 to 20.

Be as accurate as possible when drawing the projection lines.

- Plot triangle ABC with corners at points A(1, 1), B(3, 1) and C(1, 4).

  Use the construction method to enlarge triangle ABC by scale factor 2, with the origin (0, 0) as the centre of enlargement.

  Label the corners of the enlarged triangle A´, B´ and C´.

  Write down the coordinates of points A´, B´ and C´.

- On the same grid, enlarge triangle ABC by scale factor 3 from (0, 0).

  Label the corners of the enlargement A´´, B´´ and C´´.

  Write down the coordinates of points A´´, B´´ and C´´.

- On the same grid, enlarge triangle ABC by scale factor 5 from (0, 0).

  Label the enlargement A´´´, B´´´ and C´´´.

  Write down the coordinates of points A´´´, B´´´ and C´´´.

What is the connection between the coordinates of the original triangle ABC and the coordinates of each enlarged triangle?

Exercise 9

1 Without using a grid, copy and complete this table for enlargements of the quadrilateral PQRS.

Enlargement	Coordinates of corners			
Original quadrilateral	P(5, 4)	Q(3, 7)	R($^-$1, 6)	S($2\frac{1}{2}$, 1)
Scale factor 2 from (0, 0)				
Scale factor 3 from (0, 0)				
Scale factor 10 from (0, 0)				

2 Draw a grid with both axes numbered from $^-$5 to 10.

(a) Plot the triangle JKL with corners at points J(2, 1), K($^-$1, 2) and L($1\frac{1}{2}$, $^-$1).

(b) Triangle JKL is enlarged by scale factor 2 from the point (0, 0). Plot the enlargement on the same grid. Label the corners J′, K′ and L′.

(c) Triangle JKL is enlarged by scale factor 5 from the point (0, 0). Plot this enlargement on the same grid and label the corners J″, K″ and L″.

3 Draw a grid. Number the x-axis from $^-$4 to 6, and the y-axis from $^-$1 to 12.

(a) Plot the triangle XYZ with corners at points X(1, 1), Y(2, 1) and Z(1, 3).

(b) Triangle XYZ is enlarged by scale factor 4 from the point (1, 1). Plot the enlargement on the same grid. Label the corners X′, Y′ and Z′.

(c) Triangle XYZ is enlarged by scale factor 2 from the point (4, 2). Plot this enlargement on the same grid and label the corners X″, Y″ and Z″.

(d) Triangle XYZ is enlarged by scale factor 3 from the point (3, $^-$1). Plot this enlargement on the same grid and label the corners X‴, Y‴ and Z‴.

Review Exercise

1 Look at these shapes.

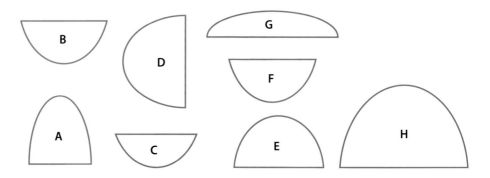

    (a) Which shapes are congruent?

    (b) Which shapes are similar?

2 Enlarge this drawing onto a grid of 1-cm squares.

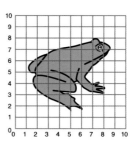

3 You will need 5-mm squared paper.
The diagram shows the start of an enlargement by scale factor 2.
Copy and complete the enlargement.

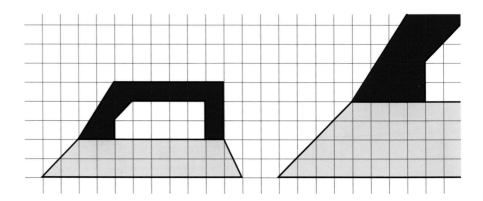

4 Rectangles P, Q and R are enlargements of the shaded rectangle. What are their scale factors of enlargement?

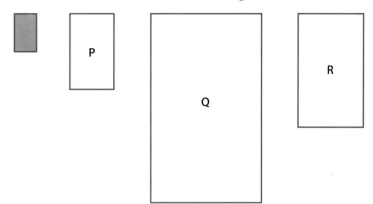

5 (a) Copy this diagram.

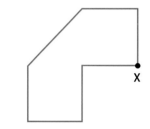

(b) Enlarge the shape by scale factor 2 using the point X as centre of enlargement.

(c) On the same diagram, enlarge the original shape by scale factor 3, this time using point Y as the centre of enlargement.

6 Draw a grid with both axes numbered from ⁻5 to 10.

(a) Plot triangle ABC with corners at the points A(2, 1), B(1, 2$\frac{1}{2}$) and C(⁻1, ⁻1).

(b) Triangle ABC is enlarged by scale factor 3 from the origin (0, 0). Plot the enlargement on the same grid. Label the corners A´, B´ and C´.

(c) Triangle ABC is enlarged by scale factor 4 from the origin (0, 0). Plot this enlargement on the grid and label the corners A´´, B´´, C´´.

Review chapter

In this chapter you will revisit earlier work on:

→ **writing down large numbers**
→ **addition, subtraction, multiplication and division with large numbers**
→ **probability**
→ **finding the area and volume of simple shapes**

Starting points

Before starting this chapter you will need to know how to:

• write down a number, putting the digits in their correct position

• use a calculator efficiently

• solve problems involving simple probability

• calculate the area of simple rectangular shapes

• calculate the volume of simple cuboid shapes.

Handling large numbers

For the first exercise, you may only use one number card from each pile each time.

For example, to make the largest 3-digit number you would select

Exercise 1

1 Which three cards would you select to make:

(a) the second largest 3-digit number?

(b) the largest even number?

(c) the largest number which can be divided exactly by 3?

(d) the largest number which can be divided exactly by 5?

(e) the smallest 3-digit number which is greater than 100?

(f) the largest number which can be divided by 4?

(g) the smallest 3-digit prime number?

2 Look at this pattern.

$$\square \ \square \ \square \ + \ \square \ \square \ \square \ =$$

Using this pattern:

(a) select six cards to make the largest answer in the sum

(b) select six cards to make the smallest answer.

3 Look at this pattern.

$$\square \ \square \ \square$$
$$- \ \square \ \square \ \square$$
$$\overline{}$$

Using this pattern:

(a) select six cards to make the largest difference in the subtraction sum

(b) select six cards to make the smallest difference

(c) select six cards to make the smallest difference which is an even number.

Exercise 2

1 These numbers have been written in words. Write them down as digits.

(a) nine hundred and twenty-seven   (b) seven hundred and eight

(c) two thousand and thirty-five   (d) six thousand and four

(e) four thousand two hundred and twenty

(f) eighteen thousand and ninety-four

(g) sixty thousand four hundred and eight

(h) forty-five thousand and eighty-nine

(i) thirty-three thousand and thirty-three

(j) fifty thousand and fifty

(k) sixty-four thousand nine hundred and ninety-five

(l) thirty-six thousand two hundred and forty-six

(m) fifty-four thousand three hundred and twenty-one

(n) one hundred and sixty-three thousand two hundred and thirty-one

(o) one hundred thousand one hundred and one

Assignment 1   Magic squares

6	1	8
7	5	3
2	9	4

In this magic square every row, column and diagonal adds up to 15.

It is possible to make other magic squares.

Palandromic numbers look the same when the digits are reversed, e.g. 747.

• On copies of these two magic squares, complete the empty boxes, using only palandromic numbers.

This one adds to 666

333		
	343	111

This one adds to 999

	131	
151		
		343

Assignment 2 Calculator highs

On your calculator, use only these keys.

You may only press each key once.

You are not allowed to press the = key immediately after the × key.

- In what order should you press the keys so that you reach the largest total?

- If you include the 6 key to the keys you can use, what order of key pressing would give you the highest total?

- Is it possible to predict the sequence of key pressing which will create the largest number when using these keys once only?

Assignment 3 Hundreds and thousands

Use the digits 1, 2, 3, 4, 5 and 6 once only to create four different sums.

- What arrangement gives the *highest* total for an addition?

  $$+ \; \bigcirc \bigcirc \bigcirc \atop \bigcirc \bigcirc \bigcirc$$

- What arrangement gives the *lowest* total for a subtraction?

  $$- \; \bigcirc \bigcirc \bigcirc \atop \bigcirc \bigcirc \bigcirc$$

- What arrangement gives the *highest even* total for a multiplication?

  $$\times \; \bigcirc \bigcirc \bigcirc \atop \bigcirc \bigcirc \bigcirc$$

- What arrangement gives the *smallest whole number* total for a division?

  $$\bigcirc \bigcirc \bigcirc \atop \bigcirc \bigcirc \bigcirc$$

Assignment 4   Making 100 from 1 to 9

It is possible to make 100 using the keys for the digits 1 to 9 in sequence and only the ⊞ , ⊟ and ⊜ keys on your calculator.

For example, pressing the keys

gives

$123 + 4 - 5 + 67 - 89 = 100$

Here is another example:

This gives

$-1 + 2 - 3 + 4 + 5 + 6 + 78 + 9 = 100$

- Press the keys for the digits 1 to 9 *in order* on your calculator, together with the ⊞ , ⊟ and ⊜ and keys.

  See what results you get.

- How many different ways can you make 100?

- Is it possible to make 100 by pressing the keys for the digits 1 to 9 *in the reverse order*

and only the ⊞ , ⊟ and ⊜ keys?

Assignment 5   Calendar multiplication

Here is the calendar for the month of January 1996.

January 1996

S	M	T	W	T	F	S
	1	2	3	4	5	6
7	8	9	10	11	12	13
14	15	16	17	18	19	20
21	22	23	24	25	26	27
28	29	30	31			

- Choose any 2×2 square from the calendar month of January. Multiply the diagonals.

1	2
8	9

  $1 \times 9 = 9$ $8 \times 2 = 16$

- Repeat this for several other 2×2 squares. What do you notice?

January 1996

S	M	T	W	T	F	S
	1	2	3	4	5	6
7	8	9	10	11	12	13
14	15	16	17	18	19	20
21	22	23	24	25	26	27
28	29	30	31			

- Choose any 3×3 square. Multiply the diagonal corner numbers.

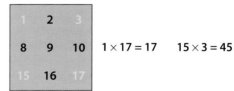

$1 \times 17 = 17$ $15 \times 3 = 45$

- Repeat this for several other 3×3 squares.

  Comment on the results you have obtained.

- Is there any connection between your findings for the 2×2 squares, 3×3 squares and 4×4 squares?

| Assignment 6 | **A million seconds** |

Look at this clock.

> **1 million is 1 000 000.**

- What will be the date and time in a million seconds?

Probability

| Exercise 3 |

1 The probability of throwing a six with a fair dice is $\frac{1}{6}$.

How many sixes would you expect to get if you throw the dice 150 times?

2 What is the probability of getting an even number with a fair dice?

3 What is the probability of not getting a 1 with a fair dice?

4 A dice is thrown and scores a 6. It is then thrown again.

What is the probability of getting a 6 this time? Explain your working.

5 Two dice are thrown and their scores are added together.

The lowest score is 2.

The highest score is 12.

Are all total scores equally likely?

Explain your answer.

Calculating probability

Exercise 4

1 A bag contains coloured beads: 7 red, 5 blue, 4 green, 3 yellow and 1 white bead.

Calculate these probabilities.

> p(green) is a short way of writing 'the probability of picking a green bead'.

(a) p(green)

(b) p(red)

(c) p(white)

(d) p(yellow)

(e) p(blue or yellow)

(f) p(red or white)

(g) p(green or yellow or blue)

(h) p(any colour except blue)

2 An ordinary pack of playing cards contains 52 cards divided into 4 suits: clubs, diamonds, hearts and spades.

> Diamonds ♦ and hearts ♥ are red. Clubs ♣ and spades ♠ are black.

The 52 cards are all mixed up and placed face down on a table.

What is the probability of turning over

(a) a King?

(b) a club?

(c) the 8 of hearts?

(d) a red card?

(e) a '10' card?

(f) a picture card?

> A picture card can be either a King, or a Queen, or a Jack.

(g) a red 3?

Perimeters, areas and volume

Exercise 5

1 Look at these shapes. All units are in centimetres.

(a)

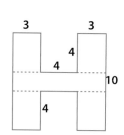

(b)

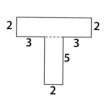

(c)

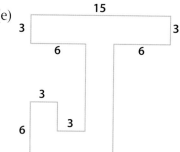

(d)

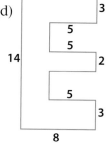

(e)

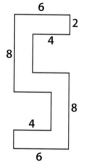

(f)

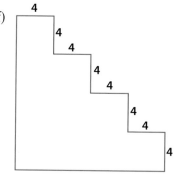

(g)

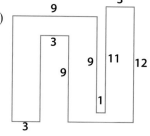

(h)

First **divide** each shape into parts.

For each shape find the perimeter and the area.

2 For each of these shapes, find the area by counting the squares or otherwise.

(a)

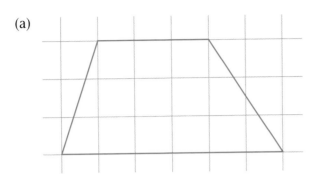

(b)

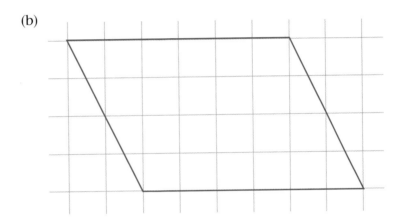

(c)

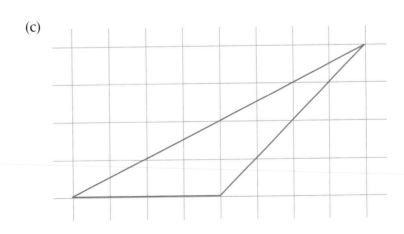

3 How many cubes are there in each of these shapes?

(a)

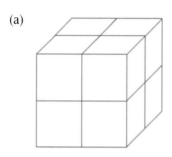

(b)

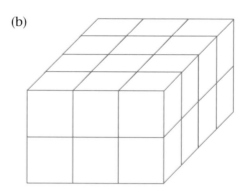

(c)

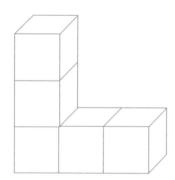

(d)

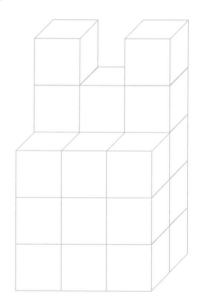

4 Work out the volume of each of these shapes.
Write down how you worked out your answers.

(a)

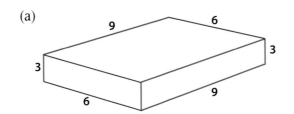

(b)

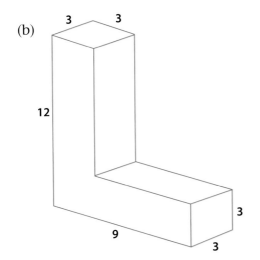

(c)

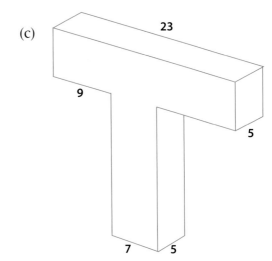

(d)

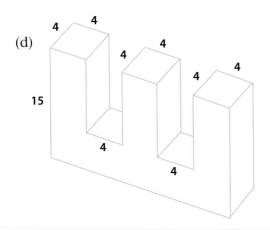

(e)

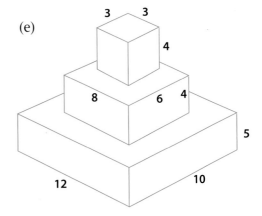

| Assignment 7 | Snooker |

This 2 by 8 snooker table has four pockets, one at each corner. Only one snooker ball is used and it is hit each time from the bottom left-hand pocket (marked A) at 45°.

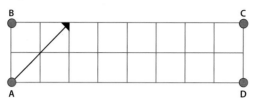

The ball rebounds off each cushion at 45° and keeps moving until it falls into a pocket.

• Complete the path of this ball until it drops into a pocket.

• This snooker table is 2 by 9. Which pocket will this ball fall into?

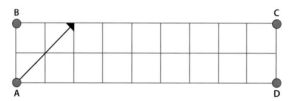

• Draw a set of eight snooker tables with size 1 by 10, 2 by 10, 3 by 10 and so on to 8 by 10.

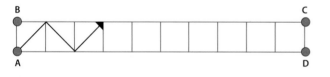

• The ball is hit from the bottom left-hand corner (marked A) in each case. Draw the path of the ball on each table.

• Which table has the simplest path?

• Which table has the most complicated path?

• Do the dimensions of the tables give a clue about when to expect a simple or complicated path?

• Now draw a set of seven snooker tables with size 1 by 7, 2 by 7, 3 by 7 and so on to 7 by 7.

• Investigate what happens and write about what you have found out.

• Will the ball ever finish in the starting corner?

Assignment 8 It grows on you!

- Colour in one square in the centre of a sheet of paper.

- Using a different colour, fill in all squares which touch the first square along just one side.

- Now use your first colour again to fill in any squares which touch your second colour along just one side.

- Continue following the same rules.

- Copy and complete this table to record your results.

Go	New squares	Total number of squares
1	1	1
2	4	5
3	4	9

- What patterns can you find?

- What happens if you use triangled paper?

- Try your own rule for 'growing'!

Assignment 9	Spots in a square

- Draw a square and mark three spots inside the square. (Make sure that the three spots are *not* in a straight line.)

  Join each spot to each other (to form a triangle). Then join each spot to any corner of the square you can, *without* crossing another line.

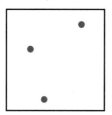 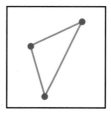 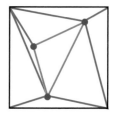

  The inside of the square has been split into triangles.
  Count the triangles.

- Start again, but this time mark five spots and join them to make a pentagon.

  Add lines *inside* the pentagon to join all points to other points, without crossing any lines already drawn.

  Add lines *outside* the pentagon to join points to the corners of the square, again without crossing any lines already drawn.

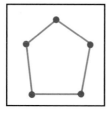 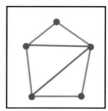 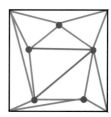

  Count the triangles.

- Is there a connection between the number of spots and the number of triangles?

- If there were 20 spots inside the square, how many triangles would there be? Explain why.

- What if there were 100 triangles? How many spots would there be? Explain why.